Out *Inn* CHESHIRE

The definitive guide to all the county's pubs

GW00368054

Editors: **George Symes & Simon Scott**

Distribution: Cheshire CAMRA Branches
Dee Services

Printing: Thornton & Pearson Ltd.

Published by Cheshire CAMRA Branches © CAMRA Ltd 1998
ISBN: 1 85249 144 2

CREDITS

This book is dedicated to the scores of CAMRA members in ten branches in and around Cheshire who gave so freely of their time and enthusiasm, in surveying and photographing the pubs they care for so much. We are also most grateful to the licensees who put up with being pestered. With one or two notable exceptions they were courteous, helpful and clearly dedicated to their vocation.

Branch contacts are as follows:

Chester	Brian Vardy	01244-373298
High Peak	Tom Lord	0161-427-7099
Macclesfield & E Cheshire	Keith Farman	01625-572460
Merseyside	Dave Cunningham	01925-224203
South Cheshire	Tony Bates	01270-764219
South East Lancs	Steve Prescott	01942-719037
Stockport & S Manchester	Rhys Jones	0161-231-6465
Trafford & Hulme	Roger Wood	0161-747-3987
Warrington & N Cheshire	Mark Enderby	01925-602809
Wirral	Dave Goodwin	0151-334-6549

Articles (A), maps (M) and photographs (P) were provided by the following:

Ian Bray	(P)
Jan Codling	(A)
Roland Domleo	(P)
Mark Enderby	(A)(M)
Jim Flynn	(A)
Scott French	(M)
Dave Hall	(A)
John Hallas	(M)
Dave Hasler	(P)
Rhys Jones	(A)
Roger Lowe	(A)
David & Wendy Scott	(A)
Simon Scott	(A)(M)(P)
George Symes	(A)(M)(P)
Robert Symes	(M)
Nicholas Winterton	(A)

Special thanks are due to the following individuals, for contributions above and beyond the call of duty:

Adrian Cavinder, Jan Codling, Roland Domleo, Ron Elder, Mark Enderby, Dave Goodwin, David Hair, Brian Marples, Jeremy Nuttall, David Scott, Robert Symes, Brian Vardy.

We apologise if we have inadvertently omitted anyone, we nevertheless extend our thanks to you.

We also wish to acknowledge the assistance and patience of the many licensees who provided much of the information contained in these pages.

The details in this guide were compiled from survey visits made by local CAMRA members in their own time, and the information is believed to be accurate and complete. However, we are reliant on licensees for providing some details, and there can of course be changes. Please do not hesitate to advise your local branch of any updates, errors or omissions.

FOREWORD BY MARTIN BELL M.P.

It has been one of the advantages of my accidental political career that it enabled me to make the acquaintance of some of the best pubs in the country. Those pubs happen to lie in the Tatton constituency, although there are others as appealing elsewhere in the country. Cheshire is as rich in pubs as it is in history.

It is not my purpose here to be political; indeed I am about as non-political as any politician can get. But I note with pride that John Sweeney of the Observer, the historian of my election, described it as not so much a political campaign, rather a pub crawl with attitude. He then went on to list in his book's acknowledgements every single pub in Alderley Edge, Wilmslow and Knutsford, which had made their contribution.

Cheshire has been fortunate. It still has small pubs alongside the large pubs, small brewers competing with the large brewers and liquid assets which still include many and splendid varieties of real ale. Of course there are threats to the country pub – an institution which lies at the very heart of country life. I am absolutely no defender of drunk driving, but I believe the proposed changes in the law on alcohol limits to be unnecessary. They could actually put the country pubs out of business.

I took part in a huge Countryside Rally in London for reasons which had nothing to do with foxhunting, but a great deal to do with the plight of our farmers and the future of our pubs. My father was a farmer, a notable writer on country life and an expert and erudite pub goer. From him I learned an affection for real ale, and for a mixture known as "old and mild", which is nowadays hard to find.

Of course not all pubs are equal and not all beers are equal. Since my father is no longer with us, I too need expert guidance – especially of the pubs of Cheshire. This book provides it, and I am delighted to be associated with such a refreshing enterprise.

My fondness for the English pub is matched by a fondness for the poet of the English pub – who is of course G. K. Chesterton. One of his verses was surely dedicated to the George and Dragon in Great Budworth; or it may have been the George and Dragon in Macclesfield; or other Georges and Dragons in our great country.

> *"King George he was for England,*
> *And before he slew the dragon,*
> *He drank a pint of English ale,*
> *Out of an English flagon."*

It was real ale of course.
In those days that was the only kind there was.

Out *Inn* CHESHIRE

This guide is for all Cheshire pub goers, be they casual visitors or regulars. We have attempted to provide details of every pub, and hope that all our readers will find in its pages much that is of value We could have aimed it exclusively at CAMRA members and beer buffs, but felt it would be more useful to write for a wider audience. If you are just as likely to go to a wine bar for a drink, a restaurant for a meal or to a burger joint to amuse the kids, we hope that the descriptions within will encourage you instead to visit some of Cheshire's historic inns. They are a real alternative. They have stood the test of time, and are part of our cultural heritage.

Within these pages you will find venues to suit every taste and every mood. Quiet pubs for a reflective or romantic evening, inns with the best of British food, roaring fires or talkative locals; country hostelries with a welcome for families and lovely gardens for those sunny afternoons.

We provide full details of all **1000 plus** of the county's pubs, and additionally we have chosen to showcase the **very best 100** of these, with detailed descriptions and specially-commissioned photographs and drawings. These **"flagship"** entries have been selected by local branches of CAMRA, who know and love them, as your introduction to all that is best in the traditional British pub. We indicate these flagships with the following flag symbol, throughout the book, in maps and text. Each one is a worthwhile destination in its own right. We hope you will agree with our choices.

The editors' award for the **Best Pub in Cheshire** goes to the **Bhurtpore Inn** in Aston. Read the entry to find out why, or better still, go there!

Although we believe all our chosen flagships serve good beer (and in fact many of them feature in CAMRA's national Good Beer Guide), it is not our main purpose in these pages to pass judgement on the quality of beer or meals. For the first you will find the Good Beer Guide itself invaluable; for the latter, the CAMRA's Good Pub Food Guide by Susan Nowak is recommended.

We have defined "Cheshire" as the county existed in late 1997, without being unduly pedantic.

We include the best of the neighbouring pubs in our "Over the Border" article.

We hope you enjoy using this guide as much as we enjoyed compiling it.

Simon Scott & George Symes

How to use this guide...

We attempt to provide directions to hard to find pubs, and provide a number of maps. For a rural county like Cheshire, a decent road map is a must, and an O.S. map or A to Z guide is best.

The editors hard at work!

TATTON
GEORGE & DRAGON
Knutsford Road (A56, from Tabley roundabout head down Stanley Road)
⏲APH

Bells Battleaxe <u>Bitter</u> (denoted as **B** in this guide), **Mischievous May Mild, White Suit Original, guest beers [H] Parliamentary Cider [H]**
This is one of Cheshire's classic pubs, well deserving of its status as one of our top 100 "flagships". Always welcoming to visitors, it is also very much a focus of the community. Recently taken over by the independent, Bells.

A warren of tiny rooms with low ceilings and exposed beams, it exudes character. The public bar is festooned with hops and decorated with an impressive display of pump clips. Toby, the pub cat is usually ensconced next to the open fire. The charming snug is non-smoking, as is the comfortable lounge, which admits well-behaved children. This adjoins the patio and garden, as well as the toilets which are wheelchair friendly. The sheltered garden is well fenced and set away from the road. Phil & Phyllis, the pubs tame pheasants will keep younger visitors amused.

The excellent traditional food is freshly made on the premises from local produce. Deservedly, the George features in CAMRAs Good Pub Food Guide. Situated close to the Middlestone Trail and Knutsford Canal, this is the perfect spot for a break during a day out in Cheshire. It is served by local buses and is ten minutes walk from the railway station.

The guest beer range is one of the pubs finest points, with over 2000 real ales from independent brewers over the last four years. It always stocks a cask mild and real cider, and has been in each of the first 25 editions of CAMRA's national Good Beer Guide. **GBG**

❶❷ ☡ ♿ ✿ ⇌ P 🚭

[H]　　We list only traditional beer (real ale) in the pub entries. **[H]** denotes the familiar hand pump, usually your guarantee of real ale. A handful of pubs use electric pumps **[E]** to serve real ale – look for the words "Cask Conditioned".

⏲　　Following the victory which CAMRA helped to bring about in the relaxation of the absurd restrictions in opening hours, it is a lot easier to find a pub open. It would be even easier if Publicans displayed their new hours. We have asked every one for details. Where we show "APH", this means that the pub, like Mr Arkwright, is open All Permitted Hours.
As we went to press, these were 11am to 11pm, except Sunday, which is 12 noon to 10.30pm.

❶❷　　We show when hot meals can be obtained; although bar snacks of various kinds can be had at other times in many pubs. The two symbols represent the two halves of a plate, for lunch and evening meals respectively. We have chosen not to provide telephone numbers, as we find they are rarely used. You can of course find these fairly readily in the phone book if you wish to book a table or travel to a distant pub.

🐎　　We do not mention Children's Certificates, as the application of the rules has been controversial, and prefer to deal with the realities as reported to us by the licensee. The symbol is shown only where we are told that children can be taken into at least one room without asking permission or ordering a meal. Parents will be aware that greater flexibility is occasionally possible.

♿　　The disabled access symbol is only awarded where there are disabled toilets and easy access to at least one bar. In other circumstances, much can be achieved given a considerate attitude from the staff.

✿　　The garden symbol is used sparingly; a bench in the yard is not enough!

⇌　　The railway symbol means that a station is less than a mile or so away.

🚭　　We indicate where a no-smoking room or area is provided.

GBG　　This indicates that the pub is in the 1998 Good Beer Guide, an accolade to the consistently high quality of its beer.

ACTON BRIDGE

HAZEL PEAR
1 Hilltop Road
⏰12-3, 5.30-11 Mon-Fri; 12-11 Sat; 12-10.30 Sun
Greenalls B, Original, guest beer [H]
The Hazel Pear is a large pub opposite the railway station. The staff are particularly attentive and friendly. It has three rooms of which one is used for dining. The front bar has wood panelling, plush seating, a blazing open fire and a parquet floor, with walls decorated with brass and prints of local sights. On the left is a lounge and at the rear is the dining room with a plate rack all the way round. The lively games room on the right of the pub has its own entrance, a pool table and dart board.

A recent development has been live jazz on Sunday evenings in the upstairs room which can seat sixty. Outside is a bowling green and a large children's play area. There are hazel pear trees in the grounds. The food is excellent, comes in very satisfying portions and includes fish specialities. There is no food on Mondays.

ACTON

STAR
Chester Road (main road through village)
⏰11.30-3, 7-11 Mon-Wed; 4-11 Thu-Sat; 12-10.30 Sun
Draught Bass, guest beer (occasional) [H]
Village local near Dorford Hall.

MAYPOLE
Hilltop Road
⏰11.30-11, 6-11 Mon-Sat;
12-3, 6.45-10.30 Sun
Greenalls Mild, B, guest beer [H]
Food-orientated pub with large lounge and separate small bar. Open fire. Children allowed in for meals.

RHEINGOLD
No real ale.

RIVERSIDE
Warrington Road (A49)
⏰ 11.30-11 Mon-Sat; 12-10.30 Sun
**Marstons B, Pedigree,
Head Brewers Choice [H]**
Large, recently converted pub on banks of Weaver Navigation. Concentrates on food and family trade.

ADLINGTON

LEGH ARMS
London Road
⏰Unknown
Beers Unknown
Once pleasant local, totally gutted in late 1997 and due to re-open in early 1998 as a Wacky Warehouse. Try as a last resort.

AGDEN BROW

WHEATSHEAF
Higher Lane, Broomedge
⏰ 11.30-3, 5.30-11 Mon-Fri; 11-11 Sat; 12-4, 6-10.30 Sun
Hydes Mild, B [E & H]
Comfortable roadside pub overlooking the western outskirts of Manchester. Popular with locals but lacks atmosphere when not busy. Evening food Thursday to Sunday only. Lined glasses ensure a full pint.

ALDERLEY EDGE

COUNTY HOTEL
Wilmslow Road, Harden Park (off A34)
⏰12-11 Mon-Sat; 12-10.30 Sun
Marstons Pedigree, Tetley B, guest beer [H]
Wacky Warehouse theme pub on main road.

DE TRAFFORD ARMS
London Road (A34)
⏰APH
Boddingtons B, Greenalls B [H]
Pub on edge of town with Hotel attached.

MOSS ROSE
Moss Rose (off Heyes Lane)
⏰11-3, 5-11 Mon-Fri; 11-11 Sat; 12-3, 7-10.30 (11-11 in summer) Sun
Robinsons Hatters Mild, Best B [E]
Welcoming pub that must be looked for off main road. Bowling green. (Pub open all day on match days!).

OAKWOOD
Brook Lane (B5085)
⏰11-3, 5-11 Mon-Sat; 12-10.30 Sun
Boddingtons B, 5 guest beers [H]
Busy pub on road from Alderley Edge to Mobberley. Open fire. Guest beers usually from major breweries.

QUEENSGATE (aka BRISINGAMENS)
No real ale.

ROYAL OAK HOTEL
28 Heyes Lane
⏰11.30-3, 5-11 Mon-Sat; 12-10.30 Sun
Boddingtons B, guest beer [H]
Large brick Victorian pub. Thai restaurant upstairs. No food Monday. Bowling green. Guest beer usually from independent breweries.

ALLGREAVE

ROSE AND CROWN
On a sharp bend on the A54 Congleton to Buxton Road near Wildboarclough
⏰12-3, 7-11 Mon-Sat; 12-3, 7-10.30 Sun
Robinsons Best B [H]
Stone-built, roadside country pub in a quiet part of Peak District, close to footpaths, youth hostel, and scout camp. Understandably popular with walkers. Tremendous views of the rolling hills around. Pinewood settles, three real coal fires and a friendly greeting make this family-run, oak-beamed pub worth a visit. Good, traditional evening meals, with sandwiches at lunch-times. No food Monday, except Bank Holidays. Children welcome in small room to left of the bar. Accommodation & function room available.

AGDEN BROW

JOLLY THRESHER
Higher Lane, Broomedge (A56)
⊘11.30-3, 5 .30-11 Mon-Thu; 11.30-4, 5.30-11 Fri; 11.30-4, 6-11 Sat; 12-3, 7-10.30 Sun
Hydes Mild, B, seasonal beer [H]
The Thresher was extensively refurbished around 1996, and is very presentable. A large roadside pub, it concentrates on food, and can therefore be very busy at lunch times, serving both bar food and full meals in a separate restaurant. The dining clientele can be somewhat mature and on the occasion of the editorial visit, I was made to feel quite young! Intending visitors should be aware that there is no food available on Sunday evenings.

The name of the pub is said not to be a simple rural term, but a reference to Lord de Trafford, who disguised himself from his creditors and undertook agricultural labouring until the coast was clear. Despite the strong emphasis on dining, it retains some of its pub atmosphere, with a bar and two drinking areas by the entrance, with stained glass windows. There is a vault to the rear with its own entrance. The pub has a good local trade, with a darts team and four bowling teams, and quarterly charity fund raising events for the Adventure Farm Trust. A bowling green, overlooked by a patio, and a function room are both hirable. There is a quiz on Monday evenings.

This is one of a relatively small number of Hydes outlets in the county (one of the others is the next entry!). This small, family-owned independent brewery in Manchester has a loyal following for its traditional ales. It started a programme of brewing seasonal beers in the nineties, in tune with growing demand for more choice in speciality beers. Its 4X strong winter ale should be tried; a classic winter warmer!

ALLOSTOCK

DROVERS ARMS
London Road (A50)
⊘11.30-3, 4.30-11 Mon-Fri; 11.30-11 Sat;
12-10.30 Sun
Boddingtons B, Flowers Original,
guest beer (summer) [H]
Recently extended and refurbished in rural style with various farm implements. Once a farmhouse, it became an inn early this century as evidenced by the wonderful photo in the side porch. The front room houses leather settees and an impressive open fire. Bowling green available to visiting parties. Pool also popular. Large restaurant. Free child's meal with adult order. Weekday evening meals in summer only.

THREE GREYHOUNDS
Holmes Chapel Road (Junction B5081/B5082)
⊘12-3, 5-11 Mon-Fri; 12-3, 6-11 Sat;
12-3.30, 7-10.30 Sun
Greenalls B, Tetley B [H]
Smart, clean and large establishment which became a pub in 1757. Despite some emphasis on food, landlord is keen to keep the dedicated tap room for local drinkers and the darts team. The extensive lounge is heavily beamed and houses comfortable leather settees. There is an impressive 200 year old yew tree by the front door. The function room also serves real ale.

ALPRAHAM

TOLLEMACHE ARMS
Chester Road
(A51 in the middle of the village.)
⊘12-3, 6.30-11 Mon-Sat; 12-3, 7-10.30 Sun
Boddingtons B, Tetley B [H]
Big mock-Tudor roadside local. Pool, darts, dominoes, quiz and theme nights, and boasts a football team. Straightforward pub grub.

TRAVELLERS REST
Chester Road (A51, outskirts of village)
⊘6-11 Mon-Sat; 12-3, 7-10.30 Sun
McEwans 70/-, Tetley Mild, B [H]
A unique pub fixed in a 1950s time warp; utterly unspoilt by progress, it is listed in CAMRA's National Inventory of Heritage Pubs and has consistently been in the Good

ALDFORD

GROSVENOR ARMS
Chester Road
⊘11.30-2.30, 5-11 Mon-Sat; 12-10.30 Sun
Boddingtons B, Crown Buckley B, guest beers [H]
This is a spacious, well-lit, multi-roomed pub full of character, from its stone, tiled and wooden floors, to its settles and sunny conservatory. It has been described as stylish, well-run and unashamedly upmarket. It was refurbished a couple of years ago and has attracted customers from Chester as well as locals. The overall décor could be described as 'modern-traditional', with bare boards, lots of pictures and chalkboards. There are interesting collections of prints, bottles, plates and house-plants. There is also a cosy bar-billiard area with wood-burning stove at the front.

A conservatory has been added to the rear, and the large garden is a welcome spot on a sunny afternoon. The extensive food and wine menu is available nearly all day, and the Grosvenor is well known for good food. They also serve pies as snacks, and you can get £1 off a 4 pint jug of beer. Several constantly-changing, guest beers from independent breweries feature. There are occasional beer festivals too.

Beer Guide for many years. The Travellers was South Cheshire CAMRA's Pub of the Year 1997/98. It has no music or electronic gadgets and is not child-friendly. There is a bowling green and a strong darts/dominoes/pub games following. Although it appears quiet, it can be busy and smoky at lunchtimes. GBG

ALSAGER
ALSAGER ARMS
Sandbach Road South
⏰12-11 Mon-Sat; 12-10.30 Sun
Tetley B [H]
Large pub by railway station. Multiple pool tables and bowling green.
≢ P

DEVONSHIRE ARMS
No real ale.

LINLEY
Talke Road
⏰12-3.45, 7.30-11 Mon-Sat;
12-3.45, 7.30-10.30 Sun
Robinsons Hatters Mild, Best B [H]
Modern, single room pub. Lunch Tue-Sun.
◖ ⛺ ≢ P

LODGE
88 Crewe Road
⏰APH
Greene King Abbot, Tetley B, Titanic Premium, guest beer [H]
Popular, two room pub. Student haunt. A rare Cheshire outlet for Stoke's Titanic brewery.
≢

MANOR HOUSE HOTEL
Audley Road
⏰11.30-3, 6.30-11 Mon-Sat; 12-3, 7-10.30 Sun
Wadworths 6X, Flowers Original [H]
Public bar attached to modern hotel and restaurant. Good to see real ales being served in an environment where keg beers usually dominate.
◖ ◗ ⛺ ♿ ≢ P ⊗

MERE
58 Crewe Road
⏰APH
Greenalls B, Original [H]
Small building opposite Alsager Mere. Popular with students.
● ≢ P

PLOUGH
Crewe Road
⏰APH
Marstons Pedigree, Tetley B [H]
This 300-year old pub has been transformed into a Big Steak House/Wacky Warehouse. So much for our heritage. Meals all day.
◖ ◗ ⛺ ● P

POACHERS POCKET
Crewe Road
⏰APH
Banks B, Marstons Pedigree [H]
The former name, the Old Mill gives a clue to the history of the building. Now a family pub with a children's play area downstairs, and adults only upstairs. Meals all day.
◖ ◗ ⛺ P

WILBRAHAM ARMS
Sandbach Road North
⏰11.30-3, 6-11 Mon-Sat; 12-3, 7-10.30 Sun
Robinsons Hatters Mild, Old Stockport B, Hartleys XB, Best B, Frederics [H]
A large modern pub/restaurant, with a good range of Robbies beers.
◖ ◗ ⛺ ● P ⊗

YEOMAN
Audley Road
⏰APH
Ind Coope Burton Ale, Tetley B [H]
Two-roomed Victorian local, formerly called The Railway. With Damocles' Sword hanging over Burton Ale, try it while you can...!
● ≢ P

ALVANLEY
WHITE LION
Manley Road
⏰11.30-3, 5.30-11 Mon-Fri; 11-11 Sat; 12-10.30 Sun
Boddingtons B, Greenalls B, Original, guest beer [H]
The White Lion is a comfortable, attractive and welcoming large hostelry set in a quiet village. It has been recently extended and now provides a 100-seat restaurant. In common with many Greenalls pubs, it offers a guest beer, although the licensee has to choose this from lists provided by the company.
◖ ◗ ⛺ ● P ⊗

ANDERTON
STANLEY ARMS
Old Road
⏰12-3, 6-11 Mon-Sat; 12-3, 7-10.30 Sun (winter); 12-11 Mon-Sat; 12-10.30 Sun (summer)
Greenalls Mild, B, Tetley B [H]
Plain, but cosy, two-room pub high above the Weaver. Adjacent to the famous Anderton boat lift, which is currently being renovated. Putting and bowling green.
◖ ◗ ⛺ ● P

ANTROBUS
ANTROBUS ARMS
Warrington Road
⏰ 12-3, 5.30-11 Mon-Sat; 12-4,7-10.30 Sun (winter); 12-10.30 Sun (summer)
Greenalls B [H]
Rustic country pub with public bar. Children's play area outside. Tuesday is Piano Night!
◖ ◗ ● P

APPLETON THORN
APPLETON THORN VILLAGE HALL
Stretton Road
⏰8.30-11 Thu-Sat, 8.30-10.30 Sun
6 guest beers [H]
This is an attractive sandstone building; a former schoolhouse converted to a village hall, although the draw is the beer rather than the setting. It has a small comfortable lounge to the left, with a high ceiling. To the right is the village hall itself, with TV and darts. This area may be inaccessible during community functions. There are regular functions including quiz nights and it is the home to various societies. There is a garden to the rear. This is a real ale haven for the area offering a much-needed choice from regional and micro-breweries. It was selected as 1995 CAMRA Club of the Year, and is also listed in the national Good Beer Guide. It holds a popular beer festival in October each year. Intending visitors should take careful note of the restricted opening hours. It also opens 12-3 on 1st and 3rd Sunday of the month. **GBG**
⛺ ● P

THORN
Grappenhall Lane
⏰11.30-3, 5.30-11 Mon-Wed; 11.30-11 Thu-Sat ; 12-10.30 Sun
Greenalls B, Original, Tetley B [H]
Popular village-centre inn with separate bar and function room. Undergoing major Refurbishment; due to re-open March 98.
◖ ◗ ⛺ P

ARCLID
ROSE & CROWN
Newcastle Road (at A50/A534 junction)
⏰12-3, 6.30-11 Mon-Fri; 12-11 Sat; 12-10.30 Sun
Burtonwood B [H]
A traditional pub in an area where there are few. Being situated on a busy crossroads this pub attracts a lot of passing trade. However locals are well catered for and pool and dominoes are popular. Single-roomed, with an outdoor play area for children. The food is home-cooked and includes a vegetarian option. Occasional seasonal beers from Burtonwood.
◖ ◗ ● P

ASHLEY
GREYHOUND
Cow Lane
⏰11.30-11 Mon-Sat; 12-10.30 Sun
Greenalls B, Original, Tetley B, guest beer [H]
Set in a quiet village only two miles from suburban Altrincham, with the resulting mix of customers. The food is home-cooked but can be expensive, as can the guest beers. Food served noon till 8.30 on Sunday. The licensee has been here for 38 years!
◖ ◗ ⛺ ● ≢ P

8

ASHTON
GOLDEN LION
Kelsall Road (B5393 off A54)
⏰12-3, 5.30-11 Mon-Fri; 12-1 Sat; 12-10.30 Sun
Draught Bass, Greenalls Mild, B, guest beer [H]
Comfortable and friendly village centre local, popular with locals and visitors, including regular parties of walkers and cyclists from the Delamere Forest. It is a short walk from Mouldsworth station on the main Chester to Manchester line. The building was once a farmhouse as evidenced by the framed photos opposite the bar, and is thought to be about 300 years old. It is the only survivor of the three original village inns. The smart interior is beamed and has copper-topped tables and a warming open fire in Winter. There is a separate public bar, a games room with a pool table and a separate restaurant. Good value food is served daily and all day Sunday, when there can sometimes be a bit of a wait. The pub cats are called Whisky and Soda!

ASTBURY
EGERTON ARMS
Audley Road (just off the A34)
⏰11.30-11, Mon-Sat; 12-3, 7-10.30 Sun
Robinsons Best B [E], Frederics [H]
A 15th century country inn set opposite Saint Mary's church in a pretty village just south of Congleton. Large, multi-roomed, and beamed, the Egerton boasts 6 bedrooms and a menu of home-cooked food in a separate restaurant including good vegetarian options. The comfortable interior has displays of brewing paraphernalia. This is a good place to sit and enjoy the pleasures of conversation. Children will enjoy the play area, in the garden, which is fenced and safe. A convenient spot for a number of local attractions, including Jodrell Bank science centre and Little Moreton Hall, said to be the best example of a timber-framed house in the country

Out *Inn* CHESHIRE

ASTON
BHURTPORE INN
(See Overleaf)

AUDLEM
BRIDGE
12 Shropshire Street (A525)
⏰APH
Banks Mild, Marstons B, Pedigree [H]
An unpretentious village pub next to the canal bridge. A local which can get busy in summer. Meals served all day in summer when the canal is open. Proud of using local produce to make proper pub grub. Opens at 10 for morning coffee; children's menu.

LORD COMBERMERE
The Square
⏰APH
John Smiths B, Marstons Pedigree [H]
Large building dominating the village centre. Rather shabby at present, but due a major refurbishment imminently. Many-roomed, including vault and two snugs. Lovely etched door and wood-panelled hallway. Lunch, evening meals and a guest beer promised.

SHROPPIE FLY
(See Overleaf)

BARBRIDGE
BARBRIDGE INN
Old Chester Road (signposted from the A51)
⏰11.30-11 Mon-Sat; 12-10.30 Sun
Boddingtons B, Cains B, guest beer [H]
Large and comfortable with canal-side garden, and enclosed children's play area. Airy and well-furnished with imitation-coal gas fires. Unashamedly family-friendly chain pub, perhaps a little short on originality and atmosphere. Purpose-built disabled access. Busy when the canal is open (there is mooring right outside) and bedlam on hot Summer weekends. A fence will keep stray children and dogs from a watery grave. Meals are served through from noon every day, and there is a barbecue in summer. Jazz Thursdays, quiz Mondays. Interesting choice of changing guest beer.

BARNTON
BARN OWL
No real ale.

BEECH TREE
Runcorn Road (A533)
Times not known.
Greenalls Mild, B [H]
Estate pub with large lounge and bar. Shabby exterior but well-maintained inside. Refurbishment/theming expected.

BARROW
STAMFORD BRIDGE
Barrow Lane
⏰APH
Boddingtons B, Greenalls Original [H]
Food-oriented theme pub with fake beams and other olde worlde fittings.

ASTON

BHURTPORE INN
Wrenbury Road (just off A530, south of Nantwich)
☺12-2.30, 6.30-11 Mon-Fri; 12-3, 6.30-11 Sat; 12-3, 7-10.30 Sun
Hanby Drawwell B, at least 9 guest beers [H] cask cider or perry [H]
The best real ale outlet in Cheshire! CAMRA members and beer lovers for miles around are drawn to the Bhurtpore. Named after Bharatpor, a city in India, shown in colour photos in side snug, besieged in the Nineteenth century by a local gentleman, on whose land the building stood. Some of decor reflects this oriental theme too. Photos of old Aston/Wrenbury area and pub-through-the-years and old field maps adorn the walls, and a collection of whisky jugs hangs from the beams. There is a very cosy interior with four drinking areas and a separate dining room. Wooden settles and gorgeous grandfather clock are complemented by two lovely fires, to the left a large brick one with intricately carved Indian figure and porcelain Indian elephant at side, to right a black-leaded and tiled Victorian grate (with Charge of the Light Brigade print above). A pool table and original pub sign feature in the back room.
The Bhurtpore was originally opened by the current landlord's grandfather, and is now back in the family after a few years absence. Formerly a small-holding, it is now a very popular local with a separate restaurant. The Bhurtpore is about fifteen minutes walk from Wrenbury station, and a bus service is occasionally sighted, so public transport is a possibility if you want to sample a few of the magnificent range of beers.
There is a good variety of quality bar food, from snacks (some of which are complimentary!) to full home-made meals which can also be eaten in the separate restaurant. Not surprisingly, curries are a speciality. There have been 1400 guest beers in the last 5 years, including regular milds, stouts and porters. Numerous foreign beers both on draught and in bottles are featured, as evidenced by the menu and the pub holds its own annual pub Beer & Cider Festival around Easter. It is of course a Good Beer Guide stalwart. A regularly changing range of real ciders and perries are also available.
The Bhurtpore receives the Editors' award for Best Pub in Cheshire. Well worth a visit. **GBG**
◖◗ ⚞ ♿ ❀ ⇌ P

BARTON
COCK O' BARTON
No real ale

BEESTON
WILD BOAR HOTEL
No real ale

BEESTON CASTLE HOTEL
A49 (1½ miles east of Castle, near Tiverton)
☺11-3.30, 7-11 Mon, Tues, Thurs;
11-11 Wed, Fri, Sat; 12-10.30 Sun
Draught Bass, Worthington Draught B, guest beer [H]
Roadside pub near local agricultural market, with separate no smoking restaurant. Real fire.
◖◗ ❀ P

SHADY OAK
8 Bate's Mill Lane (near Tiverton & Huxley)
☺APH
Courage Directors, Theakston Best B [H]
Beside the Shropshire Union Canal and close to the Sandstone Trail. The children's play area includes a small pets enclosure. Meals all day, every day. Welcomes boaters and caravanners.
◖◗ ⚞ ♿ ❀ P

BETCHTON
NEW INN
Newcastle Road
☺11.30-3, 6-11 Mon-Sat; 12-3, 7-10.30 Sun
Marstons Burton B, Pedigree [H]
A modernised roadside inn with the emphasis on food, including Sunday roasts.
◖◗ ❀ P ⊗

BEWSEY
IMPERIAL
No real ale.

BICKERTON
BICKERTON POACHER
On the A534 midway between the A41 & A49
☺Not provided
Greenalls beer, guest beer H]
Built in 1642, now, very much a cloned but inoffensive theme venue. Open plan, but with the beams retained, the interior is lifted by a black-leaded range. The barbecue and the function room/skittle alley can be hired. There is a play area and patio, but no garden as such. The mild and bitter may be keg. We cannot supply full details of the beers or the opening hours, as the licensee declines to co-operate with this guide. Draw your own conclusions.
◖◗ ⚞ P

BLACKBROOK
GREENWOOD
No real ale.

BORN TO BE MILD?!

Have you ever been into a pub, seen the clip on the handpump advertising "Mild", wondered what this strange beverage was, but decided to stick with something you knew? Same here. Until a friend bought me one...which left me pleasantly suprised...very pleasantly suprised.

Unlike many bitters and lagers, mild is thirst-quenching but without the sharp "hoppiness" some find rather unpalatable. It can range from pale and straw-coloured to almost black and has an array of tastes to match, from dry and clean to roasted and almost smoky! All have a nice, distinctive malty flavour. Milds are usually slightly lower in alcohol than other beers (worth noting if you're out for a drive in the countryside). They'll also lighten your wallet less quickly. You can expect to save the best part of a pound a pint if you switch from lager or Guinness to Mild!

We are lucky in Cheshire, in that there are a number of excellent Milds to be had. The most common of these are the lightly fruity **Greenall's Mild**, **Tetley's Mild** and **Dark Mild** and the dry, refreshing **Robinson's Hatters Mild** (there is also the rare **Robinson's Dark Mild** that's well worth seeking out, at the Red Lion in Lower Withington for instance). Try a pint of the rapidly disappearing **Boddington's Mild** (at the Farmers Arms in Wilmslow is a good place).

Marston's pubs often stock either the superb, amber-hued **Banks's** or the gorgeous, deeply roasted, ruby/black **Bateman's Dark Mild** (current Champion Mild of Britain). Most Holts pubs keep their unusually hoppy **Holt's Dark Mild** (pop in for one at the Angel in Knutsford or the Cock O' Budworth in Great Budworth).

Cheshire brewer **Burtonwood** also produces a smooth, rich brown **Mild** with caramel over-tones (where better to taste it than at the Bridge Inn near the brewery itself). Likewise (though slightly more difficult to find in Cheshire), Manchester's **J.W. Lees** has **GB Mild** (try the Spread Eagle in Lymm or the Golden Pheasant in Plumley), **Thwaites** produce a **Best Mild** (served at the White Lion in Childer Thornton), **Whitbread** brew **Chester's Best Mild** (a good drop is to be found at the Olde Harp Inn in Little Neston and the Crown in Lower Peover), **Ansells** have their own (as seen at the Royal Oak in Rode Heath) and **Hydes** turn out three (**Mild, Dark Mild and Light**)! Congleton's **Beartown** microbrewery are due to launch their new ale, a strong mild called **Black Bear**, at the Macclesfield Beer Festival this year. This should also be for sale as a guest in the locality and will be brewed regularly if it "goes down" well. So seek it out! Last, but by no means least, is the wonderful **Gunpowder Mild** of Warrington's **Coach House** brewery. Too good to just drink on Bonfire Night!

Appetite whetted? Go on, take a walk on the Mild side!

THE SHROPPIE FLY - AUDLEM

AUDLEM
SHROPPIE FLY
The Wharf (on the canal bank; follow the lane from the bridge where the A525 crosses the canal.)
🕑12-3, 6.30-11 Mon-Sat; 12-10.30 Sun
Boddingtons B, Castle Eden Ale, Flowers Original [H]
This large open-plan pub is popular with canal users, and can be busy in summer. The opening hours may be reduced from those shown above during the winter months. It has a spacious bar and a dining area which is distinguished mostly by a change in the style of furnishing. The food is straightforward pub grub. Meals are served 12 to 2.30 and 6.30 to 9.30. As we went to press, Country & Western acts were featuring on Friday evenings.
The outside drinking area runs alongside the locks; although it has limited seating it is an excellent spot to watch the narrow-boats as they navigate the lock (or the antics of amateur crews as they attempt to navigate the locks!). On a cautionary note, this very proximity to an active lock brings danger for unsupervised children or dogs. This is a lovely spot, and the only reservation is the uninspiring choice of beers. With guest beers from independent breweries, this would be idyllic.

BARTHOMLEY
WHITE LION
Audley Road (in the village centre, a mile from M6 junction 16)
🕑11.30-11 Mon-Wed, Fri-Sat, 5-11 Thu, 12-10.30 Sun
Burtonwood B, James Forshaws B, Top Hat, Buccaneer [H]
This gorgeous half-timbered Tudor, thatched inn, dating from 1614 is a veritable time-capsule. With open fires, beams, settles and scrubbed tables, it provides the perfect setting for a quiet pint. Its name derives from the crest of the Crewe family, the silver lion. The building faces the elevated prospect of St. Bertoline's church, the scene of a Royalist massacre in the Civil war. Ale was sold here by the Parish Clerks as early as the 16th century, when it was known as the Clerk's Cottage. Having obeyed the injunction to enter by the "other door", you find yourself in a small room looking much as it has done for hundreds of years. To the left, down a step is the quarry-tiled bar where the beams are low enough to catch unwary tall visitors. Don't miss the tiny back room with its stove. Although the White Lion can be busy, especially when lunch is being taken, it has its peaceful spells, when the presence of sleeping cats testifies to the relaxed atmosphere. Two outdoor drinking areas overlook a small stream in the centre of this quiet and attractive village.
Meals are served from noon till 2.15 daily, except Thursday, when there is no lunchtime session. Coffee is available at all times, handy for drivers. The gents are across the yard near the accommodation (a new bunkhouse is available for visitors providing their own sleeping bag!) and a centrally heated meeting room is available. The beers are consistently good enough to merit an entry in CAMRA's Good Beer Guide. It is difficult to fault this classic unspoilt country pub. **GBG**

BOLLINGTON
BULLS HEAD
2 Oak Lane
(Kerridge, ½ mile south of the village)
🕑12-2.30, 6-11 Mon-Thu;
12-3.30, 6-11 Fri,Sat; 12-3.30, 7-10.30 Sun
Robinsons Hatters Mild, Best B [H]
Stone built pub in an elevated position. The car park is very small and roadside parking can be a little tight.

CHESHIRE HUNT
Spuley Lane
(from Pott Shrigley church, head towards Bollington, and take left fork to Rainow)
🕑11-3; 5:30-11 Tues-Sat;
12-3; 7-10.30 Sun
Boddingtons Bitter, guest beers [H]
Traditional, unspoilt 300-year old country pub, concentrating on English and Continental food. On the Gritstone Trail, there are three patios with lovely country views. Bar meals, plus separate restaurant with its own a la carte menu. No smoking in third, quiet room with no music. Sunday lunch carvery is popular. Former cattle auction house, when women were not allowed, hence the original pub name of the Quiet Woman. Bass and Marston's Pedigree are almost permanent guest beers. There is level access for wheelchairs.

COCK AND PHEASANT
Bollington Road (Bollington Cross)
🕑11:30-11 Mon-Sat; 12-10:30 Sun
Boddingtons B, Greenalls B [H]
Once an excellent, thriving community pub. Unfortunately, renovation has changed this. Amazingly the pub enlargement was at the expense of the cellar which is now too small to store sufficient drink for even the current demand. The lack of guest beer is a direct result. Conservatory and large garden with good facilities for children

COTTON TREE
Ingersley Road
🕑12-11 Mon-Fri; 11-11 Sat; 12-10.30 Sun
Vaux Mild, B, Samson [H]
This stone built corner local has recently been renovated tastefully. Vaux is an unusual brew for Cheshire.

CROWN
Church Street (south of bus terminus)
🕑5-11 Mon-Thu; 11-11 Fri-Sat; 12-10.30 Sun
Boddingtons B [H]
Pleasant, quiet, single room local offering pool, darts, large screen satellite TV, and Rolly and Stan, the ghosts of two ex-landlords! Bar snacks always available. Children welcome afternoons. Flat entrance for wheelchairs.

DOG & PARTRIDGE
97 Palmerston Street
🕑APH
Robinsons Hatters Mild, Best B [H]
Unusual, cosy pub with central bar surrounded by a series of small rooms. A former Bells pub, this is very much part of the community, with a Light Opera group, Folk on Fridays and a
presence on the Internet! Bar snacks.

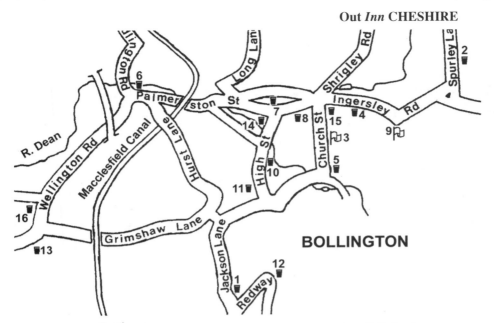

BOLLINGTON

1 – **Bulls Head**
2 – **Cheshire Hunt**
3 – **Church House Inn**
4 – **Cotton Tree**
5 – **Crown**
6 – **Dog & Partridge**
7 – **Holly Bush**
8 – **Meridian**
9 – **Poachers**
10 – **Queens Arms**
11 – **Red Lion**
12 – **Redway Tavern**
13 – **Royal Oak**
14 – **Spinners Arms**
15 – **Turners Arms**
16 – **Waggon & Horses**

HOLLY BUSH
75 Palmerston Street
⏱12-2, 5-11 Mon; 5-11 Tu-Fri; 12-11Sat;
12-4, 7-10.30 Sun
Robinsons Hatters Mild, Best B [H]
The Holly Bush is a small mock-Tudor pub in
the centre of Bollington, retaining many of its
1930s features. Quiet pub with unusual wood
panelling in the lounge at the back. Two other
rooms provide diversity. Casual visitors should
note that the Bush is closed several lunchtimes
in the week. Satellite TV on the bar for most
sporting occasions. It also offers a reliably
good pint of Robinsons.

CHURCH HOUSE INN
Chapel Street (corner of Church Street)
⏱12-2.30, 5.30-11 Mon-Fri; 12-3, 5.30-11 Sat; 12-3, 7-10.30 Sun
Flowers IPA,Theakston Best B, Wadworth 6X[H]
Situated on a quiet side street at the top end of Bollington, the Church House occupies a corner site
in a row of traditional cottages, close to the open countryside of the Peak District. The Church
House is very popular, with both the open plan bar area with its blazing fire in winter, and a smaller
back room providing comfortable seating for diners and drinkers alike. It is also one of the few pubs
in the area to provide accommodation, meriting three Crowns.
 The pub specialises in excellent food. Indeed, the pub has been listed by Egon Ronay and
appears in CAMRA's Good Pub Food Guide. Consequently, booking ahead for meals is advisable at
peak times, as the Church House is both small and well known in the locality for its varied menu.
The car park is very small, but street parking is possible.

THE CHESHIRE CANAL RING

Though the water usually associated with Cheshire is the plentiful rain, which keeps its fields characteristically lush for cattle grazing, there is a wide variety of more accessible water within the county boundary. Rivers, streams, meres and canals form a playground for many of the young-at-heart. It is the latter however, with which Cheshire is most justifiably famous. The **BRIDGEWATER CANAL** was opened in 1759 by the eponymous Duke, Francis Egerton, as the world's first modern canal, being independent of all existing natural waterways. It now forms part of the renowed **CHESHIRE RING**, which consists of six canals, and travels in a rough circle for 97 miles (excluding side-branches) and contains no less than 92 locks! About three-quarters of the Ring is in Cheshire, and it is the wide variety of public houses on, or near, this portion with which we are concerned in this article. Pubs by towpaths were originally built to slake the thirst of busy canal workers. Nowadays, their customers are more likely to be walkers or day-trippers as well as boaters. We hope you will find this to be a useful guide to recommended refreshment stops along the Ring, whatever your pursuit. For further details, see the pub entries in Out *Inn* CHESHIRE. Access points from the canals are given where possible, but an Ordnance Survey map may also prove useful.

We shall travel clockwise round the Ring, starting at border with the County of Greater Manchester on the **MACCLESFIELD CANAL**, where the route criss-crosses the county boundary a couple of times before delving deep into Cheshire.

Firstly, an honourable mention must go to that short section of the **PEAK FOREST CANAL** which lies in Cheshire. The canal passes both **Disley**, where the *Dandy Cock Inn* is your best bet, and is accessible from *Bridge 26 (Br26)*. Next is the *Sportsman's Arms* at **Strines** *(Br24)*. This canal then meets the true Cheshire Ring at Marple, where the **MACCLESFIELD CANAL** leads you to the *Royal Oak* at **High Lane** which serves beers from Cheshire's Burtonwood Brewery. See our "Over The Border" article for further details of these latter two pubs.

Into Cheshire proper now. After some miles we recommend a stop in **Bollington.** Getting off at *Bridge 27* or the nearby aqueduct, try the *Holly Bush* or *Queens* or, a little further, the *Meridian* and *Church House.* In **Higher Hurdsfield**, the *George & Dragon* freehouse is a worthy stop *(Br34)* despite the uphill walk. One of the few major conurbations on the Ring is **Macclesfield**. A walk from *Bridge 37* will take you into the centre for supplies, where both the *Waters Green Tavern* and the *Castle* should be visited. Diverting from the same bridge down Brook St. on the left will lead you to the *Boarhound.* Another worthwhile trip from *Bridge 40* down Black Rd. and Gunco Lane is the excellent *Railway View.* Once into open country we come very near the lovely *Sutton Hall* pub/hotel *(Br45)*, which is an obligatory stop for those of a historical bent. Several miles later at the foothills of the Peak District we pass Oakgrove and Bosley, shortly followed by an aqueduct over the

HOLLY BUSH · BOLLINGTON

River Dane. After curving round the isolated peak, known as The Cloud, we reach **Congleton**. Getting off at *Bridge 75*, the ***Moss Inn***, and further away the ***Waggon & Horses*** can be investigated. A fine example of a "snake" bridge *(Br76)* is met soon. A three-quarter mile stroll West from the *Bridge 79* or *80* will take you to the superb ***Egerton Arms*** in the quaint village of **Astbury**. Passing the National Trust-owned Tudor mansion of Little Moreton Hall *(Br86)*, the Victorian ***Rising Sun*** at **Scholar Green** *(Br94)* may also provide a welcome place of rest. Alternatively, you could stop and observe locking techniques at Red Bull.

The **TRENT AND MERSEY CANAL** is joined at the Kidsgrove canal loop, involving a brief step into Staffordshire. Re-entering Cheshire, you could visit the ***Lawton Arms Hotel*** in **Church Lawton** *(Br135)*. A few miles further the beer oasis that is the ***Royal Oak*** at **Rode Heath** is reached *(Br139)*. At **Wheelock** *(Br154)*, the CAMRA Heritage Pub designated ***Commercial Hotel***, where real cider is served, should be visited. If any provisions are needed, then frequent buses travel from here to **Sandbach** where the ***Lower Chequer*** on Crown Banks or **Crewe**, where the *Albion* on Mill St. is a worthwhile short walk from the station.

Restocked, we carry on through to **Middlewich**, passing the junction with the **SHROPSHIRE UNION CANAL**, where the ***Boar's Head*** *(Br172)* or ***Big Lock*** may be worth popping in. Crossing over the Dane again, the canal runs alongside for a couple of miles passing Broken Cross, Wincham and the ***Salt Barge*** at **Marston** *(Br193)*. The next important landmark is the impressive Anderton Lift, which used to carry boats down into the Weaver Navigation and is currently being restored. The centre of Northwich is only 2 miles away by bus from here. Further along, **Little Leigh** *(Br209)* may provide refreshments in the form of the ***Holly Bush*** (north) and ***Leigh Arms*** (south).

Following the almost mile long Preston Brook tunnel we join the **BRIDGEWATER CANAL**, passing the Runcorn side-branch to the River Mersey. Continuing on the Ring however, passing the ***Ring 'O' Bells*** in **Daresbury** *(Br5)* and two ***Red Lions*** at **Moore** *(Br7)* and **Stockton Heath** *(Br15)*. Bypassing Warrington, the ***Parr Arms*** at **Grappenhall** *(Br17)* beckons. In the pretty village of **Lymm** we find the *Spread Eagle (Br23)*. Finally, we can call in at the ***Swan With Two Nicks*** **Little Bollington** *(Br26A)* for a pint from Cheshire's own Coach House brewery, and maybe to stretch our legs in the National Trust's Dunham Park, before crossing the border into Greater Manchester once again.

Last, but not least, some watering-holes on the Ring's canal side-branches for your consideration:

SHROPSHIRE UNION CANAL: *Bunbury Arms* - Stoak *(Br 138)*, *Harkers Arms/Mill Hotel/ Telfords Warehouse* - Chester, *Old Trooper* - Christleton *(Br122)*, *Shady Oak* - Tiverton *(Br109)*, *Dysart Arms* - Bunbury *(Br105)*, *Travellers Rest* - Alphraham *(Br105)*, *Barbridge Inn* - Barbridge *(Br100)*, *Red Cow/Wilbraham Arms* - Nantwich *(Aquaeduct 20)*, *Shroppie Fly* - Audlem *(Lock 13)*.

Middlewich Branch: *Verdin Arms* - Wimboldsley *(Br19)*, *Badger* - Church Minshull *(Br13)* and *Royal Oak* - Worleston *(Br8)*.

Llangollen Branch: *Dusty Miller* - Wrenbury *(Br20)*, *Bhurtpore Inn* - Aston (a well spent half mile walk from *Br17*), *Swan* - Marbury *(Br23)*, *Willey Moor Lock Tavern* - Willey Moor Lock.*(Br25)*.

BOLLINGTON

POACHERS

Ingersley Road. (From the bus terminus head up the hill to Rainow (not Pott Shrigley).
⏰12-2:30; 5:30-11 Mon-Fri; 12-2:30; 7-11 Sat; 12-2:30; 7-10.30 Sun
Boddingtons Bitter, Marstons Pedigree, Taylor Landlord [H]
The Poachers is a pleasant and very friendly pub with a rapidly growing reputation for good quality, fresh home-made food. Formerly known as the Masonic Arms, it has been created by merging half a dozen terraced cottages. Occupying a corner site it is solidly built from local stone and blends well with its surroundings. Well known for its window boxes and hanging baskets, the Poachers has won the "Bollington in Bloom" award three times. It is situated on the very edge of the village, at the foot of Blaze Hill, a hundred yards from the Peak District National Park. Both the Gritstone Trail and the Middlewood Way pass nearby.

Although a single room, it manages to combine the interests of diverse groups in a way which defeats modern designers. In the centre, diners and drinkers mix affably around the bar. By the door, the comfortable lounge chairs and open fire provide a warm, relaxing and surprisingly quiet niche, where you can stare into the fire while enjoying a pint of real ale. The games area features a pool table and attracts a younger clientele.

You may care to know that there are Wednesday barbecues in Summer, and around once a month these are enlivened by live entertainment. Sheltered from the wind, but overlooking the fields, they are invariably well attended. Winter has its counterpart in the popular Bonfire night.

LORD CLYDE INN

Clarke Lane (leave A523 from Macclesfield at roundabout with the B5090, turn right in 50m).
⏰12-11 Mon-Sat; 12-10.30 Sun
Greenall Mild, B, Draught Bass, guest beer (occasional) [H]
Compact, homely, single bar country inn, offering a cheerful, traditional atmosphere. This listed building was originally built as a weaver's cottage in the 17th century and is reputedly haunted by the friendly ghost of a young girl in a mop cap. A host of pub games are popular including; dominoes, cards, league topping darts, and on Friday nights, skittles. Live singer once a month. Small dining area provides good food at reasonable prices. Flat access for wheelchairs, and toilets on request.

MERIDIAN

Palmerston Street
⏰11-3, 7-11 Mon-Sat; 12-3, 7-10.30 Sun
Boddingtons B, Theakstons Mild, Wilsons Original [H]
Originally two cottages, the internal layout has not changed since. Entering by way of the splendid half-glazed door with its two brass rails, the visitor sees an attractive black and white tiled floor bar area with low-ceilinged rooms off, comprising a public bar with pool, a smaller basic room for darts and an even smaller room with the rare sight of bar skittles. Rear lounge, with leather settles, coal burning stove and piano. Original etched windows and wooden benches. The original bell pushes which were used to summon service are still in evidence throughout, and still function, although they are often unplugged to avoid the landlady being plagued by the insatiably curious, or late night humorists.

The Meridian is a friendly and community-based basic town local. Its beer is served in oversize lined glasses, to guarantee you a full pint. A rare Cheshire outlet for Theakstons Mild. Well kept too. **GBG**

QUEENS ARMS

High Street
⏰2-11 Mon-Thurs; 12-11 Sat; 12-3, 7-10.30 Sun
Robinsons Hatters Mild, Best B [H]
Solidly built, stone pub which is well worth seeking out. Modernised, but comfortable and friendly, with a cosy lounge. There is plenty of space in the main bar area for pub games such as darts, pool, cards and dominoes. Bar snacks are always available. Quizzes every alternate Sunday. Near canal and popular country walk routes. Beer garden in Summer.

RED LION

High Street (up the hill from Palmerston St.)
⏰12-11 Mon-Sat; 12-10.30 Sun
Burtonwood B, plus one other [H]
A friendly back street local set high above the village, with a panoramic view of Bollington from the front step. Meals noon till 9pm (7 at weekends).

REDWAY TAVERN

Redway Lane
(Kerridge, ½ mile south of the village)
⏰12-3, 5.30-11 Mon-Sat; 12-10.30 Sun
Boddingtons B, Courage Directors, guest beer (occasional) [H]
Popular pub with a lot of food-related trade, at the foot of Kerridge Hill, near White Nancy. Promotes itself as a conference centre and wedding venue, with a large car park and accommodation. Extensive children's facilities, both inside and out, including garden, which can get crowded in Summer. Also, across the car park, are pens of chickens, ducks, sheep and rabbits. In the evenings there is regular live entertainment (i.e. music, comedy, cabaret nights), Monday quizzes and "Dance 'n 'Dine" nights, with a 1am licence. Meals served all day Sunday.

ROYAL OAK

9 Princess Street
⏰11.30-3, 5-11 Mon-Thu; 11.30-11 Fri; 11-11 Sat; 12-10.30 Sun
Marstons B, Pedigree [H]
A popular terraced local , tucked away just off the main road. Pool, darts, cards and dominoes played. The worryingly high turnover of landlords has not prevented a consistently friendly welcome being extended to both locals and travellers. Real fire. Yard seating only outside. Snacks available at all times.

SPINNERS ARMS

Palmerston Street
⏰11.30-11 Mon, Fri, Sat; 11.30-3.30, 5.30-11 Tue-Thu; 12-10.30 Sun
Draught Bass, Boddingtons B [H]
A loud, smoky and busy main street local. The many amusements on offer include darts, dominoes, pool and crib. There is a free public car park opposite. Bar snacks available all day.

16

TURNERS ARMS

Church Street (at corner of Ingersley Road)
⏰11-2.30, 7-11 Mon-Fri; 11-3.30, 7-11 Sat;
12-3, 7-10.30 Sun
Marstons Pedigree [H]

A popular community pub opposite the bus
station. Two basic rooms, one of which is
largely a games room with pool table. Up for
sale as we went to press; details may change.

WAGGON AND HORSES

127 Wellington Road.
⏰5.30-11 Mon; 12-3, 5.30-11 Tue-Thu;
12-11 Fri-Sat; 12-3, 7-10.30 Sun
Boddingtons B, guest beers [H]

Pleasant pub with high ceilings dating from
the turn of the century. Friendly, welcoming
and roomy local, which has avoided refurbishment ruin so far. Real fire, darts, pool and satellite TV and benches outside. Jazz nights,
quiz, Sunday disco. One or two, often unusual,
guest beers. Such is Greenall's local reputation
that the wise will probably visit now before the
owners unfeelingly replace yet another favourite pub serving interesting guest beers with a
bland eatery.

BOSLEY

HARRINGTON ARMS

London Road (A523, ¾ mile south of A54)
⏰12-3, 5.30-11 Mon-Sat; 12-10.30 Sun
Robinsons Best B [H]

Family pub catering for all tastes. Friendly,
helpful service and home-cooked food. Open
plan with open fire. Pool room. Garden
provides good, safe play area for children,
including tractor and boat! Coaches welcome.

QUEENS ARMS

London Road (A523, 1 mile south of A54)
⏰5.30-11 Mon; 12-3; 5.30-11 Tues-Fri;
12-11 Sat; 12-10.30 Sun
Boddingtons B, guest beer (Summer) [H]

Fairly small and friendly 17th century pub.
Emphasis on food. No smoking in the separate
dining room. Regular live music, quizzes and
karaoke. Set in lovely surroundings with
pleasant beer garden including childrens' play
area. Kitchen closes 8pm on Sundays.

BOUGHTON

BELLS

1 Boughton
⏰12-11 Mon-Sat, 12-10.30 Sun
Beer range varies [H]

Live music Fridays.

CROSS FOXES

No real ale.

ENGINE HOUSE

No real ale.

GARDENERS ARMS

On the gyratory system at the end of Boughton.
⏰ 5-11 Mon-Fri; 11-11 Sat, 12-10.30 Sun
Banks Mild, B [H]

Popular local, with pool, darts & dominoes.
Thursday folk nights. Real fires and excellent
wood panelling.

BOTTOM OF THE OVEN

STANLEY ARMS

Ankers Lane (off A537 Buxton New Road near Cat & Fiddle Inn)
⏰12-3, 5.30-11 Mon-Fri; 12-11 Sat; 12-10.30 Sun
Marstons B, Pedigree [H]

Friendly and welcoming, the Stanley Arms is an excellent rural pub, set in a small valley just off the
main Buxton road in the Peak District outside Macclesfield. Directly opposite is the start of the
road through the beautiful Wildboarclough on the edge of what remains of Macclesfield Forest and
the foot of Shutlingsloe. The building retains a cottage-style atmosphere. To the left is a dining room
and to the right the bar, leading on to two further rooms. Three coal fires in stone fireplaces generate
a warm, cosy feel, and there are padded settles around the walls.

The separate restaurant, renowned for its duck dishes, closes at 9:30p.m. You can catch
occasional live music, and outside jazz in Summer. Indoor amusements include dominoes and darts
while there is a large garden to the rear with views of the surrounding hills. In fine weather, visitors
can use tables at the front too, and there are even two tables in the porch! The large car park often
fills up on summer weekends, when the well-deserved reputation for good food brings diners from
far and wide. Sadly, this excellent pub is often overlooked by visitors to the nearby and better-
known Cat & Fiddle Inn. A ramp for disabled access should be installed shortly.

LITTLE OAK

99-101 Boughton
⏰11-3, 5.30-11 Mon-Sat; 12-10.30 Sun
**Draught Bass, Greenalls B, Original,
guest beer [H]**

Extended a few years ago, but not spoilt.
Popular, particularly with Law College
Students. Tuesday quiz, jazz on Sunday.
Aquarium. Breakfasts a speciality!

LOCK VAULTS

Hoole Lane
⏰12-11 Mon-Sat, 12-10.30 Sun
Tetley Mild, B [H]

Large canalside pub with big screen TV.
Entertainment most nights.

MOUNT INN

11 The Mount (on Tarvin Rd.)
⏰APH
Boddingtons B, Greenalls B [H]

Friendly, old-fashioned inn with views of the
River Dee. Elevated patio.

WATERLOO

67 Boughton
⏰APH
Tetley B [H]

Small but welcoming pub with a bagatelle
table, pool and darts. Karaoke on Tuesdays.
Disco alternate Saturdays. *Beware the fake
handpump serving keg cider.*

BRADFIELD GREEN

COACH & HORSES

Middlewich Road (A530 at B5076 junction)
⏰12-11 Mon-Sat; 12-10.30 Sun
Greenalls B, Original H]

Recently renovated roadhouse. Spacious open
plan interior with a dining room.

WHAT IS "REAL ALE"? MORE TO THE POINT, WHAT ISN'T?

Personally, I prefer to call it Traditional Beer, but the term Real Ale was coined in the Sixties by the fledgling CAMRA to alert the public to the danger that what had always been known simply as "beer", was on the point of disappearing. The big brewers of the time, motivated as ever by the bottom line rather than any sense of responsibility to their customers or to centuries of culture, were intent on phasing out traditional beer, and replacing it with "keg". The advantages to them (but no-one else) included an infinite "shelf life, no variation in quality, and the fact that no cellarmanship skills were needed.

As ever, Joe Public was losing out, paying over the odds to finance expensive advertising campaigns, and drinking a bland, chilled and uninteresting factory-produced fizz. This was a poor, fake substitute for the real thing, and hence the term Real Ale for the proper stuff.

CAMRA won that particular battle, and real beer is widely available in Britain, with the remaining *No Go "Keg Zones"* being restricted largely to clubs, hotels and a minority of pubs. This does not mean the war is over; keg beer is still with us, but in an updated, even more insidious nineties disguise; 'smoothflow' or 'nitrokeg'.

Typified by the likes of pseudo-Irish/traditional Caffreys and Kilkenny, and promoted as ever by lavish advertising budgets (funded by you!) these are springing up on bars everywhere. Despite the implied tradition in much of the advertising, these are not traditional beers, they are not real ale. Like keg beer, they are pasteurised and dead, so as to prevent the maturation which is essential for quality in beer, and are then given the fake appearance of life by having a mixture of gases pumped into them. *They are the zombies of the beer world, and like such horrors, should be avoided.* They may have the dubious virtue of never being truly bad, but they are consistently bland and insipid. Real Ale can vary, and this is where your discernment comes in. You can enjoy experimenting with dozens of styles, hundreds of different brews, and luxuriate in the sheer variety of traditional beers to be found. The Good Beer Guide is recommended as the best place to find good quality real ale.

Real Ale is a natural living product. It contains yeast which continues to develop flavour in the barrel, producing complex flavours, and ensuring that your ale has character and variety. **"Cask" or "Cask-Conditioned"** are commonly used terms for real beer. Taking care of this needs commitment from the publican, but we think that quality is worth working for. Incidentally, the fermentation of the yeast produces Carbon Dioxide, which gives the beer its 'condition', and a modest natural head. In contrast when a gas cylinder is hooked up to a keg beer, a much greater volume of gas is forced to dissolve, making keg beer fizzy. This can bloat you and have anti-social consequences.
More tea, Vicar?

How can I tell whether I am buying Real Ale?

If in doubt **look for a hand pump**. There are very few fake hand pumps around, and the familiar manual pull should be your guarantee. The picture is less clear where electric pumps are used , but there are few of these in the county. Most 'illuminated boxes' on the bar will contain an aerosol which will squirt something horrid into your glass.

Alternatively, you can ask; your friends or the regulars should be aware, and a good landlord will be proud of his beer (although undertrained staff can be ignorant of the most basic details). Most pubs in the county sell Real Ale, although it must be said that some of it comprises the uninspired offerings of larger brewers.

Out *Inn* CHESHIRE will point you to some of the tastier and rarer brews.

BRERETON
BEARS HEAD HOTEL
Newcastle Road South
⏰ subject to change
**Burtonwood B, Draught Bass,
Theakstons Best B [H]
(Beer range likely to change)**
A superb Grade II listed black and white building dating back to 1615. It is worth a visit just to see it. Whilst it is a hotel with an up-market restaurant, non residents are most welcome to the bar and restaurant . There is an outside cobbled area with "parasols", a delightful setting to sup a pint on a warm summer's evening and feel at peace with the world. It's good to see three real ales in a hotel.It was closed for major refurbishment as we went to press
 P

BRIDGE TRAFFORD
NAGS HEAD
Chester Road (A56)
⏰APH
Greenalls B, guest beer [H]
Food is served all day at the weekend from a varied menu. The dining area is non-smoking. Has a children's menu and a large play area; one for the family.
 P

BROKEN CROSS
BULLS HEAD
Broken Cross (A537, on western fringe of Macclesfield, by roundabout)
⏰11-4, 5-11 Mon-Fri; 11-5, 6.30-11 Sat; 12-5, 7-10.30 Sun
Boddingtons B, Tetley B, guest beer [H]
A two-roomed pub with dining, lounge and games areas. Leaded lights & etched windows. Children only admitted at lunchtimes, if eating. Car park can be difficult to find: left when facing roundabout, then first right.
 P

PACKHORSE
12 Chelford Road (A537, by the roundabout)
⏰11.30-11 Mon-Sat; 12-10.30 Sun
Boddingtons B [H]
This ex-hotel has a public bar, large lounge, quiet room and a varied menu. There are also two dart boards! Children are allowed at lunchtimes.
 P

BROWNLOW
BROWNLOW INN
Wallhill Lane (near Smallwood)
⏰ 12-3, 5.30-11 Mon-Sat; 12-3,7-10.30 Sun
**Boddingtons B, Marstons Pedigree,
guest beer (occasional) [H]**
A busy and popular pub that has a great emphasis on catering, but it is still very much a pub. You will find no lager louts here, which may explain why it is very popular with older people who enjoy the food and the relaxed atmosphere. No food Monday.
 P

BROXTON
BROXTON HALL COUNTRY HOUSE HOTEL
No real ale

BUNBURY
DYSART ARMS
Bowe's Gate Road (opposite the church in the centre of the village)
⏰11.30-3, 5.30-11 Mon-Fri; 11.30-11 Sat; 12-10.30 Sun
Boddingtons B, Fullers London Pride, Taylors Landlord, guest beer [H]
Named after local family, the Dysart Arms is situated opposite the impressively large and ornate red sandstone church in a very picturesque village. This ex-police station has come on in leaps and bounds in the last year under new management. The small, slightly plain, brick exterior, belies an Grade II-listed inn which extends into former outbuildings at the rear. Much converted and extended in recent times, it still manages to retain some of the character of the old pub. The whole renovation has been carried out with consummate taste and respect, a lesson many other planners could learn. The interior is now open and furnished in a rustic style with a multitude of interesting wall prints, display cases and old books. Ancient beams adorned with dried flowers run throughout and there is lovely, brick inglenook fireplace in one of the six rooms. The interior itself, although open-plan and well-lit by the many windows, is in the form of separate areas clustered round the central bar, and thus maintains intimacy. It is heavily timbered throughout, with old wooden furniture and pot plants everywhere.

It is a wonderful place, with tasteful decor, a high standard of food and a good range of well-kept cask ales (the guest being from a small, independent brewery). Both the menu (which includes cheeses from nearby Beeston) and wine list are extensive, though many just pop in for a quiet pint. It has been a Cheshire Life Pub of the Year recently. Food is served all day at weekends, but parents should be aware that children are not permitted in the pub in the evening. The attractive garden overlooks the church. Opening hours may extend in the Summer. The local, working Mill is worth a visit too. Definitely one for a special occasion.

THE COPPER MINE
Nantwich Road (A534, east of A41)
⏰12-3, 7-11 Mon-Sat; 12-3, 7-10.30 Sun
Draught Bass, Burtonwood B [H]
Regular Egon Ronay Guide entry. Live country music Monday evenings.

DURHAM HEIFER
Nantwich Road (A534, ½ mile east of A41T)
⏰ 1.30-3, 5.30-11 Mon-Sat; 12-3, 5.30-10.30 Sun
Banks B, Marstons Pedigree [H]
Former farmhouse, with separate restaurant, pool room. Caravan and camping site.

EGERTON ARMS
Whitchurch Road (junction of A41 & A534)
⏰APH
**Burtonwood B, Forshaws, Top Hat,
seasonal beers [H]**
Large pub with restaurant and outdoor play area. Accommodation available. A good range of Cheshire's Burtonwood beers.

BUCKLOW HILL
SWAN
Chester Road (prominently sited at traffic lights on the busy A556 at the A5034 junction)
⏰12-11 Mon-Sat; 12-10.30 Sun
Greenall B, Original, Tetley B [H]
A 69 room Motel; not a typical pub, but it is good to see a hotel selling three cask beers.

BURLEYDAM
COMBERMERE ARMS

Lodmore Lane (A525, 1/2 mile east of the A530)
⏱12-11 Mon-Sat; 12-10.30 Sun
Draught Bass, Worthington Draught B, 2 guest beers [H]
A large multi-roomed 16th Century pub, with original oak panelling and timbers. The tall wooden bar is decorated with dried hops and winds its way through the various drinking areas. There is an open fire to the low-beamed front room and a pool room at the rear. The building is also reputed to be haunted by the spirit of a monk from the local Abbey, who is apparently buried in a bottle under the front steps! Certainly the locals believe in him.
 The pub holds regular quiz nights and has a substantial following in the local community. The straightforward pub grub is served all day at weekends and there is a separate dining room. Thursday is Steak Night, with a soup and rump for £8.50. The small paved garden features a purpose-built children's play barn with soft adventure apparatus and similar facilities are also available in the back room - seeing is believing! The pub features an interesting range of well-kept guest beers. The Combermere Arms is one of those classic old country pubs you stumble across once in a blue moon. Well worth the drive. GBG
◖ ▶ ⛺ P

BUNBURY
NAGS HEAD
Vicarage Lane (next to the village hall)
⏱6-11 Mon-Fri; 12-12 Sat; 12-10.30 Sun
Boddingtons B, Greenalls B [H]
Original beams, open fires and wattle & daub give character to this 17th century inn. Very much a local, and can be very busy at weekend. Food at weekend only.
▶ ⛺ ᗾ ● P

BURTONWOOD
BRIDGE INN
Phipps Lane (in the centre of the village)
⏱11.30-11 Mon-Sat; 12-10.30 Sun
Burtonwood Mild, B [H]
A sport-oriented pub, with a variety of teams including Ladies' Rounders. The pub has 4 rooms, and children are admitted into the conservatory. It has a bowling green and a play area in the garden. Mementoes of the landlord's Rugby League playing days are displayed. There is a room for hire, and the car park is shared with the Elm Tree. Food weekday lunchtimes only. A Good Beer Guide listed pub, it is close to the Burtonwood Brewery. GBG
◖ ⛺ ● P

CHAPEL HOUSE
No real ale.

ELM TREE
Chapel Lane, corner of Phipps Lane.
⏱7-11 Mon-Thu; 4-11 Fri; 2-11 Sat; 12-10.30 Sun
Burtonwood B [H]
A small two-roomer with a dartboard in the public bar. The Elm Tree shares the car park with the neighbouring Bridge Inn.

FIDDLE I' TH' BAG
Alder Lane (a mile from Burtonwood village, east toward Winwick).
⏱11.30-3, 7-11 Mon-Sat; 12-3, 7-10.30 Sun
Greenalls B [H]
A one roomed pub with several distinct areas giving the impression of separate rooms. There is also a separate restaurant open at busy times, mainly weekends. Fresh meals are home-cooked daily. A play area will keep the children amused.

BUTLEY
ASH TREE
London Road (A523 near Prestbury)
⏱11.30-3, 5.30-11 Mon-Thurs; 11.30-11 Fri-Sat; 12-10.30 Sun
Boddingtons B, Greenalls Original, Theakston Best B [H]
Yet another pleasant local pub recently given the treatment and left with all the individuality of a McDonald's (having been built in 1749 as a coach house). It apparently does not encourage children. The result of the internal restructuring is mainly open plan, but with plenty of small self-contained areas providing an acceptable if slightly medicinal atmosphere, though the bar lacks intimacy. Snacks only in afternoons. No smoking in part of restaurant area. Sadly, the excellent collection of clocks is no longer on display.

CALVELEY
DAVENPORT ARMS
Chester Road (A51, by canal bridge on bend)
⏱6-11 Mon-Fri; 12-2, 6-11 Sat; 12-3, 7-10.30 Sun
Boddingtons B, guest beer (summer) [H]
Inoffensive roadside pub, not long in new hands and trying to become a restaurant pub. Beware when trying to get in and out of the car park.

CHELFORD
DIXON ARMS
Knutsford Road (A537)
⏱11.30-3, 5.30-11 Mon-Fri; 11.30-11 Sat; 12-3, 7-10.30 Sun
Greenalls B, Tetley B [H]
Large, roadside hotel near railway station. Two comfortable drinking areas and a separate dining room. Function room and bowling green, with child's play area nearby. Wheelchair friendly.

EGERTON ARMS
Knutsford Road
⏱APH
Courage Directors, Theakstons Best B, 2 guest beers [H]
A huge, food-oriented establishment, which was tastefully refurbished recently. Despite the largely open-plan nature of the building, the low-lighting, table candles and rustic decor manages to convey some sense of intimacy. Meals served all day. Well-behaved children admitted. Good to see four real ales served in this kind of pub. The guests are from major brewers.

CHESTER

ABBOTS WELL INN
No real ale.

ALEXANDERS
Rufus Court, Northgate Street
(from Odeon cinema, 50yds on right)
⏰11-12pm Mon-Thurs, 11-12.30am Fri-Sat,
12-10.30 Sun
**Courage Directors, Theakstons Best B,
guest beer [H]**
Music or comedy nightly (admission charge).
Guest beer changes weekly.

BAR COAST
No real ale.

BEAR & BILLET
(See overleaf)

BLOSSOMS HOTEL
St John Street
⏰APH
Draught Bass [H]
Typical upmarket provincial hotel bar, compact and comfortable. The walls are strewn with prints of over-muscled livestock in the style of Stubbs. A pianist plays in the foyer six nights a week.

BOATHOUSE
The Groves
⏰APH
**Marsons Pedigree, Theakstons Best B,
Old Peculier, guest beers [H]**
Superbly located riverside hostelry close to picturesque Grosvenor Park. Large windows make the most of the view. No-smoking family room. Food served all day. Beware that guest beer is only in the 'Ale Taster' bar, open only in the evenings. Old Peculier is not commonly found in Cheshire.

BOOT INN
9 Eastgate Row, Eastgate St.
(under the clock, up steps on right, to Rows)
⏰11-11 Mon-Sat, 12-10.30 Sun
Samuel Smiths Old Brewery Bitter [H]
City centre pub dating from 1643; the oldest continuous licence in Chester. Original beams, fireplace and wooden furniture are complemented by a display of the 'wattle & daub' construction.

BOUVERIE
Bouverie Street
⏰APH
Greenalls B, guest beer [H]
Cosy local in the heart of bed-sit land. While the taproom is convivial, the lounge is dominated by a large screen TV.

ALBION
Park Street (next to the city walls on the south-east)
⏰11-3, 5-11 Mon-Sat; 12-3, 7-10.30 Sun
Cains Traditional B, Greenalls Mild, B, Original, guest beer [H]
This is a Victorian street corner local whose three rooms include a snug. Flags, enamel signs and other memorabilia from the First World War are on display, including patriotic posters and part of an old wooden aircraft propeller. An open fire in a tiled fireplace in the snug keeps the chill away, and when this room is used for diners in the evenings, the tables are candle-lit to provide atmosphere. Some of the more unusual artefacts include old 78 records in a display case, and illuminated "Shell" petrol pump tops over the bar. Chocoholics will be particularly taken by the large enamel advertising sign for Fry's chocolate. Many of the tables are converted from treadle sewing machines. The Albion is inevitably popular with tourists thanks to its position adjacent to the City Walls. The food includes home-cooked dishes, and is available until 8pm, except on Mondays. The pub is well known for not using pre-packaged frozen portions, which is one of the reasons it appears in CAMRA's Good Pub Food Guide.
It is encouraging to see traditional mild on sale. Much has been said in criticism of Greenalls in recent years, given their insensitivity to their pub stock, but it must be said in their favour that a large proportion of their estate provides real ale, much of it sells guest beers, albeit from a list, and they still show commitment to cask mild. The Albion is a long-standing Good Beer Guide entry, with a very good reputation for its standard and guest beers. **GBG**

BRANNIGANS
No real ale

BRIDGE INN
Tarvin Road
⏰12-11 Mon-Sat; 12-10.30 Sun
Boddingtons B [H]
Comfortable, opened out pub with 2 pool tables and occasional live acts. Fireplace dominates the lounge area. Has a patio next to the Shropshire Union Canal.

BRIDGEWATER ARMS
16 Crewe Street (off City Road)
⏰12-11 Mon-Sat; 12-10.30 Sun
Greenalls Mild, B [H]
Unpretentious two roomed local near the station with comfortable lounge and bar with TV and pool. Fine Wilderspool Brewery etched windows.

BULL & STIRRUP
8 Upper Northgate St. (between Fountain roundabout and Walls Arch)
⏰APH
Boddingtons B, Cains Traditional B [H]
Traditional pub, no quizzes or entertainment.

CARLTON TAVERN
1 Hartington Street
⏰APH
Worthington Draught B [H]
Large imposing local with a central bar. Fascinating prints and artefacts of the City; a history lesson in itself. The beer, from Bass is unremarkable.

CESTRIAN HOTEL
City Road
⏰6-11 Mon; 12-2.15, 5-11 Tue-Fri;
12-11 Sat; 12-10.30 Sun
Boddingtons B, Flowers IPA, Original [H]
Mainly over 25's meeting place, with function room. A small family run hotel with eight rooms.

CHERRY ORCHARD
Tarvin Road
⏰APH
John Smiths B [H]
Lively and popular suburban pub with frequent events. Open plan and welcoming, it features entertainment Monday, Thursday, Saturday, Sunday.

CHESTER BELLS
21 Grosvenor Street
(next to Grosvenor Museum)
⏰11-11 Mon-Sat; 12-3, 7-10.30 Sun
Boddingtons B, Greenalls B, guest beer [H]
Large brick pub boasting 'quality
accommodation', with numerous drinking
areas and patio. Worth a visit. The guest beer
is from a Greenalls list.

CHICHESTER ARMS
Garden Lane
⏰11.30-11 Mon-Sat; 12-10.30 Sun
Greenalls B [H]
A traditional back street community pub
known locally as the "Chi". A pleasant lounge,
with pool and darts in the public bar.

CLAVERTONS
Lower Bridge Street
⏰APH
Lees B [H]
Café bar restaurant with predominantly Medi-
terranean dishes on the menu. Wood block
floors and wood panelling together with low
beamed ceilings, arches and murals evoke the
Mediterranean theme. Discos and live music.

COACH & HORSES
Town Hall Square
⏰APH
Greenalls B, Original, guest beer [H]
Boisterous pub with a central bar. Plenty of
activities and loud music create the ambience.
The guest beer is from the Greenalls list, but
quality is a problem.

COMMERCIAL HOTEL
St Peter's Courtyard (behind Northgate Street)
⏰APH
Greenalls B, Stones B, guest beer [H]
Quiet, cosy andtucked away from the bustle of
the city. It still has some of the quality of a
small, old-fashioned, chintzy hotel. Patio for
those who wish to lunch or drink alfresco.

CROSS KEYS
Lower Bridge Street (near the Dee bridge)
⏰APH
Boddingtons B, Greenalls B [H]
One room pub with split level lounge. Beware
of the Boddingtons Mild, which is keg. For
real Mild, try one of the other pubs in these
pages.

DEE MILLER
Kingsway
⏰11.30-11 Mon-Sat; 12-3, 7-10.30 Sun
Worthington Draught B [H]
Lively estate pub with large screen TV and
regular event evenings. Bar snacks.
P

DUBLIN PACKET
Northgate Street
⏰APH
**Greenalls B, Original, Stones B, guest beer
[H]**
Long narrow pub off the Town Hall square.
Refurbished in fake Victoriana. Note the
etched windows.

BEAR & BILLET
Lower Bridge Street
⏰APH

Boddingtons B, Lees B, Tetley B, Theakstons Best B, guest beers [H]
This is a large timber framed Black and White Elizabethan building by the old Dee bridge.
Attractive and historic, it is the former town house of the Earls of Shrewsbury. The name has its
origins in the ancient and barbaric practice of bear baiting. Built in 1644, it inevitably has a number
of associated legends, including the inevitable ghost. This one is said to have starved to death.
Having broached the subject of food, you may care to know that the Bear serves only lunchtime
snacks and light meals, but the inner man and woman are catered for by an Indian restaurant, under
separate management, which operates from the upper floor in the evenings. The beer range may vary
somewhat, but the Lees beer is rare in both city and county. Wooden floors and an open fireplace
make this feel like a traditional pub, but the effect is sometimes spoiled by Sky TV and a loud jukebox. Often busy, the Bear is close to the river and the Groves riverside walk. It attracts locals and
visitors at all times of day.

EDWARDS
No real ale.

EGERTON ARMS
Brook Street
⏰APH
Boddingtons B, Tetley B [H]
Small local with a collection of horse
prints. Pool and bagatelle tables.

EIGHT RIGHTS
East Countess Way
⏰11.30-11 Mon-Sat; 12-3, 7-10.30 Sun
**Banks B [E] Camerons Strongarm, guest
beers (summer) [H]**
Large open plan pub on two levels. Popular
with families in summer, not least because of
the play area. Special offers on food most
weeks. Prints of old Chester adorn the walls.
Rare Cheshire outlet for Strongarm.

CHESTER

1 -	Albion	22 -	Falcon	42 -	Shropshire Arms
2 -	Alexanders	23 -	Fat Cat	43 -	Stafford Hotel
3 -	Bear & Billet	24 -	Fortress & Firkin	44 -	Stanley Arms
4 -	Boathouse	25 -	George & Dragon	45 -	Talbot
5 -	Boot Inn	26 -	Golden Eagle	46 -	Telfords Warehouse
6 -	Bouverie	27 -	Jones Wine Bar	47 -	Temple Bar
7 -	Bridgewater Arms	28 -	Liverpool Arms	48 -	Town Crier
8 -	Bull & Stirrup	29 -	Marbororough Arms	49 -	Union Vaults
9 -	Cestrian Hotel	30 -	Mill Hotel	50 -	Victoria
10 -	Chester Bells	31 -	Northgate Arms	51 -	Watergate Inn
11 -	Chichester Arms	32 -	Oddfellows Arms	52 -	Watergates Wine Bar
12 -	Clavertons	33 -	Off the Wall	53 -	Waterloo Inn
13 -	Coach & Horses	34 -	Old Cottage Inn	54 -	Wetherspoons
14 -	Commercial Hotel	35 -	Old Harkers Arms	55 -	Yates Wine Bar
15 -	Cross Keys	36 -	Old Kings Head	56 -	Ye Deva
16 -	Custom House	37 -	Old Vaults		
17 -	Dublin Packet	38 -	Pied Bull Hotel		
18 -	Egerton Arms	39 -	Railway Inn		
19 -	Ermine	40 -	Ryans		
20 -	Fagins	41 -	Ship Victory		
21 -	Falchion & Firkin				

FALCON

Lower Bridge Street, at Grosvenor Street.
☺ APH
Samuel Smiths Old Brewery B [H]

The Falcon is a famous Chester landmark, easy to find, being a striking half-timbered substantial building set on a large crossroads in the town centre. A traditional style pub in an impressive black and white building which is the surviving half of a Twelfth century mediaeval town house. Situated within the city walls on the edge of the main shopping area, it attracts a varied clientele. Reasonably priced meals are available in the front bar. The two-roomed back bar has a stairway leading to an upstairs function room.

Purchased by the Grosvenor family in the 1600s, the building was extensively modified and haphazardly repaired in the 19th century. It was then that it was first used an an inn and a "cocoa house". In 1979 the Grosvenor estate donated the building to the Falcon Trust. After extensive restoration work, the Falcon was re-opened in 1992 by the Duke of Westminster.

Of particular historic note are the large stone piers and a late mediaeval timber partition in the front bar which are the remnants of an elevated "Row" similar to those which can still be seen in Chester's main streets.

Possessed of a spacious bar, with traditional surroundings, it serves traditional beer from Tadcaster in Yorkshire and traditional food. Popular with tourists and locals alike, it can be busy in the evenings and at weekends. This is one of only two outlets for Sam Smiths in Chester.

ERMINE

Hoole Road
☺11.30-11 Mon-Sat; 12-3, 7-10.30 Sun
Worthington Draught B [H]
Relatively modern roadside pub, softened a little by ivy and bench tables. Spacious public and lounge bars. Quiz night and karaoke. Food 12-7 daily.

FAGINS

Newgate Street
☺APH
Burtonwood B, James Forshaws B, Top Hat [H]
Formerly the Plumber's Arms, it has recently undergone a radical but welcome transformation. Friendly and relaxing, it boasts the only beer garden inside the city walls building a regular clientele, it is well-suited to those seeking a decent pint in comfortable surroundings.

FALCHION & FIRKIN

Watergate Street
☺APH
Dagger, Falchion, Cut-throat, Dogbolter, guest beer [H] Addlestones Cask Cider [H]
Long, narrow, non-brewing, Firkin pub with sturdy wooden furniture. Appeals to younger drinkers, with games and quizzes. Patio. Cold snacks all day. The theme beers here and at the Fortress are standard brews with different house names, and may be kept under gas.

FAT CAT

Lower Watergate Street
☺APH
Boddingtons B, Courage Directors, Flowers Original, Theakstons B, XB [H]
Upmarket bar close to the race course, with emphasis on food (all day). Stone floor, old fireplace and barrel-vaulted ceiling add atmosphere.

FORTRESS & FIRKIN

Frodsham Street
☺APH
Firkin Cast, Fortress, Moat, Dogbolter, seasonal beers [H]
Standard Firkin décor, with high ceiling from its previous use as a warehouse. Large canal-side drinking area. Giant games, live music.

GAMEKEEPER

Newall Road
☺APH
Tetley B [H]
Estate pub due to be refurbished soon. Bar billiards and pool are played.

P

GEORGE & DRAGON

1 Liverpool Road (Fountain roundabout)
☺APH
Whitbread beers, guest beers [H]
Large half-timbered pub with accommodation and restaurant. Claims to have the largest selection of real ales in Chester. Regrettably, they mostly come from a national brewer with a penchant for closing independent breweries.

 P

GOLDEN EAGLE

Castle Street
(near Cheshire Regiment museum)
☺12-11 Mon-Thu; 11.30-11 Fri, Sat; 12-3, 7-10.30 Sun
Draught Bass, Hancocks HB (occasional) [H]
Open plan pub in an ancient building with interesting prints. Pub games for the early evening set. Probably the smallest beer garden in Chester.

◀

GROSVENOR HOTEL

Eastgate
☺APH
Ruddles County [H]
Extremely elegant bar as befits the North West's only Five Star hotel. The glass panelled frontage looks out onto Eastgate. Full a la carte menu. Live music Friday and Saturday evenings.

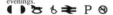

HIGHFIELD HOTEL
No real ale.

JOES WINE BAR
No real ale.

JONES WINE BAR

City Road
☺APH
Theakston Best B [H]
Wine bar with a good reputation for food (served 12 till 9pm). Relaxing decor with candlelit tables. Upstairs bar has live entertainment some evenings, real ale and an extension to 1am Thursday to Saturday. Entry must be before 11pm.

LIVER
No real ale

LIVERPOOL ARMS

Northgate Street
☺APH
Greenalls B [H]
TV dominates the bar in this street-corner boozer. The lounge is more sedate. Next to the site of the old Northgate Brewery. Note the leaded windows.

LORD BYRON
No real ale.

MARLBOROROUGH

St John Street
☺APH
Boddingtons B, Flowers IPA, guest beer [H]
Recently refurbished small city centre pub. Aimed at shoppers and tourists, and food-oriented at lunchtime. The spelling is correct!

MOATHOUSE HOTEL (RANDOLPHS BAR)
No real ale

MOUNT INN

The Mount
☺APH
Greenalls Mild, B [H]
Vibrant local with bar & lounge areas. Sweeping views of the Dee and Chester Meadows from the patio.

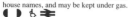

NORTHGATE ARMS
Delamere Street
🕐12-11 Mon-Sat; 12-10.30 Sun
Greenalls B [H]
A fake Irish theme pub, dominated by pool and loud music. Karaoke on Friday and Saturday.

OAKLANDS HOTEL
No real ale.

ODDFELLOWS ARMS
Frodsham Street
🕐11-11 Mon-Sat; 12-3, 7-10.30 Sun
Greenalls Mild, B [H]
A relatively unspoilt city centre local.

OFF THE WALL
St John Street
🕐APH
Boddingtons B, Greenalls B [H]
Large split-level pub catering for shoppers and tourists by day, more of a night club later, with dress restrictions.

OLD COTTAGE
Brook Street
🕐11-3, 6-11 Mon-Sat; 12-3, 7-10.30 Sun
Boddingtons B [H]
Welcoming hostelry in a street well-supplied with public houses. It only lacks a more ambitious choice or real ale! No evening meals at weekends. The garden includes an aviary.

OLD CUSTOM HOUSE
Watergate Street
🕐APH
Banks Mild, Marstons Bitter, Pedigree, Head Brewers Choice [H]
Popular 17th century pub with three distinct drinking areas, once used by the Customs and Excise. It has one of the few beer gardens in the city centre, and is in a convenient location for shoppers, tourists and race-goers alike. Meals are served noon till 8pm on Saturdays. No food on Sundays. **GBG**

OLD HARKERS ARMS
1 Russell Street
🕐11-3, 5-11 Mon-Fri; 12-11 Sat; 12-10.30 Sun
Boddingtons B, Cheriton Diggers Gold, Fullers London Pride, Taylors Landlord, guest beer [H]
Upmarket bar in converted canalside warehouse, with wooden floors, old furniture, prints and books giving a relaxing ambience. Very popular despite premium prices, possibly due to lack of loud music or amusement machines. Evening meals except Friday or Saturday. Doorman prevents overcrowding at weekends. Only regular outlet for Hampshire's Cheriton beer in Cheshire.

OLD KINGS HEAD
48 Lower Bridge Street
🕐APH
Boddingtons B, Greenalls B [H]
Attractive exterior dating from 1662, but this dimly lit pub gives a disappointing overall impression.. Large upstairs restaurant. Accommodation..

MILL HOTEL
Milton Street (To the right of the canal flyover approaching the Hoole Street roundabout)
🕐APH
Boddingtons B, Coachhouse Mill Premium, Weetwood Best Cask B, 8 varied guests [H]
As the name would suggest, this is a hotel converted from canalside mill. Iron pillars, exposed brickwork and thick, wooden beams of the original mill building are still visible. Old Chester photographs adorn the walls. Despite the outward appearance as an upmarket hotel, the large welcoming bar to the right is a haven for real ale enthusiasts, and has a genuine pub atmosphere.
It is the best real ale outlet in the city, and the long bar plays host to a variety of real ales. The range changes constantly, and you should consult the blackboard or the pumpclips on arrival to see what treats are in store. One of the guest beers is always a mild. The house beer is brewed by the local Cheshire brewer Coachhouse from Warrington, and the presence of Weetwood is encouraging support for another Cheshire micro-brewery. Sensibly, the local branch of CAMRA regularly meets at the Mill, and the hotel is a Good Beer Guide entry.
There is some pleasant outside seating on a patio by the canal. Dinner cruises on a barge are available in the summer, departing from right outside. The Mill serves both bar meals and restaurant food, both being good and reasonably priced. The bar has a large screen TV which shows major sporting events, so it can be busy and noisy during needle matches, though room for one of the many marble-topped tables can usually be found. Parking can be difficult as the car park is not big enough, but street parking is usually available outside working hours. **GBG**

OLD QUEENS HEAD
No real ale.

OLDE VAULTS
Bridge Street (a short walk from the Cross)
🕐APH
Greenalls B, Tetley B [H]
Narrow pub with front bar and comfortable rear lounge. Wood and stone floors with some excellent prints of old Chester. The upstairs lounge is accessed off the famous Rows.

PEACOCK
Christleton Road (A51)
🕐APH
Cains Traditional B, Greenalls Mild, B, Original, Tetley B [H]
Large brewer's Tudor pub opened out but retaining a public bar. Children's play area, and Sunday roasts. Good to see Cains beer in the city.

PIED BULL
Northgate Street, corner of King Street.
🕐APH
Greenalls B, Original, guest beer [H]
16th century hotel, with wood panelling and settles. Increasingly food-oriented, but the staircase, inglenook fireplace and coaching signs make a visit worthwhile.

POSTHOUSE HOTEL
No real ale.

QUEEN HOTEL
No real ale.

RAILWAY
Brook Street
🕐APH
Greenalls B [H]
Busy back street local wih old-fashioned atmosphere. Separate darts & pool room.

RED HOUSE
Dee Banks, Farndon Road
🕐11-3, 6-11 Mon-Fri; 11-11Sat; 12-3, 7-10.30 Sun
Draught Bass, Fullers London Pride, guest beer [H]
One lounge pub with an extensive garden leading down to the River Dee. Mooring for boats, but car parking is more limited!

ROSIE O'BRIEN'S
No real ale.

SCRUFFY MURPHY'S
No real ale.

SHIP VICTORY
George Street
☼APH
Tetley B, guest beer [H]
Small free-house, surrounded by car parks as a
result of demolition. Folk club Tuesday,
Karaoke Sunday. Occasionally sells the
excellent Plassey beers from nearby Wales.

SHROPSHIRE ARMS
Northgate Street
☼APH
**Boddingtons B, Flowers IPA, Wadworth
6X, Whitbread Trophy B, guest beer [H]**
Big screen TV is the main feature in this
bare-boards alehouse aimed at the younger
drinker. Despite the large cask ale range, it is
sad to see that lager is the most common
drink. Perhaps they will learn in time.

SPITAL VAULTS
Alma Street, off Boughton.
☼APH
Worthington Draught B [H]
Bagatelle played in the public bar of this local
which is close to the canal but not easy to find.

STAFFORD HOTEL
Real ale only intermittently.

STANLEYS
Brook Street
☼ 12-11 Mon-Sat; 12-10.30 Sun
Greenalls B [H]
Standard refurbished Greenalls pub with a few
remaining features and a Stan Laurel theme.

TALBOT
Walter Street
☼11-11 Mon-Fri; 11-5, 7-11 Sat;
12-5, 7-10.30 Sun
Burtonwood Mild, B [H]
Traditional back street local. Bagatelle played
in front room and pool in back room. Collection of pigs behind the bar. Good quality beer;
try the uncommon Mild.

TELFORDS WAREHOUSE
South View Road (just off the city walls)
☼APH
**Courage Directors,
Theakston Best B, XB [H]**
Live music is very popular in this brick &
beams canalside pub. Panoramic views, a red
phone box and lots of canal-themed memora-
bilia, including a large hoist. It has an upstairs
restaurant and a patio.

TEMPLE BAR
Frodsham Street
☼APH
**Cains Traditional B, John Smiths B,
Theakstons Best B [H]**
Recently extended with mediaeval and
ecclesiastical theme, including a salvaged
pulpit. Large and noisy, live bands make it
popular with younger drinkers. Doormen
used.

TOWN CRIER
City Road / Station Road.
☼APH
**Bass Worthington, Draught Bass,
Stones B [H]**
Large pub opposite the station. Disco, karaoke
& big screen TV make it popular with younger
drinkers. Meals all day Saturday,
none Sunday.

UNION VAULTS
Egerton Street
☼APH
Greenalls B. Festival, Plassey B [H]
Friendly local, with Sunday folk nights.
A former Boddingtons ale house, which due to
the perseverance of the landlord has managed
to keep stocking the splendid Plassey Bitter,
from a Welsh brewery just over the border.

VIA VITA
No real ale.

VICTORIA
Watergate Street
☼APH
Theakstons Best B [H]
A Row level pub dominated by juke box and
machines. Showing signs of wear and tear.
Raised seating area is used for meals,12-7pm.

WAGON & HORSES
No real ale.

WATERGATE INN
New Crane Street (just off the Roman Walls,
by the racecourse Grandstand)
☼11-11 Mon-Sat; 12-3, 7-10.30 Sun
Boddingtons B [H]
Basic, with walls covered by race horse prints.
Nearest pub to football ground. Pool room, TV
and outside tables. Bar snacks available.

WATERGATES WINE BAR
Watergate Street
☼APH
Boddingtons B, Greenalls B [H]
Interesting bar set in a vaulted former wine
cellar, said to be a mediaeval crypt. Extremely
noisy and busy at weekends. The beer is
reported as having a major quality problem.

CAMRA Award-winning Ales
from just over the border...

Tel: Wrexham (01978) 780922

WETHERSPOONS
Foregate Street
☼APH
**Courage Directors, Theakstons Best B,
Youngers Scotch, guest beers [H]**
Typical of its type, wide-open, well-lit and
carpeted, dedicated to mass patronage. Plus
points include non-smoking areas, no music,
and good value food served all day. The down-
side is that beer quality can sometimes
disappoint, and it smacks too much of a
formula. As theme pubs go, it could be worse.

YATES WINE BAR
Frodsham Street
☼APH
Courage Directors, John Smiths B [H]
Large, very noisy pub, popular with younger
drinkers; hence the doormen. Food 12 to 7.

YE DEVA
Watergate Street Row (close to the Cross)
☼APH.
Greenalls B, Tetleys B, guest beers [H]
A bare-boarded Row level-pub, food oriented
at lunchtimes but more boisterous at weekends. A historic building with a separate dining area. Note the inglenook fireplace and the
list of previous licensees. The two guest beers
are usually interesting examples from independent brewers.

CHILDER THORNTON
WHITE LION

New Road (100 yards off the A41, not far from junction 5 on the M53)
⏰11.30-3, 5-11 Mon-Thu; 11.30-11 Fri, Sat; 12-4, 7-10.30 Sun
Thwaites Best Mild, B [H]
This is a friendly, unspoilt, two-roomed country village pub on the outskirts of Ellesmere Port. A true community pub, it has regular customers of all ages from the village and further afield. It comprises two rooms served from a single bar, but many of the regulars prefer to drink in the corridor. Families are welcome in the snug at lunchtimes. There are no amusement machines or other noisy distractions to disturb the atmosphere. There are tables outside and a small garden with swings for the children. The meals are good value, but there is no food on Sundays. The Lion is a listed building, and we are informed that cock fighting used to be held in the loft. Now, however, it is a quiet pub with an open fire to warm the cockles of your heart.

The White Lion is handily placed for visitors to Ellesmere Port Boat Museum and is a good stopping-off point for anyone heading into Liverpool for shopping or sports fixtures. Twice a CAMRA Wirral Pub of the Year, the White Lion has a reputation for serving Thwaites beers from Blackburn at their best. The licensee is one of the most experienced in the area and the pub has appeared in nearly every edition of the national Good Beer Guide.

◖▮ 🐾 🐕 ● P

CHRISTLETON

PLOUGH
Plough Lane (at corner of Rake Lane, south-east of the village on the way to Waverton.)
⏰APH
Greenalls B, Original, Tetley B, guest beers [H]
The Plough is a rambling atmospheric pub with distinctive wooden furniture and a rather more genuine collection of bric-a-brac than a theme pub would have. It is said to have been built in 1750 on the site of a gallows, and has the obligatory ghost! The Battle of Rowton Moor in the English Civil War took place nearby. Disabled visitors will appreciate the designated parking spaces, the ramps and toilets. There is a wide range of meals, and the chef specialises in unusual dishes for the adventurous diner. Meals are served all day on Sundays. The garden boasts barbecue facilities. Despite the inevitable food emphasis in the rear extension, the front, older part of the pub retains much of its atmosphere, and is the perfect setting for a quiet pint, with photographs of old Chester, and coin displays. It features an open fire and a fantastic tiny snug. Overall, the Plough is a very good example of a food-based rural pub. The guest beer changes weekly.

◖▮ 🐾 ♿ ● P

CHILDER THORNTON
HALF WAY HOUSE
New Chester Road (A41 close to M53 Jct 5)
⏰3-11 Mon-Thu; 11-11 Fri, Sat; 12-10.30 Sun
Burtonwood B [H]
An old coaching inn with several rooms, making a compact, friendly local.

🐾 P

CHOLMONDLEY
CHOLMONDLEY ARMS
On the A49 (near Cholmondley Castle, 2½ miles south of the A534)
⏰12-3, 7-11 Mon-Sat; 12-10.30 Sun
Marstons B, Pedigree, guest beer [H]
Restaurant pub in a converted schoolhouse, hence spacious interior and high ceilings. Since its relatively recent establishment in this format, it has consistently maintained a high reputation for the quality of its food. No Sunday lunch.

◖▮ 🐾 ● P

CHRISTLETON
OLD TROOPER
Whitchurch Road (A41)
⏰APH
Boddingtons B, Flowers Original, Marstons Pedigree, Wadworth 6X [H]
Large restaurant/pub with patio by Shropshire Union Canal. Meals all day. Four well-kept real ales served by enthusiastic bar manager.

◖▮ 🐾 P

CHRISTLETON
RING O' BELLS
Village Road
⏰APH
Courage Directors, Draught Bass, Worthington Draught B, Fullers London Pride, [H]
Large two-roomed village pub with plush modern furnishings. Food-oriented but the choice of meals is unambitious. Emphasis is on catering for children and those with more basic tastes. The busy public bar is geared towards drinkers and still attracts a good local trade. Seating available outside with play area .

◖▮ 🐾 ● P 🚭

CHURCH LAWTON
RED BULL
Congleton Road South
⏰11.30-3, 5.30-11 Mon-Sat; 12-3, 7-10.30 Sun
Robinsons Hatters Mild (summer), Old Stockport B, Best B [H]
Canalside pub. Separate dining room upstairs.
◖▮ 🐾 ● P

LAWTON ARMS
Liverpool Road West
⏰11.30-3, 5.30-11 Mon-Thu; 11.30-11 Fri; 11.30-3, 6.30-11 Sat; 12-3, 7-10.30 Sun
Robinsons Hatters Mild, Best B [E]
Two roomed pub with a strong following, and a separate dining room. Traditional pub games.
◖▮ ● P

CHURCH MINSHULL
BADGER
On the B5074 in the middle of the village.
⏰12-11 Mon-Sat; 12-10.30 Sun.
Boddingtons B, Burtonwood James Forshaws B, guest beer [H]
A former pig farm, backing on to the graveyard. Due for refurbishment soon.
◖▮ 🐾 ● P 🚭

27

CHURTON
WHITE HORSE
No real ale.

CLOTTON
BULLS HEAD
Tarporley Road (off the A51)
🕐11-3, 6-11 Mon-Sat; 12-10.30 Sun
Boddingtons B [H]
Roadside eating house with limited menu.
Music can be intrusive at times.

COMBERBACH
DRUM & MONKEY
The Avenue
🕐APH
Drum & Monkey B,
Tetley Dark Mild, B [H]
A small and cosy pub with open fire and a
brass monkey! Close to Marbury Country
Park, Marbury Hall Nurseries and Budworth
Mere. Named after an old organ grinder who
used to entertain the locals here. Nowadays,
local folk groups play every second Wednes-
day. We do not know who brews the house
beer.

SPINNER & BERGAMOT
The Avenue
🕐11.30-3, 5.30-11 Mon-Sat;
12-3, 7-10.30 Sun
Greenalls B, Original [H]
Pleasant multi-room country pub named after
two racehorses once owned by Lord de Tabley
from the nearby estate. Good food and attached restaurant.

CONGLETON
ANTELOPE
No real ale.

BRADSHAWS
No real ale.

BULLS HEAD HOTEL
No real ale.

CASTLE INN
Castle Inn Road (A527, Dane in Shaw)
🕐11-3, 5.30-11 Mon-Sat; 12-3, 7-10.30 Sun
Greenalls B, Original [H]
Just outside the Congleton boundary and
adjacent to the Biddulph Valley Way, a
disused railway line trail.
Children's certificate.

CHURCH INN
Buxton Road
🕐11.30-3, 6-11 Mon-Sat; 12-3, 7-10.30 Sun
Robinsons Hatters Mild, Best B [E]
Large pub with outside facilities for children.
An ample car park and outside seating is
complemented by a pigeon cote. Excellent
bar meals.

CONGLETON
LEISURE CENTRE
Worrall Street
🕐 7-11 Mon-Fri; 7-9.30 Sat; 7.45-10.30 Sun
2 Guest Beers [H]
You can keep fit, develop and assuage a thirst
all in the same building. Ever changing good
quality guest beers, often from the local
Beartown Brewery.

DURHAM OX
West Street
🕐 APH
Tetley B [H]
Comfortable warm pub, blessed with a quiet
area at the back where it is possible to enjoy
conversation.

FARMERS ARMS
No real ale.
*Do not be fooled by the traditional ales and
guest beers sign outside.*

FORESTERS ARMS
Chapel Street (near St Peter's Church)
🕐 APH
Worthington Best B [H]
Nicely appointed pub with two separate
rooms. Children admitted daytime only.
Traditional pub games and a football team.
Town centre location.

GROVE INN
Manchester Road (A34, on traffic island at
Macclesfield & Manchester road junction)
🕐12-3, 7-11 Mon-Sat; 12-3, 7-10.30 Sun
Marstons Bitter, Pedigree [H]
Pub is due for a major refurbishment in 1998.
There is a patio but no lawn.
P

HEATH FARM
Padgbury Lane
🕐APH
**Ind Coope Burton Ale, Marstons Pedigree,
Tetley B [H]**
Large pub with Wacky Warehouse in
extensive grounds. Primarily an eating place
but with pleasant separate bar area and bar
billiards table. No smoking area. Quiz and
Karaoke nights. Food 12 until 10 all week.
A rare outlet in Cheshire for Burton Ale,
whose future is in doubt, as Carlsberg Tetley
threaten to "rationalise" their range.

LION & BELL
No real ale.

LION AND SWAN HOTEL
West Street (at the top of Swan Bank)
🕐11-2.30, 6-11 Mon-Sat;
12-2.30, 7-10.30 Sun
Courage Directors, Theakstons Best B [H]
A large black and white half-timbered 16th
century inn. Comprises hotel, restaurant,
function rooms and a bar. Meals 11-2.30 and
7-9.30. No smoking in restaurant.

MOSS INN
Canal Road
🕐 APH
**Batemans Dark Mild,
Marstons B, Pedigree [H]**
A thriving pub enjoyed by locals, cyclists and
canal usersLarge outside children's play area.
New dining room to be added in 1998.
Meals 12 until 2 all week, 6 until 8 Tuesday
to Friday. Try the excellent Mild. GBG

NEW CORNER PIN
Mill Street, Buglawton
🕐11-3; 6-11 Mon-Sat; 12-3; 7-10.30 Sun
Marstons B [H]
Large, one room traditional working man's
pub with pool, darts, and juke box. On
Saturday lunch-time there is great interest in
horse-racing. Large function hall.
P

OLD KINGS ARMS
1 High Street, near the Town Hall
🕐11-3, 5-11 Mon,Tue,Thu; 7-11 Wed;
11-11 Fri-Sat; 12-3, 7-10.30 Sun
Marstons B, Pedigree [H]
A very old black and white pub with exposed
wood and beams. Worth a visit just to see the
building. Evening food is tapas (no food
Sunday). The garden area has no lawn.
Children admitted daytime, weekdays only.

OLD WHITE LION
22 High Street (opposite town hall)
🕐11-3, 5-11 Mon-Thu; 11-11 Fri-Sat;
12-3, 7-10.30 Sun
Tetley B, guest beer [H]
Late 16th or early 17th century black and white
Tudor inn. Believed to have once been an office used by John Bradshaw, one of the signa-
tories to Charles 1st's death warrant. Open fire
in winter, patio in summer. A public car park
is nearby. Meals lunchtimes and evenings,
Sunday lunch a speciality. New management
and a return of real ale after a quarter of a century.

QUEENS HEAD HOTEL
Biddulph Road, opposite the Railway Station)
🕐 11-5, 7-11 Mon-Sat; 12-10.30 Sun
Ansells Mild, Tetley B [H]
Comfortable pub with a separate public bar.
Plans are in hand to offer B&B. Traditional
pub games. Garden backs onto canal. Food to
return early 1998.
A rare outlet in the county for Ansells.

TOURIST CHESHIRE

Cheshire is almost as well known for it's impressive stately homes as it is for it's dairy farming. As such it has been well frequented by film and television crews for use in such costume dramas as Pride and Prejudice, Moll Flanders and Granada's Sherlock Holmes series. In addition to being the traditional stages for ghost sightings, many of these venerable buildings and gardens have seen a lease of life due the popularity of open air concerts and theatre. Details of opening times and events can be obtained from Tourist Information Centres. Furthermore, some of these tourist attractions and museums now have facilities for light refreshments. However, to take advantage of another historic institution, the English pub, possibly for more substantial fare and stronger beverages (!), here are some recommended nearby haunts:

Alderley Edge & Hare Hill Gardens - *Admiral Rodney*, Prestbury

Adlington Hall - *Davenport Arms*, Woodford (details in "Over The Border" article)

Davenport Arms. (Thieves Neck) Woodford, Cheshire.

Arley Hall & gardens - *George & Dragon*, Great Budworth

Beeston Castle - *Dysart Arms*, Bunbury

Blakemere Craft Centre - *Forest View*, Oakmere

Capesthorne Hall - *Davenport Arms*, Marton

Chester Castle & Walls - *Albion/Bear & Billet/Falcon*

Chester Zoo - *Bunbury Arms*, Stoak

Delamere Forest - *Carriers*, Hatchmere/*Goshawk*, Mouldsworth

Dunham Hall, deer park & gardens [Greater Manchester]- *Swan with Two Nicks*, Little Bollington/
Vine Inn-Dunham Massey

Ellesmere Port Boat Museum - *White Swan*, Great Sutton

Gawsworth Hall - *Harrington Arms*, Gawsworth/*Chain & Gate*, North Rode

Helsby Hill - *White Lion*, Alvanley

Tattenhall Ice Cream Farm - *Sportsmans Arms*, Tattenhall

Jodrell Bank Science Centre & Arboretum- *Red Lion*, Lower Withington

Little Moreton Hall - *Egerton Arms*, Astbury/*Rising Sun*, Scholar Green

Lyme Park - *Dandy Cock*, Disley

Macclesfield Silk Museum - *Castle/Waters Green Tavern*

Mow Cop Folly - *Cheshire View*, Mow Cop

Ness Botanic Gardens - *Olde Harp Inn*, Little Neston

Nether Alderley Mill - *Stags Head*, Great Warford

Northwich Salt Museum - *Salt Barge*, Marston

Northwich, Anderton Boat Lift & museum - *Stanley Arms*, Anderton

Norton Priory Museum & Gardens - *Red Lion*, Moore/*Ring O' Bells*, Daresbury

Oulton Park & Little Budworth Country Park - *Red Lion*, *Shrewsbury Arms*, Little Budworth

Peckforton Castle - *Pheasant*, (Higher) Burwardsley

Quarry Bank Mill & Styal Country Park- Styal, *Ship*/Wilmslow, *Swan*

Stapeley Water Gardens & Yesteryear Museum - *Red Cow*, Nantwich

Tabley Hall - *Windmill*, Tabley/*Smoker* and *Golden Pheasant*, Plumley

Tatton Hall, deer park & gardens - *Angel/Cross Keys*, Knutsford

Wirral Country Park - *Red Lion*, Parkgate/*White Lion*, Childer Thornton

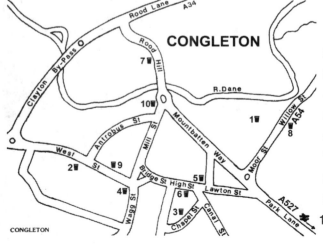

1 - Congleton Leisure Centre
2 - Durham Ox
3 - Forester's Arms
4 - Lion and Swan Hotel
5 - Old Kings Arms
6 - Old White Lion
7 - Rams Head
8 - Shakerley Arms
9 - Staffordshire Knot
10 - Three Arrows

RAILWAY

Biddulph Road (opposite the Railway Station.
① 12-2.30; 4.30-11 Mon-Fri; 12-11 Sat; 12-
10.30 Sun

**Boddingtons B, Worthington Draught B
[H]**

Large pub that is rapidly developing its catering side, but there are two rooms for drinking
only. Food all day at weekend. No smoking in
the dining area which has recently been extended. Traditional pub games and a bowling
green. Yards from the canal.

RAMS HEAD

Rood Hill. (A527, off Rood Lane, A34,
towards Manchester)
①APH

Highgate Mild, Tetley B [H]

Small busy urban neighbourhood pub with
virtually untouched interior; the last of its kind
in the town. Two rooms and an enclosed half-
covered area that is a pleasure to drink in on
hot balmy nights. Traditional pub games.
Meals planned for 1998. The car park is tiny.
The rare Highgate Mild is wonderful!

ROBIN HOOD

Buxton Road
①11.30-3, 5.30-11 Mon-Fri; 11-11 Sat;
12-10.30 Sun

**Batemans Dark Mild, Marstons B,
Pedigree, Head Brewers Choice [H]**

This friendly, family run pub is conveniently
close to the Macclesfield Canal, part of the
famous Cheshire Ring. The good beer, food
and open fire are popular with boaters and
visitors alike. Small separate restaurant.

ROSE & CROWN

West Street
①11-3, 5-11 Mon-Thu; 11-11 Fri-Sat;
12-3, 7-10.30 Sun

Burtonwood B [H]

Divided into two areas with the public bar end
having two pool tables. The lounge area has an
"olde world" atmosphere.

SHAKERLEY ARMS

Willow Street.
(follow signs to Buxton from town centre)
① APH

Bass Toby Cask, guest beer [H]

Very busy pub with a large following of
regulars. Traditional pub games and a football
team. Two separate drinking rooms.

STAFFORDSHIRE KNOT

West Street
①APH

Greenalls Bitter [H]

Large well appointed pub. Children allowed
lunchtimes only. Varied bar menu includes old
British favourites such as liver & onions.

THREE ARROWS

Mill Street (at end of main dual carriageway)
①5.30-11 Mon; 12-11 Tue-Sat; 12-10.30 Sun

Boddingtons B, guest beer (occasional) [H]

Lively pub that often has live music and
karaoke. Children admitted up to 7.30.
Outside drinking area has no lawn.
Meals 12-4.30.

COTEBROOK

ALVANLEY ARMS

Forest Road (A49)
①11.30-3, 5-11 Mon-Sat; 12-3, 6-10.30 Sun (may open all day at weekends in summer)

Robinsons Hatters Mild, Best B [H]

The Alvanley Arms is a lovely and imposing Georgian building of brick & local sandstone. Like so
many of the best rural pubs, it has been both a farmhouse and a coaching house, and indeed the
family still own the stables and surrounding farmland. As you enter through a tiled hallway from the
cobbled frontage with its mosaic star and free-standing inn sign, look out for the map of Olde
Cheshire. There is plenty of character inside with beams and an open fire. Prints of hunting scenes
and fascinating old photographs of the pub adorn the walls and there is a most impressive timber fire
surround in the back room. The brassware includes chestnut roasting pans. There is a separate
lounge dining room on the left, and the bar is on the right.

The garden includes a one acre duck pond, and the family keep Shire Horses. Food
predominates at all times and a speciality of the house at the weekend is the fresh fish menu.
The standard is such that the pub is included in the CAMRA Good Pub Food Guide.
There are also six en-suite bedrooms.

THROSTLES NEST

Buxton Road

Bass Toby

*No further details as the landlord does not
want to go into a real ale guide.
Presumably, he does not want your custom.*

UNICORN

Holmes Chapel Road
(adjacent to West Heath shopping centre)
①APH

Robinsons Hatters Mild, Best B [H]

A modern building with a separate public bar.
The lounge is quiet and peaceful; ideal if you
want to talk. Sunday lunch is a carvery. Tables
outside. Traditional pub games and a football
team.

WAGGON & HORSES

Newcastle Road
(at junction of A34, A54 & A534)
① 12-11 Mon-Sat; 12-10.30 Sun

**Batemans Dark Mild; Marstons B,
Pedigree, Head Brewers Choice [H]**

Busy bustling pub, popular with all. Pool table
and occasional special nights. No meals on
Sundays. GBG

WHARF

Canal Road
① 11.30-3, 5-11 Mon-Thu; 11-11 Fri-Sat;
12-10.30 Sun

Greenalls Mild, Bitter, Original [H]

A warm and inviting pub, popular with locals
and canal users. The dining area is no smoking
and offers an imaginative menu.
Traditional pub games.

COPPENHALL MOSS

WHITE LION

35 Warmingham Road
① 11.30, 7-11 Mon-Sat; 12-10.30 Sun

Boddingtons B, Greenalls Mild, B [H]

Welcoming country-style pub on the edge of
Crewe. There is a separate restaurant, and food
is served all day on Sundays. Pleasant garden,
5-a-side pitch & covered barbecue.

CREWE

ALBION
1 Pedley Street (at the corner of Mill Street)
⏰7-11 Mon-Thu; 2-11 Fri; 12-11 Sat; 12-3, 7-10.30 Sun
Tetley Dark Mild, B, 2 guest beers [H]
The Albion is a Victorian street corner town local, full of railway memorabilia, including logos, photos and an "Albion" engine nameplate on the chimney breast. This is hardly surprising, given the town's close association with the railways. Don't let the unprepossessing exterior put you off, this is a classic old-fashioned town pub catering for the community and visitors (particularly those waiting for a train at the famous Crewe junction). Though primarily a drinking venue, the clientele are from both sexes and all ages. Light is filtered through the original etched windows onto copper-topped tables. The lounge walls are decorated with an impressive array of beer mats, pump clips and a CAMRA mirror. There is a poolroom to the rear particularly popular with the young and a front tap-room with a dartboard. It is of course handy for the station and the town centre.

The frequently changing guest beers are from small independent breweries, as is attested to by the huge collection of pump clips framed throughout the pub. It has provided the grateful locals with over 500 different beers in two years. Current and up-coming beers are handily listed on a chalkboard next to the corner bar. The landlord is justifiable proud of the range of beers he provides, including the well-kept cask mild. As a further indication of its impeccable credentials, it is one of the rare outlets for Real Cider in the county. Needless to say, it has been a CAMRA pub of the year, and a regular entry in the Good Beer Guide. This is certainly one to visit if you have an hour between trains. Turn left out of the station, right at the lights into Mill Street, and look out for the Albion on your right. **GBG**

ANGEL
No real ale.

ASHBANK
Pym's Lane (at Minshull New Road corner)
⏰12-11 Mon-Sat; 12-10.30 Sun
Boddingtons B, Tetley Mild, B [H]
Spacious open-plan pub near the Rolls-Royce works, showing evidence of its 1930's origins. Entertainment includes Quiz (Thu), Karaoke (Sun) & live music (alternate Saturdays).

BANK
13 Nantwich Road (100 yards from railway station, near Royal Hotel)
⏰APH
Banks B, Camerons Strongarm [H]
New pub (opened 1997). One, open-plan bar area with several TV screens.
Rare Cheshire outlet for Stongarm.

BELLE VUE
No real ale.

BRIDGE
167 Broad Street (Coppenhall)
⏰APH
Greenalls Mild, B, Festival Ale [H]
A local with separate lounge and bar. Pool, darts & dominoes played. A welcome refurbishment is due in 1998.

BRITISH LION
Nantwich Road
⏰12-3, 7-11 Mon-Thu, Sat; 11-11 Fri; 12-10.30 Sun
Ind Coope Burton Ale, Tetley B, guest beer [H]
Homely pub, handy for Crewe Alexandra F.C. Try the Burton Ale before they withdraw it.

BROCKEL BANK
Weston Road (A5020 from Crewe to M6)
⏰APH
Wadworth 6X [H]
Large open plan pub near the Sorting Office. Emphasis on food, served from 10.30 to 10 every day. Admits children till 9pm, and provides play areas, including facilities for the very young.

BRUNEL ARMS
156 West Street (corner of Goddard Street)
⏰12-11 Mon-Sat; 12-10.30 Sun
Chesters Mild, Whitbread Trophy [H]
Friendly two-roomed local doing B&B.
One of the oldest pubs in the West End.
Fascinating fish tank in the bar.

BRUNSWICK
Nantwich Road
⏰APH
Boddingtons B, Whitbread Trophy, guest beer [H]
A busy, student pub.

BULLS HEAD
No real ale

CAPTAIN WEBB
Underwood Lane. (north end, in Coppenhall)
⏰1-3, 7-11 Mon-Sat; 12-3, 7-10.30 Sun
Websters B [H]
Modern pub in mature housing area. Separate public bar with pool table and pleasant lounge.
P

CHAMPIONS
No real ale.

CREWE ARMS HOTEL
No real ale.

CROSS KEYS
Romer Street
⏰APH
Marstons Pedigree, Tetley B, guest beer [H]
Large welcoming two-roomed former coaching inn with a function room upstairs. Now a steak pub with good value meals.
 P

CROWN
26 Earle Street (near the Market)
⏰11-11 Mon, Fri, Sat; 11-5.30, 7-11 Tue-Thu; 12-3.30, 7-10.30 Sun
Robinsons Hatters Mild, Best B [H]
Unspoilt four roomed pub unaltered for some time. Retains many original features.

DELAMERE ARMS
Underwood Lane (corner of Broom Street)
⏰12-4, 7-11 Mon-Fri; 11-11 Sat; 12-10.30 Sun
Tetley Dark Mild, B [H]
Known locally as the "Blazer". Friendly pub keen on darts, dominoes & pool. Has its own football team.

DUKE OF BRIDGEWATER
2 Wistaston Road
⏰12-11 Mon-Sat; 12-3, 7-10.30 Sun
Burtonwood B, James Forshaws B [H]
A friendly local near the centre of town. Good value lunches. Try the Forshaws; one of Burtonwood's harder to find brews.

EARL OF CHESTER
Wistaston Road (near the swimming baths)
⏰APH
Greenalls B, Stones B [H]
A street-corner local with good value beer.

EARL OF CREWE
Nantwich Road
⏰APH
Draught Bass, Greenalls B.
Theakstons Best B, guest beer [H]
Large old pub with regular live music at weekends. It runs its own beer festival in the spring. The garden has a children's play area.

1 - Albion
2 - Bank
3 - Bridge Inn
4 - British Lion
5 - Brocklebank
6 - Brunel Arms
7 - Brunswick
8 - Captain Webb
9 - Cross Keys
10 - Crown
11 - Delamere Arms
12 - Duke of Bridgwater
13 - Earl of Chester
14 - Earl of Crewe
15 - Express
16 - Flying Lady
17 - Hop Pole
18 - Horseshoe
19 - Kings Arms
20 - Lion and Swan
21 - Lyceum Theatre
22 - Orient Express
23 - Prince of Wales
24 - Raven
25 - Sydney Arms
26 - Three Lamps
27 - White Lion

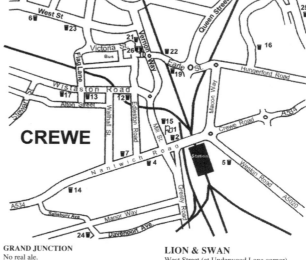

CREWE

EIGHT FARMERS
Parkers Road (near Leighton Hospital)
☺12-2.30, 5.30-11 Mon-Fri; 12-11 Sat;
12-3, 7-10.30 Sun
Banks B, Camerons B [H]
Large & welcoming modern two-roomed estate pub. Tuesday quiz. Home cooked meals, but no food Sunday evening. Camerons is an unusual brew for Cheshire.

EXPRESS
39 Mill Street (50 yards from Nantwich Road)
☺2-11 Mon-Thu; 12-11 Fri,Sat; 12-10.30 Sun
Burtonwood B [H]
Multi-roomed pub with live music Fri & Sun, sing-it-yourself on Thu & Sat. Sun lunch 12-4.

FLYING LADY
Coleridge Way
☺4-11 Mon-Thu; 12-11 Fri-Sat; 12-10.30 Sun
Boddingtons B [H]
Friendly local open plan estate pub built in the early 70's. Regular weekend entertainment.

GEORGE
645 West Street (at Sunnybank Road junction)
☺12-3, 5-11 Mon-Fri; 12-11 Sat;
12-10.30 Sun
Tetley B [H]
A welcoming two-roomed pub with large garden and play area.

GRAND JUNCTION
No real ale.

HOP POLE
Wistaston Road (near the swimming baths)
☺12-3, 7-11 Mon-Sun; 12-10.30 Sun
Greenalls B, Original [H]
An interesting multi-roomed pub, full of character, with its own bowling green. Sunday lunch available.

HORSESHOE
North Street (opposite the Methodist Chapel)
☺12-11 Mon, Fri, Sat; 6.30-11 Tue-Thur;
12-10.30 Sun
Robinsons Hatters Mild, Best B [H]
Four-roomed popular pub with lively atmosphere and a strong local following. There is a large function room upstairs.

KINGS ARMS
56 Earle Street (on the road from Crewe centre to the Grand Junction retail park)
☺11.30-11 Mon-Sat; 12-10.30 Sun
Boddingtons B, Chesters Mild, Whitbread Trophy [H]
Four roomer with public bar. Try the real, Chesters cask mild, before it disappears.

LION & SWAN
West Street (at Underwood Lane corner)
☺APH
Boddingtons Mild, B [H]
A popular corner pub in Crewe's West End. Carefully renovated in the 1980's. Try the rare Boddies Mild, before it disappears.

LYCEUM THEATRE
Heath Street (town centre)
☺APH
Ruddles County [H]
An old theatre dating from 1911. Real ale served in the cellar bar (except in the summer break). Good to see real ale in such a venue.

MERLIN
Bradfield Road, Leighton
☺12-11 Mon-Sat; 12-10.30 Sun
Boddingtons B, Greenalls Mild, B [H]
Large friendly open plan pub with a good range of meals at sensible prices.

NEW BURTON
No real ale.

ROOMS AT THE INN

Often in these pages you will see the term "multi-roomed". Clearly we see this as an advantage, but why?

Choice!

A good traditional pub will have rooms which have different characters or atmosphere. The origin, (aside from sheer architectural considerations) is in the historic social structures which led to different classes or genders being able to drink separately without the perceived discomfort of sharing space with those they would prefer to avoid. We are a little less stuffy these days, but there are still good reasons to retain such choice. Separating smokers, lovers of music, children and players of fruit machines, from those who want a quiet drink and a chat can only be a sign of good customer service.

Vast numbers of pubs have been opened out in recent years, courtesy of the steel girder and the well-meaning but misplaced views of the licensing Magistrates. Their theory that trouble will occur if customers cannot be seen from the bar is demonstrably incorrect. Troublemakers will find a quiet spot regardless of whether this is a snug, a car park or a handy bus shelter.

We can see some merit in the argument that bar staff (assuming they are not too busy) may see drunken rowdiness before it escalates, but surely this is a need for better oversight by staff as they collect glasses, or by fellow customers, rather than a wholesale demolition of a historic pub interior? Another point is that those who choose to patronise the big drinking barns on a Friday or Saturday night can testify that they are far from trouble-free.

We love multi-roomed traditional pubs This guide shows you where to find them.

SMOKING IN PUBS

Smoking, we hear may possibly be banned in pubs. This is a subject likely to generate as much heat as smoke. Many people dislike going to pubs, because "they are smoky", while smokers of course cherish their freedom to enjoy their vice.

One answer is already available – multi-roomed pubs with a smoke room. Many pubs have suffered the in-dignity and loss of character caused by "opening out", caused by the blinkered attitude of some Magistrates Benches, which insisted on all parts of the pub being capable of "supervision" from the bar. The result has been many a soulless barn, with the outpourings of smokers being shared amongst all present.

Wouldn't it be so much better if we had retained separate rooms? You could choose whether to inhale or not.

ORIENT EXPRESS
33 Earle Street
⏰APH
Hydes Light, Mild, B [H]
The ultimate final drinking stop – Chinese food served all day at takeaway prices, and accompanied by cask ale. Serves two of the three Hydes cask milds.

PRINCE OF WALES
120 West Street
⏰APH
Chesters Mild, Whitbread Trophy [H]
Large two-roomed popular pub in West End.

RAVEN
1 Brockhouse Drive
⏰APH
Boddingtons B, Cains Traditional B [H]
Recently modernised estate pub with friendly customers and reasonably priced food.

ROCKWOOD
No real ale.
Do not be fooled by the "Cask Ales" sign.

ROOKERY WOOD
Weston Gate (A5020 from Crewe to the M6)
⏰APH
Courage Directors, Marstons Pedigree, Theakstons Best B, Wadworth 6X, Worthington Draught B [H]
Large open plan pub, only recently opened. Strong emphasis on food, serving from noon to 9 or so daily. Provides massive play areas.

ROYAL SCOT
No real ale

SYDNEY
Sydney Road
⏰12-11 Mon-Sat; 12-10.30 Sun
Robinsons Hatters Mild, Best B [E]
Friendly, welcoming three-room local. Large function room, bowling green and restaurant.

THREE LAMPS
15 Earle Street (close to the market)
⏰11-3, 7-11 Mon-Thu, 11-5, 7-11 Fri, Sat;
12-3, 7-10.30 Sun
Banks B [H]
Horseshoe-shaped bar. Children admitted only at lunchtimes. You can expect full measure here in oversized glasses. Beware of the keg Hansons Bitter served on a fake handpump.

VICTORIA
No real ale.

VINE
No real ale.

WHITE LION
Ford Lane (corner of Walker Street)
⏰12-4, 7-11 Mon-Sat; 12-3, 7-10.30 Sun
Tetley Mild, B [H]
Popular West End local with open plan bar. Due for a revamp. Patio but no garden.

DARESBURY
RING O' BELLS
Old Chester Road
⏰12-11 Mon-Sat; 12-10.30 Sun
Boddingtons B, Greenalls Mild, B, Original; Marstons Pedigree, guest beer [H]
A popular pub in Lewis Carroll's birthplace, indeed, the Lewis Carroll Society meets in the parish room next door. The Ring o' Bells is very well and tastefully decorated, and is laid out on a number of levels. On the extreme left is a luxurious library-dining room with lots of paintings and a mural of the Mad Hatter's Tea Party. It was the former Sessions room, and now boasts a musicians' gallery. Behind it, the airy conservatory leads via a sunny patio to the attractive tiered garden and the sandstone out-buildings. There is a wood burning stove in the small vault to the right. Under the stairs is the highlight of the pub; a tiny alcove equipped with a variety of games and a wooden table inlaid with old coins.
This is the local for Lord Daresbury (Mr Greenall) and perhaps understandably, this could be regarded as the flagship of the company. The guest beer is from the Greenalls list and is changed every 3 months.

CROFT
HORSESHOE
Smithy Lane
⏰APH
Tetley B [H]
Comfortable pub at centre of old village. Low ceiling in lounge bar. Separate dining area.

PLOUGH
Heath Lane
⏰12-3, 5.30-11 Mon-Sat; 12-10.30 Sun
Greenalls Mild, B, Original, Marstons Pedigree, guest beers [H]
Isolated, ex-spinning mill, one mile north of village. Completely refurbished and extended recently, yet retaining cobbled frontage, beer garden and patio. A friendly locals pub.

GENERAL ELLIOT
Lord Street
⏰12-3.30, 5.30-11 Mon-Fri; 11-11 Sat;
12-10.30 Sun
Tetley Mild, B, 4 guest beers [H]
Large, multi-level, 150 year old building with separate vault, lounge and dining rooms. Play area in garden. One guest beer will be from a small independent brewery. Food served all day Sunday.

CROWTON
HARE & HOUNDS
Station Road
⏰ 12-3, 5-11 Mon-Fri; 11-11 Sat;
12-3,7-10.30 Sun
Greenalls B, guest beer [H]
Village centre pub with four separate comfy and inviting rooms. The guest beer is from the Greenalls list.

CUDDINGTON
WHITE BARN
Forest Road (A49)
⏰ 12-11 Mon-Sat; 12-10.30 Sun
Boddingtons B, Greene King Abbot, Websters Green Label [H]
Dimly lit, and full of bric-a-brac. Loud music and satellite TV. Could do with a refurbishment.

CUERDLEY
CUERDLEY CROSS
Dans Road (A562)
⏰ APH
Greenalls Mild, B [H]
Large roadside pub in shadow of Fiddler's Ferry power station. Undergoing major refurbishment.

CULCHETH

CHERRY TREE
Common Lane
⏰12-11 Mon-Sat; 12-10.30 Sun
Tetley Mild, B, 2 guest beers [H]
Large, open-plan, food-based pub in the centre
of the village. No smoking dining area. Patio
with seating at front of building.

NEW INN
474 Warrington Road
⏰12-11 Mon-Sat; 12-10.30 Sun
Tetley Mild, B [H]
Recently refurbished, two-roomed local.
Now with conservatory and dining room.
Food served right through until 7pm on
Sunday. Some outside seating.

PACK HORSE
55 Church Lane (next to parish church)
⏰11.30-11 Mon-Sat; 12-10.30 Sun
Greenalls B, guest beer [H]
Five minutes walk from the centre of the
village. Named after the animals that carried
goods over the local marshes. Upstairs
function room available.
No meals Tue, Sat, Sun.

DARNHALL

RAVEN
Swanlow Lane
Times not provided
Burtonwood B [H]
200-year old pub which has been extensively
modernised.

DEAN ROW

UNICORN INN
102 Adlington Road (A5102)
⏰11.30-11 Mon-Sat; 12-10.30 Sun
Boddingtons B, Greenalls Original [H]
One of three local Greenall's pubs extensively
"modernised" without reference to local charm
and character. Luckily, the facade of the
original attractive exterior is largely
maintained. Undeniably popular, at least
during the "honeymoon period", but must this
inevitably be at the expense of structural
alterations which destroy forever the internal
history, individuality and local character? The
equally popular, excellent Davenport Arms in
nearby Woodford (see "Over The Border" article) suggests not. Greenall's architects should
visit the Hanging Gate, Higher Sutton and
learn a thing or two.

DELAMERE

FISHPOOL
Fishpool Road
⏰12-3, 6-11 Mon-Sat; 12-10.30 Sun
Greenalls Mild, B, Original, Tetleys B [H]
Untouched country pub with five rooms,
on edge of Delamere forest.

FOURWAYS INN
Chester Road
⏰11.30-3, 6-11 Mon-Sat; 12-3, 7-10.30 Sun
Tetley B [H]
Large, modern, roadside pub – food oriented.

DAVENHAM

BULLS HEAD
465 London Road (in the centre of the village)
⏰11.30-11 Mon-Sat; 12-10.30 Sun
Greenalls B, Original; Theakstons Best B; guest beer [H]
The Bull's Head is an especially attractive grade II listed coaching inn dating back to 1764. It is set
back from the road behind a cobbled frontage, which is all too often cluttered by parked cars. The
passageway under the building, once the way into the yard for coaches, now leads to the car park.
The old stables still survive. Over one of the doors is an engraved stone bearing the initials of the
first tenant, one John Henry Royal. There are two entrances to the building. That on the left leads to
a bar and snug, created from adjoining cottages, with low ceilings, beams and a cosy atmosphere.
This is very much a social centre for the village, and this part of the pub can become very crowded,
especially when the television is on. The door on the right leads into a comfortable lounge, where
the emphasis is on the bar meals. This area has the air of a country hotel, with a flight of stairs up to
the non-smoking restaurant. All of the rooms have benefited from a restrained and tasteful refurbishment at the end of 1997, and the walls are almost covered in old prints, many with a historic aspect.
There is the inevitable ghost, although this one is obligingly quiet. She is only rarely seen, and
disappears at once.
   The home-cooked food is highly regarded locally, and the prices are not unreasonable.
Meals are available from noon till 8pm on Sundays, and at lunchtime and evening every day of the
week. The guest beer, although it is from the Greenalls list, is often interesting. Deliveries are
unfortunately only once a week, so the guest is likely to be on from Thursday evening for between
two and four days only.

VALE ROYAL ABBEY ARMS
Chester Road (A556)
⏰11.30-11 Mon-Sat; 12-10.30 Sun
**Boddingtons B, Greene King IPA, Abbot,
Websters Green Label [H]**
Large sandstone roadside pub, opposite the
road for Delamere Forest. Games room, large
through lounge and conservatory to rear.

DISLEY

ALBERT
Buxton Road
⏰APH
**Vaux Samson, Double Maxim,
Waggle Dance, Wards Best B [H]**
Small local serving excellent real ale in a
pleasant atmosphere. The food is simple but
plentiful at reasonable cost. Well worth a visit.
The Waggle Dance tastes of honey; those who
do not like their beers bitter will enjoy trying
this. So far as we know, the Albert is one of
the very few pubs serving this distinctive beer
in Cheshire.

CRESCENT
Buxton Road
⏰11.30-3, 5.30-11 Mon-Sat; 12-10.30 Sun
Robinsons Hatters Mild, Best B [H]
Traditional end-terrace on busy A6, with a
games room separate from the lounge. A
friendly local, with a real fire in winter.

DANDY COCK
(See overleaf)

DAVENHAM
ODDFELLOWS ARMS

21 London Road
⏰12-3.30, 5.30-11 Mon-Sat (except Tue lunch); 12-3, 7-10.30 Sun
Greenalls Mild, B; Tetley B [H]
Set on a bend in the road at a junction with a one-way street, your first test is to get into the car park. If you walk round to the front of the pub, instead of using the back door, you will note the cobbled frontage and the floral display. The etched windows supply a clue as to the internal layout, bearing the words 'bar' and 'smoke room'. Once inside, the visitor will notice the pleasant vault on the left. This is distinguished by a display case of OO-scale railway engines, all said to be in working order. There are a number of railway prints scattered around the walls. The vault is furnished with domino and crib tables and a TV. Beyond the bar, on the left, is a comfortable snug, while on the right are two rooms warmed by gas coal-effect fires. One of these rooms is usually set aside for diners. The food is all home cooked and is available every lunchtime except Tuesday. There is a popular Sunday roast.

        Originally operating as a beer house, with no spirits licence, the Oddfellows is now a small, cosy, village local. It plays host to a Golfing Society. The garden includes a children's play area and a patio. The Mild is a good seller, thanks to a high turnover. Davenham is now virtually a suburb of Northwich, but it is in a conservation area and still retains much of the atmosphere of a quiet village, especially since the by-pass was opened. The lanes nearby offer good walking and cycling, and the village is only a mile from the Trent & Mersey Canal and Cheshire Ring Walk, as mentioned in articles elsewhere in Out *Inn* CHESHIRE.

MOUSETRAP
Buxton Old Road, (close to A6 traffic lights)
⏰APH
Boddingtons B, Ruddles County, Websters Yorkshire B [H]
The oldest pub in the village, but the interior has been altered, a central bar serving a single room. Small front patio; mainly a young drinkers' pub.

PLOUGH BOY
Buxton Old Road
⏰ 12-11 Mon-Sat; 12-10.30 Sun
Vaux Waggle Dance, Wards Best B [H]
Small, cosy pub, up the hill a little from the A6. Can be quiet, unless singing, darts or quiz nights are in progress!

RAMS HEAD
Fountain Square (in the village centre)
⏰APH
Beer range subject to change
Large village centre pub. Closed for refurbishment as we went to press.

WHITE HORSE
Buxton Old Road
⏰11.30-3, 5.30-11 Mon-Sat;
12-3, 5-10.30 Sun
Robinsons Hatters Mild, Old Stockport B, Best B, [H]
Pleasant village pub with good food at fair prices. Not one for families.

WHITE LION
Buxton Road (¼ mile south of the centre)
⏰APH
Lees B [H]
Friendly atmosphere and intimate booths. The food is basic and inexpensive. A rare outlet in Cheshire for Lees beer.

BEHIND BARS

"*I wish to register a complaint!*" began John Cleese in that example of poor customer service, the dead parrot sketch. No guide written for consumers can omit advice on how to complain, and pub-goers can often receive poor service, even unwittingly.

- When you pay for a pint, the licensee expects to be paid in full. Similarly, you should receive a full pint, not 90%. We recommend that you politely ask them to "*squeeze a drop more in*", or "*top it up please*".
- If you think that slops or stale beer are being returned to the barrel, you should in the first instance contact your local CAMRA branch, who may be able to gather evidence so that the authorities can be approached.
- If you are given a chipped glass, dirty cutlery, bad food or sour beer, don't hesitate, but let the proprietor know, politely. During a busy session, it is easy for things to be missed, and a little courtesy and understanding on both sides should resolve matters.
- It is a legal requirement for representative price lists to be readily visible. You should not need binoculars or a crystal ball to check prices.
- If the licensee is unwilling to put things right, feel free to contact your local Trading Standards or Environmental Health Officers. (See the local phone book, public library or town hall.)

DISLEY
DANDY COCK
15 Market Street
⏰12-11 Mon-Sat; 12-10.30 Sun
Robinsons Hatters Mild, Best B [H]
This traditional pub is located in a prominent position in the centre of the village on the busy A6. The building, however, predates the trunk road and was once a home for cock-fighting, as the name suggests. The parking area to the front is small, and an equally small front patio provides the only outside drinking area. The cosy lounge bar and separate restaurant area create an admirable mix allowing drinkers and diners to co-exist without interference.

In addition to the Hatters Mild and Best Bitter, there are occasional appearances of Frederics and Old Tom, while Old Stockport Bitter makes more frequent visits to the bar. A very good selection of food is available, with specials featured on a blackboard beside the bar. Meals are not available on Mondays. Disley is an excellent centre for walking or cycling in nearby Lyme Park, or a short distance away in the Peak District. This would be an excellent place to start walking the Gritstone Trail.

DITTON
BLUNDELL ARMS
No real ale.

NEW INN
No real ale.

YEW TREE
Coronation Square
⏰APH
Tetley B [H]
Architectural gem in middle of housing estate – an imposing post-war pub.

DODLESTON
RED LION
(See opposite)

DUDDON
HEADLESS WOMAN
Tarporley Road (A51)
⏰11-2.30, 6-11 Mon-Fri; 11-11 Sat; 12-10.30 Sun
Greenalls B, Tetley B [H]
16th century roadside pub. Two rooms and a large garden in a rural location. For the curious, the story of the headless woman can be seen inside.

DUNHAM-ON-THE-HILL
DUNHAM ARMS
Chester Road (1 mile from M56 Jct14, or on A56, ½ mile from A5117 junction)
⏰11-3, 5-11 Mon-Fri; 11-11Sat; 12-3, 7-10.30 Sun
Banks B [H]
Themed 'farmhouse' interior with several eating areas, attracting a wide age range. Play area includes a rustic assault course. Large well-lit car park. Panoramic view over the Mersey basin.

WHEATSHEAF INN
Chester Road
⏰APH
Greenalls Original, Tetley B, guest beer [H]
Typical wood-panelled theme pub with the expected emphasis on food and families.

DUTTON
TALBOT
Northwich Road
⏰12-11 Mon-Sat; 12-10.30 Sun
Boddingtons B, Flowers IPA [H]
Large through lounge and separate games room. Floodlit bowling green to rear. Known as the "Tunnel Tap" as it sits above a canal tunnel.

EATON (near Congleton)
PLOUGH
(See overleaf)

WAGGON AND HORSES
Congleton Road (A34, 1½ m north of village).
⏰12-3.30, 5-11 Mon-Sat; 12-10.30 Sun
Robinsons Best B [H]
Single bar with log fire, plus separate dining and games rooms. Ten acres of gardens include an animal park, adventure playground and, at the weekend, pony rides. Imminent alterations will add a baby room and conservatory. In summer, Robinsons Frederics ale is available, and sometimes Hatters Mild.

EATON (near Tarporley)
RED LION
Beech Lane
⏰12-3, 6-11 Mon-Sat;
12-4, 6-10.30 winter Sun (12-10.30 summer)
Draught Bass, Boddingtons B, Greenalls B, Original; Tetley B [H]
Two large rooms with low partitions. Pool table in bar. Open fire and good views.

ELLESMERE PORT
BOAT MUSEUM
No real ale.

CAT
No real ale

FOXFIELDS
Poole Hall Road
⏰APH
John Smith B [H]
Lively modern pub on outskirts of Overpool.

GRACE ARMS
Stanney Lane (near Junction 7 M53)
⏰APH
Tetley B [H]
The biggest pub in town, near the Epic Leisure Centre.

GROSVENOR
Upper Mersey Street
⏰APH
Burtonwood B [H]
This had just closed as we went to press.

GUNNERS HOTEL
No real ale.

HOLIDAY INN
No real ale.

HORSE & JOCKEY
No real ale

KNOT
Whitby Road
⏰APH
John Smiths B [H]
No nonsense town centre pub with two rooms and car park at rear. Close to Asda superstore.

McGOWANS
No real ale.

DODLESTON
RED LION

Church Road
🕐12-11 Mon-Sat; 12-10.30 Sun
Draught Bass, Worthington Best B, occasional guest beer [H]
The Red Lion is a large village pub, at least three centuries old; the village dates back the
Elizabethan times. The cartoon style inn sign of an embarrassed lion is the first feature the visitor
will notice. The spacious interior has stone flagged, tiled and bare board floors together with
extensive wood panelling and exposed roof beams which combine to create a rustic ambience.
This is enhanced by numerous pictures of days gone by and various agricultural implements.
Three open fires in brick chimneys complete the effect. Outside at the rear is a patio bedecked with
hanging baskets, while further tables can be found in the children's adventure playground.
     Meals are served every day of the week from midday to 9.30. A Sunday Roast is
available all day at a reasonable cost. The theme of the establishment is good quality food, but real
ale is always available, including, it should be noted, bottle conditioned ales on occasion. See the
article elsewhere in this guide for more details of this specialised form of real ale.

ELLESMERE PORT
PRINCES
Princes Road
🕐APH
John Smiths B [H]
Standard, large inner city estate pub, with pool
and darts.

SPORTSMANS
No real ale.

STATION HOTEL
Station Road
🕐APH
Flowers IPA [H]
No frills town pub next to the station. Bare
floorboards and loud jukebox predominate.
The handpump is hidden in a clutter of
nitrokeg dispensers. Beer quality can be a
problem.

VISCOUNT
No real ale.

WESTMINSTER
No real ale.

WING HALF
No real ale.

ELTON
RIGGER
Ince Lane (from M56 jct. 14, A5117 west, first
right into Ince Lane. Pub ½ mile on right)
🕐APH
John Smiths B [H]
Modern open-plan village community pub
with one main bar. Base for Old Etonians CC
and Elton Golf Society. Large grass area
between pub and road. Bar snacks at lunchtimes. Oversize lined glasses ensure a full pint.
As we went to press, bedecked with yellow
ribbons as support for Louise Woodward.

WHEELWRIGHT ARMS
No real ale

ELLWORTH
COACHMAN
Station Road (opposite Sandbach station)
🕐12-3.30, 5.30-11 Mon-Thu; 12-11 Fri-Sat;
12-5, 7-10.30 Sun
Greenalls Mild, B [H]
Two-roomed local. Lunch Monday to Friday.

FOX
London Road (A533 towards Middlewich)
🕐12-11 Mon-Sat; 12-10.30 Sun
**Greenalls Original, Marstons Pedigree,
Tetley Dark Mild, B [H]**
Large, open-plan pub on outskirts of town.
Food served all day till 8pm. Uncommon
outlet for cask Tetley mild.

MIDLAND INN
5 New Street (opposite Sandbach station)
🕐11-3, 7-11 Mon-Thu; 12-11 Fri;
12-5, 7.30-11 Sat; 12-3, 7-10.30 Sun
Robinsons Hatters Mild, Best B [H]
Cosy, two-roomed, side street pub.

ETTILEY HEATH
ROOKERY TAVERN
Elton Road (from A533 take Abbey Rd., past
roundabout)
🕐12-11 Mon-Sat; 12-10.30 Sun
**Mansfield Grays B, Marstons Pedigree,
Tetley B [H]**
Old-fashioned local, now becoming
surrounded by new housing developments.

EATON (near Congleton)

PLOUGH

Macclesfield Road (A536,1 mile north east of Congleton)

⏲12-3, 7-11 Mon-Sat; 12-3, 7-10.30 Sun

Banks B, Beartown Bearskinful, Ruddles Best B, Marstons Pedigree, guest beer [H]

A thriving, comfortable half-timbered Elizabethan village centre freehouse , said to have been built in 1602 and revitalised in recent years by Clive Winkle, the inspiration behind the former Saxon Cross micro-brewery. The sprawling interior is centred round the horse-shoe shaped bar, and is full of old beams, wooden settles, dried flowers and leaded lights. The toilets are particularly fancy! The pub is apparently haunted by a lady whose long skirt can sometimes be heard rustling through the building.

Much of the emphasis is on food, leading to busy periods, but this does not detract from the welcoming atmosphere or the excellent beer. A separate 16th century barn spent the first four hundred years of its life in Wales before being moved in its entirety to this location where it is used as an upmarket restaurant. Meals can also be taken in the pub itself, and the quality is excellent. The Plough is licensed for civil weddings, and accommodation is also available in eight bedrooms. The Plough is one of the county's very few outlets for Congleton's tasty Beartown Brewery beers. **GBG**

◖ ◗ ✿ P

FADDILEY

THATCH

Wrexham Road (A534, midway between A49 & A51)

⏲12-3, 6.30-11 Mon-Sat; 12-3, 6.30-10.30 Sun

Courage Directors, Ruddles Best B, Theakstons Best B, Weetwood Best Cask B [H]

A stunningly attractive 15th century inn , the appropriately named Thatch oozes historical charm. It is said to be on the site of the Saxon Battle of Faddiley (AD584). It was known for many years as the Tollemache Arms, but reverted to its nickname, to avoid confusion with a nearby hostelry. Looking like everyone's idea of the classic country cottage, the low ceilings, open fires and old furniture indicate why the building is listed, as are the two yew trees outside, which are thought to be over a thousand years old. The cosily timbered rooms, with perilously low beams cluster round the central bar and open fire. The friendly atmosphere attracts both locals and visitors, and dominoes are played. The raised snug adjacent to bar area is kept as smoke-free as possible. Note the leaded grate in the dining room.

It is now very much a restaurant/pub, most space being dedicated to tables, with a small bar area, but a conservatory is shortly being built at the rear to free up the bar area for drinkers. The hanging baskets add a splendid finishing touch to a stunning exterior. The well-maintained garden covers an immense three acres, and is fenced off from road with a child's play area at rear. The Thatch has a very good reputation for food, and booking is recommended. It is currently testing the local Weetwood ales to see how they go down. We think you'll find they go down very well!

◖ ◗ 🐕 ✿ P ⊗

40

BEARTOWN BREWERY

TRADITIONAL ALES
BREWED IN CHESHIRE

Phone: Congleton 299964

42

CHESHIRE'S BREWERIES

Cheshire has four independent breweries. The largest, oldest and by far the best known is **BURTON-WOOD**. The brewery was founded by James Forshaw in 1867 and has been greatly expanded in the last decade or so. Burtonwood own around 500 public houses, with a respectable number in Cheshire itself and the majority serving real ale. Sadly, a recent merger of pub chains has resulted in some pubs now being unable to sell Burtonwood beers (the Freemasons in Knutsford and the Meridian in Bollington for instance). However, Burtonwood ales can still be tasted at some excellent, and varied hostelries such as the White Lion in Barthomley (as seen on the cover of Out *Inn* CHESHIRE), the Talbot in Chester, the White Swan in Great Sutton, the Oddfellows in Nantwich and the Bridge Inn in Burtonwood itself. In recent years their range of beers has expanded too. In addition to the **Mild** (at 3% ABV), **Bitter** (3.7%), **James Forshaw's Bitter** (4%), **Top Hat** (4.8%) and **Buccaneer** (5.2%), they have introduced seasonal ales such as **Advent Ale** (4.5%) and **Vicar's Revenge** (4.2%)! It will certainly be Cheshire's loss if the proposed boundary changes take Burtonwood out of the county.

Cheshire's second oldest brewery, **COACH HOUSE**, was founded in **Warrington** as recently as 1991 by the ex-Greenall's Head Brewer, Neil Chantrell and his wife Elayne, when they heard the news that the Greenall's Warrington plant was to close. Initially, they converted a derelict coach house behind their home to a microbrewery. However, the addition of several more ex-Greenall's employees to the team, led to an expansion and re-siting of the brewery to larger premises in 1995.

Since then Coach House has gone from strength to strength and its beers are available as guests the length and breadth of the country - a true mark of their quality and popularity.

The number of beers they have brewed is enormous! The four standards are **Coachmans Best Bitter** (3.7%), the renowned **Gunpowder Strong Mild** (3.8%)**Innkeepers Special Reserve** (4.5%) and **Post Horn Premium Ale** (5%). They also brew 3.7% and 4.2% ales which are specially "badged" for pubs (for example the Hedgehopper Bitter at the Bulls Head in Mobberley and the Mill Premium at the Mill Hotel in Chester respectively) - take note any interested landlords!

Lastly, Coach House have produced over 20 different seasonal and special occasion ales, including Four Nations beers such as St. George's Heritage Ale, Wizard's Wonder Halloween Ale, Three Kings Christmas Ale and topically, Cheshire Cat Strong Ale! There are now a number of pubs in Warrington, Chester and elsewhere in the county that stock these brews (see Out *Inn* CHESHIRE for details!). Lastly, the **Gunpowder Strong Mild** won **bronze medal** in it's category in CAMRA's Champion Beer of Britain awards last year, Post Horn was voted Champion Strong Bitter in 1994 and **Blunderbus Old Porter** has also won runner-up to Supreme Champion Beer of Britain. There are also plans to bottle Coach House beers this year, starting with the porter. Make sure you ask your local off-licence or supermarket to stock it!

The **WEETWOOD** brewery is to be found near **Tarporley** on the route of the Sandstone Trail. It was started by ex-farmer, Roger Langford, and another ex-Greenall's brewer, Adrian Slater in 1993, in an equestrian centre on Weetwood Grange. and now has about 40 regular outlets. These include the Royal Oak in Kelsall, the Black Lion in Nantwich, the Pheasant in Higher Burwardsley and the Bear & Billet in Chester. They currently produce four regular beers; **Best Cask Bitter** (3.8%), **Old Dog** (4.5%), **Oasthouse Gold** (5%) and **Eastgate Ale** (4.2%) brewed to celebrate the centenary of Chester's ornate city clock. And each one's a belter! Old Dog won Best Premium Beer at CAMRA's Bradford Beer Festival in 1995, with Oasthouse Gold being joint winner of the Wirral Beer Festival last year. Do you need any more convincing?

Last, but cetainly not least, the baby of the bunch. Congleton's **BEARTOWN BREWERY** was named after the town's ancient tradition of bearbaiting and its logo is taken from the coat-of-arms. Brewing was begun in only 1994, by Ian Burns and Andy Milligan, and was run part-time until Christmas last year. Recently, following a few personnel changes, Beartown became a limited company and is endeavouring to switch its emphasis from the guest beer market to developing local outlets. In collaboration with CAMRA enthusiasts, Beartown beers have found their way into both the Plough at Eaton, the Swettenham Arms and the Ship at Wincle. We wish to congratulate the owners of these inns for sticking their necks out and supporting local industry. Let's hope more will follow suit! Beartown produce three excellent, regular beers; **Ambeardextrous** (3.8%), **Bearskinful** (4.2%) and **Bruin's Ruin** (5%). They will also be launching a new ale, a strong mild called **Black Bear**, at this year's Macclesfield Beer Festival. This should also be available as a guest in some local pubs, so seek it out and they may make it a regular. Other occasional Beartown brews include the gorgeous Polar Eclipse Oatmeal Stout at 4.8% (which could show Guinness a thing or three!), Hoppy Rambler summer ale (4%) and the "cheeky" Bear Ass (4%)!!

If you fancy trying any of these superb beers, either call at the pubs mentioned above, scan Out *Inn* CHESHIRE for other outlets, keep your eye on the handpumps, or, better still, ask your local to get some in! *Enjoy the real taste of Cheshire!*

THE COACH HOUSE BREWING COMPANY Ltd.

Suppliers of prize-winning cask conditioned beers

Coachman's Best Bitter (3.7% ABV)   Squire's Gold Spring Ale (4.2%)
Innkeeper's Special Reserve (4.5%)   Ostler's Summer Pale Ale (3.8%)
Post Horn Premium Bitter (5.0%)   Taverner's Autumn Ale (5.0%)
Gunpowder Strong Mild (3.8%)   Blunderbus Old Porter (5.5%)

Tel. (01925) 232800   Fax. (01925) 232700

Wharf Street, Howley, Warrington, Cheshire WA1 2DQ

WEETWOOD ALES LTD

Brewers of Fine cask Beers

Contact: The Brewery, Weetwood, Tarporley, Cheshire.
Tel. 01829 752377

FARNDON

FARNDON ARMS
High Street
⏱11-3, 5-11 Mon-Sat; 11-3, 6-10.30 Sun (all day in Summer)
4-5 guest beers [H]
A 16th century coaching inn on the London to Anglesey route. Attractive etched windows advertise the old name of the Raven Hotel. Although open plan, the area to the left of the bar appears like a Victorian living room, with plush sofas, book shelves, an open fire, a large potted plant and an upright piano that apparently sees action during occasional singalongs! There is also a bar billiards table tucked in the corner.
The all-day menu is quite adventurous, and there is a separate restaurant upstairs, which has a no smoking area. The beer range sometimes features independent brewery ales amongst more mainstream offerings. There is a wheelchair ramp from the car park, but no toilets with special disabled facilities.
◖◗ ᧒ ● P

GREYHOUND HOTEL
High Street
⏱5.30-11 Mon-Fri; 12-3 Sat;
12-3, 7-10.30 Sun
Greenalls Mild, B [H]
Cosy village centre pub
● P

NAGS HEAD
High Street
⏱APH
Marstons B, Pedigree [H]
Comfortable village local
● P

FRODSHAM

ASTON ARMS
Mill Lane
⏱APH
**Burtonwood B, Top Hat;
seasonal beers [H]**
Unspoilt multi-room pub but alterations are due. Well-kept bowling green to rear. Close to River Weaver. Accommodation is available. The seasonal beer is from the Burtonwood programme of rotating speciality brews.
◖ ● P

BEARS PAW
Main Street (A56 at town centre traffic lights)
⏱APH
Boddingtons B, Greenalls Mild, B, Original, Tetley B [H]
Attractive 17th century sandstone coaching inn on the wide main street. Especially welcoming at night. Modernised twice in recent years but still retaining many original features, including exquisite carved wooden fireplaces and leaded windows. It is a wide building, with a long bar, and separate rooms at each end. Formerly an excise house, and derives its name from the bear-baiting which took place outside. It is now popular with youngsters at weekends. The patio area at the rear next to the car park does not quite qualify as a garden.
◖⇌ P

1 - Bears Paw
2 - Bellemonte
3 - Bulls Head
4 - Cheshire Cheese
5 - Golden Lion
6 - Helter Skelter
7 - Netherton Hall
8 - Queens Head
9 - Red Lion
10 - Ring O'Bells

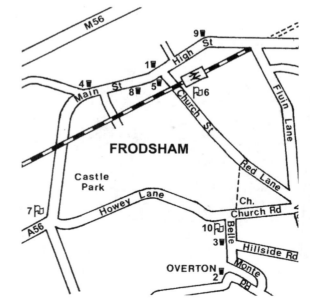

BRIDGE INN
Bridge Lane
🕐APH
Greenalls B [H]
Plain pub with bar and lounge close to River
Weaver. Accommodation is available.
🍺 ⚫

CHESHIRE CHEESE
29 Main Street
🕐APH
Greenalls M, B [H]
Open-plan pub just outside the town centre.
🍺 🐕 ⚫ 🚆 P ⊘

CHOLMONDLEY ARMS
No real ale.

GOLDEN LION
Main Street
🕐APH
Samuel Smiths Old Brewery B [H]
Locally known as the "Corner House". Busy at
weekends. Has a real fire, a large lounge and
several smaller rooms.
🍺 ⚫ 🚆

KYDDS
No real ale.

QUEENS HEAD
92 Main Street
🕐11.30-3, 7-11 Mon; 11.30-11 Tue-Wed;
11-11 Thu-Sat; 12-10.30 Sun (summer);
12-3, 7-10.30 Sun (winter)
Greenalls Mild, B; guest beer [H]
Built in 1550, this is the oldest pub in
Frodsham. Five good drinking areas, each
with its own character. Stables in rear yard
still hold a Friday night folk club. No food
Saturday. The guest ales are from the
Greenalls list. **GBG**
🍺 ⚫ 🚆 P

RED LION
17 High Street
🕐 APH
Boddingtons B; guest beers [H]
Two-roomed town pub with pool table.
Newly acquired by a national pub chain
and beer range liable to change.
⚫ 🚆 P

TRAVELLERS REST
Kingsley Road, Five Crosses (B5152)
🕐 12-2 Wed-Sat; 6-11 Mon-Sat;
12-10.30 Sun
Greenalls B [H]
Good views over Weaver Valley and Cheshire
Plain. Occasional live bands. Bar, lounge and
dining area, warmed by an open fire.
🍺 🍴 🐕 ⚫ P

HELTER SKELTER
31 Church Street
🕐APH
Boddingtons B; Weetwood Best Cask B; 4 guest beers [H] real cider [H]
Very close to Frodsham Station, and known until recently as Rowlands it always offers the
discerning drinker a good range of guest beers, and is a regular outlet for the brews of Weetwood in
Tarporley. Although the sign outside advertised it as a brasserie, this is no wine bar, but more of an
alehouse.
The Helter Skelter referred to in the name used to be on the top of Frodsham Hill, and a
reproduction of this can be seen on the menu. A very popular one roomed pub, it has a good
atmosphere. There is a raised area in one corner, and the walls are decorated with shelves of books
and bottles, but beer posters and a large collection of pumpclips predominate. These are mute
testimony to the record of more than 1600 cask ales served in seven years. This is also a measure of
the success CAMRA has had in rescuing real ale. There is also a good range of foreign bottled
beers. This is one of the few regular outlets for cask cider in the county, with Cheshire Cider from
Eddisbury being a frequent visitor.
There is car parking opposite, near the shops, and more parking to the rear. It has recently changed
hands, so food availability may change. At the time of going to press, a range of sandwiches and
baguettes was available each lunchtime, and all evenings except Friday and Saturday. There is
occasional live acoustic music. Lined glasses are used to ensure you get a full pint. **GBG**
🚆

NETHERTON HALL
Chester Road
🕐11-3, 7-11 Mon-Sat; 12-3, 7-10.30 Sun
Marstons Pedigree,Tetley B, 3 guest beers [H]
A big food pub set on a bend in the road on the western outskirts of Frodsham, on the site of the
former Whalebone Inn. Set on the edge of the town, it is worth the fifteen minute walk from the
station. This converted farmhouse is now rather open plan but derives some of its plentiful character
from the beams and bric-a-brac. This includes old sewing machines and a splendid old dentist's
chair in front of the kitchen range. It is very cosy and comfortable in the evenings, with candle-lit
tables and subdued lighting. Excellent food is served noon till 9pm Sunday to Thursday, and till
7pm on Friday and Saturdays. The chef has a well-earned rest on Mondays.
Live music is featured every Sunday evening. There is play area for children in the extensive garden.
The guest beers are from the Tetley lists, but are generally adventurous, and the quality of the
cellar-work has earned the pub an entry in the Good Beer guide. **GBG**
🍴 🐕 P ⊘

REAL CIDER IN CHESHIRE

What is Real Cider? Just as with beer, the mass-market brands of "cider" are a world away in flavour and character from the true traditional product. With beer, it is the *raw materials*, the *conditioning method* and the *dispense system* that determine whether it can be called "Real Ale"; all these elements are relevant to cider production too, though the emphasis placed on them differs.

Good quality fruit is indispensable for the making of good cider, and the type of fruit used has a major influence on the style that results. While it may be acceptable to use small quantities of apple concentrate to eke out apple supplies in a year of poor yield, the importance of the fruit is such that CAMRA does not recognise ciders made solely from concentrates as "Real Cider".

The conditioning process, crucial to the concept of Real Ale, is of less importance to Cider. The maturation of traditional cider is a long complex process, commencing when the first drops of juice trickle out of the cider press in the autumn, and continuing until the cider is ready to drink in the spring. While some real ciders are advertised as 'Cask Conditioned', in many cases the process takes place predominantly at the cider-maker's premises.

When it comes to the dispense method, however, the concepts of Real Ale and Real Cider are as one. A good cider should be served naturally, either direct from the cask (most often these days a 5 gallon plastic polycask) or by hand or electric pump from a cool cellar. Real cider, though it may have a modicum of natural 'condition', is essentially a still drink, and to drive it to the bar by applied gas, or still worse to pasteurise it and seal it in a pressurised keg; is to destroy its character.

WHERE TO FIND REAL CIDER IN CHESHIRE
Back in 1987 when this guide's predecessor "Cheshire Ale" was published, the above discussion would have been largely academic, for there was only one Cheshire pub where Real Cider could be had; the delightful Commercial at Wheelock, still a real cider outlet today. Since then, however, largely as a result of CAMRA's efforts in bringing to public notice the virtues of Real Cider, the choice is wider; and though some parts of the county are still far from a Real Cider House, the trend is definitely upward. Specialist Real Ale pubs such as the **Bhurtpore at Aston** are increasingly likely to sell Real Cider, while other regular outlets are **Helter Skelter in Frodsham**, the **Lodestar in Neston** and the **Old Town House in Warrington**. Real Cider is increasingly available on the "guest" portfolios of the big pub operators. If your local doesn't stock it, ask for it! In addition, as you will see below, Real Cider is generally available at **CAMRA Beer Festivals**.

REAL CHESHIRE CIDER
Most remarkably of all, in 1997, Real Cheshire Cider became available again, after a gap longer than most people can remember. Mike Dykes of **"CHESHIRE CIDER"** at Eddisbury Fruit Farm in Delamere Forest started making cider in 1996, and initially sold through the farm shop. The cider reached a wider public at Frodsham Beer & Cider Festival in May 1997, and shortly afterwards won the Cider of the Festival Award at the highly-regarded Stockport Beer & Cider Festival. A variety of different ciders has been produced to date, including Golden Oak and Sunrise. One of his ciders has an alcohol level of only 4.3%, much lower than most. We salute this splendid enterprise, and hope to see more cider makers appearing in the years to come.

FAKE CIDER
Things are not always all they seem, particularly when they are handpumps serving cider. Some "hand-pumped" cider is in fact keg, served by a real or imitation handpump, to masquerade as a traditional product. This squalid deception shames those responsible. *Scrumpy Jack* and *Cidermaster* are always keg, despite being seen regularly on misleading handpumps and should be avoided. CAMRA policy is to exclude from listing in the Good Beer Guide any pub which cons its customers in this way. *Addlestones*, usually seen on handpump is designed to be served using a high pressure of applied gas. **BULMER'S** handpumped **OLD HAZY** , despite using the term "scrumpy jack" in its branding, is a real cider!

Perry
If you ever see a traditional Perry, try it. Cider's sister drink, made from pears instead of apples, is now very rare in its traditional form. (The mass-market travesties of perry often seen in supermarkets can best be likened to debased copies of *Babycham,* and should be left well alone.) Sometimes subtle, sometimes insistent, Real Perry is one of the glories of the nation; seek it out!

Cheshire Cider

Made From The Finest Quality Apples Grown on rich Cheshire Soils At Haworth's Of Eddisbury Fruit Farm Yeld Lane, Kelsall Cheshire

GAWSWORTH

HARRINGTON ARMS

Church Lane (just off A536 main Congleton to Macclesfield road, 500 yards from church)
⏰12-3, 6-10.30 Mon-Sun
Robinsons Hatters Mild, Best B [H]
Presided over by the matriarchal Mrs Bailey, the Harrington Arms is a strong echo of the typical rural pub from the inter-war years. A virtually untouched rural inn, it is part of a working farm owned by Robinsons and is still decorated in 1930's style. This is a 400 year old farmhouse, full of character, with wooden settles and scrubbed tables throughout the several small, basic rooms. Popular with local farmers, there is even an old framed veterinary advert in the front room on the left near the darts board. On the right is the bar, leading to a tiny snug at the end, with another sitting room off. Some people regret the alterations carried out in the Seventies, involving the replacement of gravity stillages by handpumps and an old wooden bar by a fake antique one, but the bar area looks somewhat like an old shop counter, and it is still one of the most unspoilt and characterful pubs in the county. There are seats outside on the cobbled frontage, enhanced by the hanging baskets. Samuel Johnson is said to be buried in the nearby wood. Finally, the Harrington is convenient for Gawsworth Hall, and a handy watering hole for walkers and cyclists.
◖◗ P

RISING SUN

Congleton Road (A536, north of the village, near Macclesfield)
⏰11.30-11 Mon-Sat; 12-10.30 Sun
Boddingtons B, Greenalls B, Original , guest beer [H]
Large pub, revamped on the Miller's Kitchen theme, catering for business people and families. Unusually, offers full table service for diners. Garden is small, but includes children's play area.
◖◗ 🐎 🔥 🌼 P 🚭

GLAZEBURY

CHATMOSS HOTEL

207 Warrington Road
⏰7-11 Mon; 12-2, 7-11 Tue; 12-2, 5.30-11 Wed, Thu; 12-11 Fri, Sat; 12-10.30 Sun
Burtonwood Mild, B, Top Hat, guest beer [H]
Situated next to the world's first railway built in 1830 between Manchester and Liverpool. Originally the site office for the head engineer, Stephenson, later a waiting room and ticket office. Nowadays, a comfortable pub with separate games area. Food served until 9pm daily. One of a dwindling number of Burtonwood pubs serving their tasty mild.
◖◗ 🐎 🌼 P

COMFORTABLE GILL

458 Warrington Road (opposite garden centre)
⏰12-11 Mon-Sat; 12-10.30 Sun
Greenalls Mild, B [H]
Pub with two long rooms, vault at the front, comfy lounge at back. Children not allowed inside, though a play area is provided in the garden. Food served throughout the day, all week.
◖◗ 🌼 P

FORESTERS ARMS

384 Warrington Rd (off A580/East Lancs road)
⏰12-3, 7-11 Mon-Fri; 12-11 Sat; 12-10.30 Sun
Lees B, Tetley B, Marstons Pedigree [H]
Black & white pub with tap room and bright lounge. A rare Cheshire outlet for Lees beer.
◖ 🐎 P

GREY HORSE

Warrington Road
⏰APH
Boddingtons B, John Smiths B, Worthington Draught B [H]
Open-plan with central bar and various, comfy drinking areas. No food Sunday evening.
◖◗ 🐎 P

RAVEN

Warrington Road
⏰12-3, 6-11 Mon-Sat; 12-10.30 Sun
Burtonwood B, guest beer [H]
Attractive, 16th century, timber-framed inn, with several rooms and upstairs restaurant. The name derives from a local story in which a sword was removed from the body of a wounded civil war soldier by a raven, which proceeded to carry it to the roof of the pub!
◖◗ 🐎 🌼 P

GRAPPENHALL

PARR ARMS

Church Lane

⏰11.30-3, 5.30-11 Mon-Fri; 11.30-11 Sat; 12-10.30 Sun

Greenalls B, Original; guest beer [H]

The Parr Arms is a quiet and historic pub set in a picturesque old village on a cobbled street by the church. It is popular with locals and food plays an important part in its trade. There are several rooms, including a public bar. The interior is complemented by lots of brass and bric-a-brac, and there is a fine grandfather clock in the lounge. A noteworthy feature is the many pictures and models of bulldogs.

Beware of the limited parking on the frontage; if you need it, there is overflow space at the Rams Head just up the road. The Parr Arms is set very close to the Bridgewater Canal and the associated Cheshire Ring Walk. This is a lovely spot, yet it is just outside Warrington and is easily accessible by the motorway network. The guest ales come from the Greenalls list.

◖ ◗ P

GOOSTREY

CROWN INN

Main Rd

⏰11.30-3, 5.30-11 Mon-Sat;
12-3,6-10.30 Sun

Marstons B, Pedigree [H]

Archetypal English country pub in the front, with a swish separate restaurant in the rear, but retaining pubby atmosphere with beams, antique furniture and open fires. Originally a combined 19th century farm cum pub. Separate vault and a tap room with its own entrance. Function room. The restaurant has a no smoking area. Baby changing room illustrates commitment to the family trade.

◖ ◗ ⛺ ⚘ ☕ ⇌ P

RED LION

Main Rd

⏰ 12-3, 5-11 Mon-Thu; 12-11 Fri, Sat;
12-10.30 Sun

Tetley B, Coachmans Best B

Morland Old Speckled Hen (occasional) [H]

Surprisingly large pub for a village, catering for most people, with very smart dining area at the front, and a games room at the rear. The building dates back to the 17th century and has many exposed beams. The good menu is and the prices are reasonable. The games room offers two pool tables, darts, chess and table football.

◖ ◗ ⛺ ⚘ ⇌ P

GORSE COVERT

POACHER

From M62 jct 11, signs for local services

⏰12-11 Mon-Sat; 12-10.30 Sun

Tetley B, guest beer [H]

Huge, open-plan building with a number of drinking areas on various levels. There is a family area to one end, decorated to look like a rural, village pub! Lunches served Mon-Fri.

◖ ⛺ ⚘ P

GORSTAGE

OAKLANDS

Millington Lane (off A49)

⏰APH

John Smiths B, Theakstons Best B [H]

Large country house, now pub with restaurant and accommodation. Open plan, but has several areas at different levels with comfortable seating. Function room available. Children welcome until early evening. Beware keg cider on real handpump.

◖ ◗ ⛺ ⚘ P

What I don't like about pubs...

I am not a drinker, although I must admit that the occasional sip of my husband's beer can be quite tasty. Our social life involves going to pubs on occasion, although I tend to be reluctant. The reason is that some pubs can be very smoky. I have no problem with smokers pursuing their addiction in private, but I do object to them making my eyes sting, and my hair and clothes smell. Why on earth have so many pubs been opened out into one big room, where one smoker can irritate a hundred non-smokers (and diners)? The benefit of a multi-roomed pub is that it caters to all needs. A non-smoking room, or better still, a smoking room can accommodate everyone's wishes. – JC

GRAPPENHALL

BRINDLEY
Knutsford Old Road
⏰7-11 Mon-Fri; 12-3, 5.30-11 Sat
Flowers IPA, guest beer [H]
Open-plan bar attached to Fir Grove Hotel.
Guest beer from Whitbread.

DOG & DART
Knutsford Road (A50)
⏰11.30-11 Mon-Sat; 12-10.30 Sun
Greenalls B, Original; guest beers [H]
Large children-friendly and food-oriented pub
with raised areas and alcoves plus separate
dining area. Guest beer (from Greenall's list)
changes monthly.

GRAPPENHALL COMMUNITY CENTRE
Bellhouse Lane
⏰7.30-11 Mon-Fri; 12-5, 7.30-11 Sat;
12-10.30 Sun
Ruddles B, Websters Yorkshire B, guest beers [H]
Large private club and social centre converted
from an old farm. Recent refurbishment has
formed a central bar serving a bar area and
hall. Home to many societies. Usually two
guest beers. A CAMRA membership card
allows entrance. GBG

RAMS HEAD
Church Lane
⏰11-3, 5.30-11 Mon-Sat; 12-10.30 Sun
Greenalls Mild, B, Marstons Pedigree [H]
Timber and sandstone exterior village inn with
two ash-panelled lounges and a central bar.
Rooms are available.

ROCKFIELD HOTEL
No real ale.

SPRING BROOK
Stockport Road (A50/A56 intersection)
⏰11.30-11 Mon-Sat; 12-10.30 Sun
Banks's B; Marstons Pedigree [H]
New, well-equipped pub. Children welcome.
Lift for disabled customers to restaurant on
upper level. Beware of the smoothflow keg
mild.

GREAT BARROW

WHITE HORSE
Main Street
⏰Opening times not available
Banks Mild, B, Wadworth 6X [H]
A cosy village local with a real fire and a
no-smoking dining area. A feature is made of
cartwheels and brass ornaments.

GREAT BUDWORTH

GEORGE & DRAGON
(See overleaf)

GREAT BUDWORTH

COCK O' BUDWORTH
Warrington Road (A559)
⏰APH
Holts Mild, B [H]

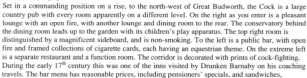

Set in a commanding position on a rise, to the north-west of Great Budworth, the Cock is a large
country pub with every room apparently on a different level. On the right as you enter is a pleasant
lounge with an open fire, with another lounge and dining room to the rear. The conservatory behind
the dining room leads up to the garden with its children's play apparatus. The top right room is
distinguished by a magnificent sideboard, and is non-smoking. To the left is a public bar, with open
fire and framed collections of cigarette cards, each having an equestrian theme. On the extreme left
is a separate restaurant and a function room. The corridor is decorated with prints of cock-fighting.
During the early 17th century this was one of the inns visited by Drunken Barnaby on his coaching
travels. The bar menu has reasonable prices, including pensioners' specials, and sandwiches,
baguettes and jacket potatoes providing a lighter option. This is one of the regrettably few Holts
pubs in Cheshire, providing a welcome combination of low prices and distinctively hoppy beers
from this well-loved Manchester brewer.

GREAT SANKEY

BUTCHERS ARMS
Liverpool Road
⏰12-11 Mon-Sat; 12-10.30 Sun
Greenalls Mild, guest beer [H]
Lively and popular pub. Lounge is food-
dominated and bar is smoky. Depressingly, the
guest beer is usually one of Stones bitter,
Tetley bitter or Greenall's Original.
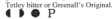

CHAPEL HOUSE
380 Liverpool Road
⏰11-11 Mon-Sat; 12-3,7-10.30 Sun
Greenalls Mild, B, Tetley B [H]
Pleasant pub in village centre. Formerly a
coaching inn and before that a mortuary!

SANKEY ARMS
No real ale.

TRIGGER POND
Liverpool Road
⏰APH
Banks Mild, B [E],
Camerons Strongarm [H]
Large modern estate pub on edge of ever-
expanding new town. Emphasis on food
(a 'Milestone' pub). Conservatory at front
looks towards the power station.

WOODLANDS
Liverpool Road
⏰12-3,5.30-11 Mon-Thu; 11-11 Fri-Sat;
12-10.30 Sun
Tetley B [H]
A pleasant roadhouse with public bar, saved
by a local campaign from being knocked
through into a "Wacky Warehouse".
The willow tree was also saved. However, we
hear that a major refurbishment is due in
spring 1998, with a 'Mr Q's theme! We really
have to watch these people.

GREAT SUTTON

BULLS HEAD
⏰APH
Draught Bass, Worthington Draught B [H]
A games-oriented locals' bar on the edge of
Ellesmere Port. The lounge is open at week-
ends with live music (Fri) and Disco (Sat).

WHITE SWAN
(See overleaf)

GREAT WARFORD
FROZEN MOP
Faulkner's Lane
(off Knutsford Road at Knolls Green)
⏰ APH

Boddingtons B, 2 guest beers [H]
Huge, family- and food-oriented theme pub. Once a row of cottages as evidenced by the old beams. Known as the Warford Arms up to about 50 years ago, now virtually unrecognisable. Large play area and patio outside. Guest beers from major breweries.
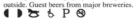

STAGS HEAD HOTEL
Mill Lane
(near Mary Denby Hospital off A535)
⏰ 12-3, 5-11 Mon-Sat; 12-3, 7-10.30 Sun
Boddingtons B, Greenalls B [H]
Up-market Victorian, brick pub with flower-filled, cobbled frontage and retaining original etched windows and front door. Inside, there are three main rooms with high ceilings and moulded cornices, the front containing a lovely black-leaded open fire, the rear an impressive ornate mirror. Food is a feature, though the bar area has a cosy atmosphere for drinkers, and stools made from old milk churns! There is no accommodation despite the name.
No food Sunday evening. More interesting beer would make this a classic.

GRESTY
CHESHIRE CHEESE
332 Crewe Road
⏰ APH
Boddingtons B, Greenalls Original, Tetley B, guest beer [H]
Friendly pub, attracting a varied clientele. Heavily themed.
Well kept garden.

GEORGE & DRAGON
High Street (off the A559 Northwich to Warrington road)
⏰ 11.30-3, 6-11 Mon-Thu; 11.30-11 Fri-Sat; 12-10.30 Sun
Tetley B; 2 guest beers [H] Addlestones Cask Cider [H]
The George is a popular Edwardian brick-built pub in what must be the most picturesque village in Cheshire. It is set opposite the striking red sandstone church and a photogenic row of cottages. Look out for the unusual pub sign (a rarity these days) of Saint George slaying the beast. The exterior is noteworthy for the intriguing inscriptions on the garden fence. The timbered entrance lobby leads into a comfortable lounge, which is divided into four areas round the central bar. To the left you will find an open fire and beyond the bar a cosy snug is tucked in the corner. To the right is a non-smoking section for drinkers and diners. Low ceilings, exposed beams and a lovely old clock add atmosphere. Newspapers are provided; a most civilised touch. The large public bar to the rear has a pool table, darts, TV and table football, providing a good locals' atmosphere. Catering is important to the trade, and the extensive menu includes adventurous daily specials and Sunday roasts. You can eat either in the pub or in the upstairs forty-seater restaurant. The latter can be booked for functions.

The George has been voted Pub of the Year by the local branch of CAMRA, and is a particular favourite of the writer of our foreword. The beer range includes one guest from Tetley's "Tapsters Choice" range and another often from local micro-breweries such as Weetwood of Tarporley and Coach House of Warrington. Great Budworth is convenient for Arley Hall, Pickmere and Marbury Country Park.

GREAT SUTTON
WHITE SWAN
A Road
⏰ APH

Burtonwood B, 2 guest beers [H]
The White Swan, dating from the nineteenth century, is a fine Burtonwood house, where imaginative guest beers nestle alongside the host brewery's ales. With a traditional bar and split-level lounge with prints of old Ellesmere Port and a vintage model vehicle collection, a warm welcome is guaranteed. The pub has its own football team and a strong golfing section. Plans are in hand to refurbish the interior without spoiling its character, and the facilities will be supplemented in July 1998 by the addition of a conservatory and beer garden. Food is available all day on Sunday, but there are no meals on Tuesdays.

The Swan is an oasis in an area where beer choice is at a premium. The licensee's enthusiasm, together with a praiseworthy guest beer supply contract approved by the brewery, means that almost any British beer can be ordered. In three years, the Swan's customers have enjoyed over 300 brews, and it is a favourite port of call for discerning drinkers visiting the area.

GUILDEN SUTTON
BIRD IN HAND
Church Lane (off Station Lane, signposted from main village road)
⏱11.30-3, 6-11 Mon-Sat; 12-3, 7-10.30 Sun
Boddingtons B, Flowers IPA, 2 guest beers [H]
Tucked away on a no through road past the church, this white-washed and pebble-dashed pub provides a welcome rural retreat from the nearby hustle and bustle of Chester. Once an unassuming village local, the Bird in Hand has been so transformed that it is now probably more restaurant than pub. Certainly the menu reflects this with Thai specialities and an extensive range of sophisticated fish, meat, pasta and vegetarian dishes, while barmen in white shirts and black ties serving at the cloth covered tables at every seating point confirm its *raison d'etre*. It remains a relatively small establishment, however, and this, together with low ceilings and simple furnishings make for a cosy atmosphere. Weaving around the flower tubs, you enter via a porch on the side of the building. The smart interior has comfortable seats and sofas. The open-plan areas are well-lit through the leaded lights of the surrounding bow windows. A quiet pub, suitable for those usually irritated by youngsters playing fruit-machines and juke-boxes.

Secreted down a quiet lane in one of Cheshire's more affluent outlying villages, it is the sort of place where you might take a loved one
(or maybe somebody else's). Very popular on St Valentine's Day, one would imagine.

HANDLEY
CALVELEY ARMS
Whitchurch Road (off A41, in the village)
⏱12-2.30, 5.30-11 Mon-Sat;
12-3, 7-10.30 Sun
Boddingtons Mild, B, guest beer[H]
This is a single-roomed 16th Century coaching inn set at the centre of a peaceful rural village. A distinctly family and food-oriented pub, it has beamed ceilings with some original timbers, which are hung with water jugs and dried hops. There is a multitude of postcards above the bar, while at the side are old photos depicting various stages of pub and village history. A large beer barrel (a hogshead) sits in the middle of the long, single room, which has an attractive brick fireplace at one end. The whole pub interior is light and airy with light from the extensive row of leaded side windows. The healthy pot plants certainly seem to appreciate this!

The Calveley Arms boasts a good selection of freshly prepared meals at a reasonable price, always including a number of interesting fish dishes. The amusements inside involve bar skittles, Shove Ha'penny and other traditional pub games, while outside diversions in the large gardens include a Boules pitch. The garden is entered via the car park through a large arch in the high conifer hedge. Well-behaved children only, please.

The guest beers come from a fairly predictable range of mainstream guests, including Castle Eden, Draught Bass, Flowers IPA and Original, Greene King Abbot,

GURNETT
OLD KINGS HEAD
Byron's Lane (less than 100 yards east of canal on Macclesfield to Sutton road)
⏱11-2.30 Mon-Fri; 11-11 Sat; 12-10.30 Sun
**Banks B, Boddingtons B,
guest beer (occasional) [H]**
Dating from 1695, this former coaching house, smithy and wheelwrights on the old Manchester to London road provides a friendly welcome. Though open-plan, it has traditional oak beams and a real fire. Haunted too!
The "hot beef baguette" enjoys an enviable reputation. No main meals Tue-Fri evenings in Winter. Outdoors, there are benches by the road. Accommodation is available.

HALE
CHILDE OF HALE
Church End
⏱12-11 Mon-Sat; 12-10.30 Sun
**Burtonwood B, Higsons Mild,
guest beer (occasional) [H]**
Named after the famous, early seventeenth century nine foot giant, who lived, died and is buried in the village. There are three rooms, including a public bar. A rare Cheshire outlet for Higsons, especially so for the mild.

WELLINGTON HOTEL
Town Lane
⏱12-11 Mon-Sat; 12-10.30 Sun
**Burtonwood Mild, B, Top Hat, Buccaneer,
guest beer [H]**
A food-based tavern with two lounges, a public bar and separate restaurant. Bowling green at rear. Children admitted on Sunday. Good range of Cheshire's Burtonwood beers.

Marstons Pedigree, Morlands Old Speckled Hen, Ruddles Best and County and Wadworth 6X. The choice of cask mild changes occasionally, all being well kept. However, beware of the keg Scrumpy Jack cider falsely served via a real handpump. The beer quality is considered to be good, and the availability of cask mild is good news for drivers.

HALE BANK
COCK & TRUMPET
Halebank Road
⊘11.30-11 Mon-Sat; 12-10.30 Sun
Burtonwood Top Hat; 2 guest beers [H]
Large split-level room. Pleasant and
comfortable pub on edge of countryside.
◖◗ ☙ ▦ P ◉

MERSEY VIEW
No real ale.

HAMPTON HEATH
NEW INN
No real ale

HASLINGTON
HAWK
137 Crewe Road
⊘APH
Robinsons Hatters Mild, Best B, Frederics [E]
A 15th century, roadside Tudor inn, with eye-catching graffiti such as *"The Hawk Inn, be it known of good ale and dry stables 1510 AD"* carved into the outer timbers. The inside presents a warren of cosy rooms, on different levels and with different characters, most featuring their own real fire. Throughout there are low ceilings, crooked beams and characterful lop-sided walls. Brasswork of every description permeates the rooms, even including a large hawk by the old bar entrance.
A watercolour of another hawk gazes down from the wall of another room. Comfy, upholstered seats are clustered around the numerous wood and copper-topped tables in the bar area. A large brick, coal fire roars in the grate during Winter. The room to the left of the entrance is given over to diners, while the hall itself houses a rather tempting chaise-longue! The inter-linking doors have barn door-style latches, reflecting the age of building. Dick Turpin is reputed to have found the Hawk hospitable enough to stay at!
    The wide-ranging menu includes a buffet, children's portions and, on Friday evenings, Asian specials. Food is served every lunchtime, in addition to Wed-Sat evenings. There is a paved, backyard with seating for warmer weather. Several function rooms are available at no charge, provided there is a reasonable number of customers. Beer is served from metered electric pumps into oversized glasses.
◖◗ ☙ P

HATCHMERE
CARRIERS INN
Delamere Road
⊘12-3, 6-11 Mon-Fri; 12-4, 6-11 Sat; 12-10.30 Sun
Burtonwood B, Forshaws B, Buccaneer, Top Hat, seasonal beers [H]
The Carriers is much extended from its original form. It was built three hundred years ago as a stopping point on the Salt Trail. A carrier is a flat bedded cart, and there was a time when these were used to carry oak from Delamere Forest to the Liverpool ship-building yards. At a later date it fell into disrepute as a gypsy pub and venue for bare-knuckle fights. The neighbouring cottage is reputed to be haunted by the shade of a poor girl who had a child out of wedlock. The pub has been left on the outskirts now that the centre of Norley has migrated eastward, but is still an integral part of village life. It was once known as the Snig Foot, a reference to the trail through the forest which was said to resemble the shape of a snig, or eel.
Live music plays an important role, with blues and a folk club alternating on Tuesdays, bluegrass on Mondays, contemporary music on Thursdays, and traditional folk music on Sunday lunchtimes. Some of the more unusual activities are occasional Laser 'clay pigeon' shooting, and demonstrations of hawks and game birds on the evening of the last Friday in the month in summer. Barbecues are held on Sundays too.
    The open plan layout is broken up into different levels. On your right as you enter is the lively games room with pool and darts teams. Dominoes are also played. A small lounge area on the left has a brick fireplace and a video projection system. This leads on into a bar area where jugs, books, plates and fish tanks add pleasing detail. On the walls are nostalgic prints of the area. There is a quiet rear bar, then steps down to a small dining area overlooking the garden, and the Mere itself.
    Typically, there will be three beers from the range of Cheshire's own Burtonwood brewery, and these will vary. The licensee would like to serve real mild, but is defeated by the low turnover. Apparently the summer hordes are more interested in lager than the real thing. Pity.
◖◗ ☙ ◉ P

HATTON

HATTON ARMS
Hatton Lane
⏰11.30-11 Mon-Fri; 11-11 Sat; 12-10.30 Sun
Greenalls Mild, B, Original, plus either Marstons Pedigree or Theakstons B [H]
A picturesque pub set in a 17th Century row of cottages with a cobbled frontage. Once known as the Red Lion, the Hatton Arms has recently been extended into the adjoining Post Office to provide en-suite accommodation, a restaurant and residential facilities. What has emerged is entirely in keeping. The pub retains a pleasant cottage atmosphere with low beams, brasses, small windows and real fires. Look for the old handpumps displayed above the door to the separate taproom, which has a timeless country pub atmosphere, well away from the diners. The Hatton Arms is still very much a country pub serving locals and visitors alike. There are disabled toilets accessible from the restaurant.

The landlord takes his guest beers from Greenalls, but feels that alternating Pedigree and Theakstons fits the bill. Some might feel that a more adventurous policy would be preferable.

 P

HANDBRIDGE

GROSVENOR ARMS
32 Handbridge
⏰APH
Greenalls Mild, B [H]
A multi-roomed down to earth pub popular with the local community.

 P

RED LION
37 Overleigh Road.
⏰APH
Draught Bass, Ferry B, Greenalls B, Tetley B, [H]
Well refurbished pub with drinking areas round a central bar. Basic meals, no food on Mondays. The house beer is from Tetley.

SHIP
18 Handbridge (by the old Dee Bridge)
⏰APH
Greenalls Mild, B [H]
Two roomed friendly local with B&B adjacent to the river and historic Edgar's Field.

WHITE HORSE
66 Handbridge
⏰11.30-4, 6-11 Mon-Fri; 11.30-11 Sat; 12-3, 7-10.30 Sun
Tetley B [H]
Roomy local with games emphasis, including bagatelle. Separate TV bar.

HANDFORTH

BULLS HEAD
Manchester Road (A34)
⏰APH
Theakstons Best B, guest beers [H]
Multi-room, country-style, food-based pub on main road. Guest beers from the large Scottish & Newcastle brewery.

FREEMASON
Manchester Road (A34)
⏰APH
Boddingtons Mild, B [H]
Cosy, mock Tudor local in centre of town. No food weekends. A rare outlet for Boddington's Mild in Cheshire, or indeed anywhere.

GREYHOUND
Wilmslow Road (A34)
⏰12-11 Mon-Thurs; 11-11 Fri & Sat; 12-10.30 Sun
Holts B, John Smiths B [H]
Open plan pub in town centre. Try the Holts bitter, you don't see it much in Cheshire, and it's lovely!

MERMAID
No real ale.

RAILWAY HOTEL
Station Road (B5358 off A34)
⏰11.45-3, 530-11 Mon-Fri; 11.45-3.30, 6.30-11 Sat; 12-3, 7-10.30 Sun
Robinsons Hatters Mild, Best B [E], Old Stockport, Frederics [H], Old Tom [G]
Large, multi-room pub facing the station. A thriving local which is popular with all, and a perennial Good Beer Guide entry. No food weekends. Traditional pub games. It is encouraging to see a pub serving five of Robinsons' seven beers. The Old Tom strong ale is particularly rare and like liquid fruitcake! Only usually available as a winter warmer, here it's thankfully all year round. Oversized lined glasses are used to ensure full measure. **GBG**

WAGGON & HORSES
231 Wilmslow Road
⏰11.30-11 Mon-Sat; 12-10.30 Sun
Boddingtons B, Tetley B, Theakston XB [H]
Theme pub with food all day and indoor play area. Live music on Thursdays.

HAUGHTON MOSS

NAGS HEAD

Long Lane (a minor road between Bunbury and Burland)
⏲11-3, 6-11 Mon-Sat; 12-3, 7-10.30 Sun
Marstons Best B, Pedigree, guest beer [H]

A picturesque, black and white, early 17th century coaching inn which acted as the mid-way staging post on the route between The Swan at Tarporley and The Crown in Nantwich. Indeed, the room which now serves as a restaurant area was once a smithy. It has been an inn ever since licences were first issued. Almost inevitably, there are rumours of hauntings! The building has an impressively ornate entrance and there are exposed beams and brickwork throughout the three main rooms.

The snug, to the left of the bar, houses a carved, old church pew as seating and a stone candle-holder built into the brick pillar. In winter, the lounge has a welcoming fire. There is a friendly atmosphere with a modern but intelligent attitude towards children.

Good quality, home-cooked, restaurant and bar food are served, and while the emphasis can seem to be on dining, especially on a busy weekend, this does not detract from the "pub" side of things, and the Nag is a good place to visit just for a drink. The large, award winning gardens can be a lovely place to sit, especially as they are set well away from the road. They feature a sturdy climbing frame for children, and there is a well-tended bowling-green for hire! Beeston, Peckforton and Cholmondley castles are all nearby for those with a historical bent. **GBG**

◖ ◗ ⛺ ⑂ ● P ⊗

HEATLEY

RAILWAY

42 Mill Lane
⏲12-11 Mon-Fri; 11.30-11 Sat; 12-10.30 Sun
Boddingtons B; Timothy Taylors Landlord, guest beer [H]

Set a couple of miles east of Lymm, the Railway is now no longer aptly named; the line in question has long gone, and forms part of the route of the Trans-Pennine trail for walkers and cyclists. It is still decorated with many items of railway memorabilia, including a magnificent watercolour of a station scene over the fireplace in the bar. A substantial four-square building, it is very much a traditional community pub. The layout has changed little over the years; it still has four different rooms in addition to the bar, and a function room. There is a TV in one of the pool rooms.

Folk music is featured on Thursdays, and the list of clubs and societies is impressive, including two fishing clubs, a Budgie club (presumably for their owners), a Hawkers club, and local farmers' meetings. The pub also hosts regular meetings of bikers. Time is called by the ringing of a mighty brass bell behind the bar. The large garden includes a play area for children. The good value lunches are served daily except Sundays. **GBG**

◖ ◗ ⛺ ● P

HANKELOW

WHITE LION

Audlem Rd. (opposite green and pond)
⏲12-2, 7-11 Mon-Sat; 12-2, 7-10.30 Sun
Greenalls B, Original [H]
Two-roomed local with games room and lounge adjoining restaurant. Excellent and extensive menu. Lunchtime food only until 1.30 Mon-Sat.
◖ ◗ ⑂ P ⊗

HARTFORD

COACHMAN

286 Chester Road
⏲APH
Greenalls Mild, B, Original, Tetley B [H]
Large former coaching inn opposite station. Separate public bar and pool rooms. Dining area in conservatory. Accommodation in old stables. Children's play area.

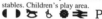

◖ ◗ ⛺ ⑂ ● ⇌ P

HARTFORD HALL HOTEL

No real ale.

RED LION

Chester Road
⏲11.30-3, 4.30-11 Mon-Fri; 11.30-11 Sat; 12-10.30 Sun
Boddingtons B, Greenalls B [H]
Popular multi-roomed pub with comfy lounge. The landlord's name really is Julio Iglesias!
◖ ◗ ● ⇌ P

HASLINGTON

BROUGHTON ARMS

No real ale.

FOX

56 Crewe Road
⏲11.30-3, 5-11 Mon-Fri; 11.30-3, 6-11 Sat; 12-10.30 Sun
Boddingtons B, Flowers Original, Marstons Pedigree, guest beer [H]
Modern, open plan roadhouse with the emphasis on food. Food all day Sunday.
◖ ◗ ⛺ P

HASSAL GREEN

ROMPING DONKEY

No real ale

HEATLEY

ADMIRAL BENBOW

Agden Wharf, Warrington Lane
⏲12-11 Mon-Sat, 12-10.30 Sun
Draught Bass, Worthington Draught B, guest beer (occasional) [H]
Popular canalside pub with its own barge offering a variety of cruise packages
◖ ◗ ⛺ ⑂ ● P

GREEN DRAGON
Mill Lane
⏰ 11.30-11 Mon-Sat; 12-10.30
Draught Bass, Worthington Draught B [H]
Modernised country pub with partly tiled floor
and wood panelling throughout. Popular for
food and with families. Open fire and bric-a-
brac from local farming traditions.

HELSBY
HELSBY ARMS
No real ale.

HORSE & JOCKEY
Chester Road
⏰ 11.30-11 Mon-Sat; 12-10.30 Sun
Greenalls B [H]
Multi-roomed pub with bar and restaurant.
Popular with climbers from Helsby Hill. Ac-
commodation available.

RAILWAY
Chester Road
⏰ 11-3,5.30-11 Mon-Thu; 11-11 Fri-Sat; 12-
10.30 Sun
Greenalls Mild, B, Original; guest beer [H]
Large multi-room pub with restaurant and
comfortable bar. Handy for Helsby Hill. Pub
games and real fire.

ROBIN HOOD
163 Chester Road
⏰ 11.30-11 Mon-Sat; 12-10.30 Sun
Marstons B, Pedigree [H]
Large open-plan pub with leaded windows at
front. Function room and accommodation
available. Open fire.

HENBURY
BLACKSMITH'S ARMS
Chelford Rd
⏰ 11-11 Mon-Sat; 12-10.30 Sun
Boddingtons B; guest beer(s) [H]
Family-oriented themed food pub with chil-
dren's play area. Also Sky TV. Meals 12-9.30
Sun-Thu, 12-10 Fri and Sat.

COCK INN
Chelford Rd
⏰ 11-3, 5.30-11 Mon-Fri; 11-11 Sat; 12-10.30
Sun
**Robinsons Hatters Mild, Best B; guest beer
[H]**
Food-oriented pub with access for disabled.
Play area for children outside. Sky sport for
adults inside. Meals 12-3, 7-10 Monday-
Saturday; 12-10 Sunday.

HERMITAGE GREEN
HERMIT
Golborne Road
⏰ 12-11 Mon-Sat; 12-10.30 Sun
Tetley B; guest beer [H]
Well-appointed pub set back from the road.
Extensive and adventurous menu (e.g. croco-
dile!), including food theme nights and all day
availability on Sunday. Regular entertainment
evenings.

HIGHER BURWARDSLEY

PHEASANT
Rock Lane (take road to Burwardsley from Tattenhall, turn left at the top of the hill by post office,
and follow the sign for the pub)
⏰ 12-3, 7-11 Mon-Fri; 12-11 Sat; 12-10.30 Sun
Guest beers (usually Draught Bass plus one independent) [H]
The Pheasant is a 300 year old half-timbered, sandstone inn, nestling on top of the Peckforton Hills.
The lounge has the biggest log fire in Cheshire, while the restaurant was formerly the farmhouse
kitchen and retains the old range. Pictures of Highland cattle, and rosettes from successful shows
decorate the walls. Enjoy the superb views over the Cheshire Plain toward the Welsh hills. Set mid-
way along the Sandstone Trail, in magnificent countryside, the Pheasant is ideal for walkers, and a
leaflet detailing four circular walks from the pub has been specially commissioned. The castles of
Beeston, Cholmondley and Peckforton are within easy reach, while other attractions include Oulton
Park racing circuit six miles away, and Cheshire Candle Workshops close by. Ten en-suite rooms
are situated in an award-winning converted barn, with Bed & Breakfast available. The food is of
such a high standard that the Pheasant is listed in CAMRA's prestige Good Pub Food Guide. Only
eight miles from Chester, this is an excellent spot for visitors to Cheshire or North Wales.

HIGHER HURDSFIELD
GEORGE & DRAGON
61 Rainow Road
⏰ 12-3, 7-11 Mon-Fri; 7-11 Sat; 7.30-10.30 Sun
Theakston Black Bull B, 2 guest beers [H]
The George & Dragon is the last of half a dozen or so pubs set along the road out to Whaley Bridge.
Part of the pub is reputed to be 400 years old, and it was once the home for a school of privileged
girls. It is now open to a wider public, the privileged real ale drinkers of Macclesfield. Once called
the Nag's Head, it then served home-brewed beer and was a Free House until purchased by
Lonsdale & Adshead of Macclesfield in 1927. It is now a free house once again, providing an ever
changing range of traditional beers, as evidenced by the absorbing display of pump clips which fills
and overflows the wall space behind the bar.
　　　　The front part of the pub is divided into three. On the left as you enter is the cosy bar room
with its inviting row of handpumps. The middle room acts as a wide lobby with a few tables, while
on the right is a long narrow room with a dartboard and television at one end. When big matches are
being televised, the pub may stay open all day Sunday for football in the afternoon. There is also a
separate pool-room and a snug. The George is very much a community local, with the landlady of
13 years standing ensuring that the atmosphere is friendly.
◖ P

HIGH LEGH

BEARS PAW
Warrington Road (A50)
⏰11.30-11 Mon-Sat; 12-10.30 Sun
Boddingtons B, Greenalls B [H]
Country cottage style road house with public
bar and separate dining room. Comfortable
and welcoming. Evening meals Sat and Sun.
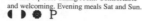

HIGHER HURDSFIELD

BRITANNIA
260 Hurdsfield Road (on B5470 400 yards
past the church, near the canal)
⏰12-3, 6-11 Mon-Fri; 11-11 Sat;
12-10.30 Sun
Burtonwood B [H]
Small but rewarding stone-built terrace on the
Macclesfield to Whaley Bridge road.
Multi-roomed locals pub, convenient for
Macclesfield Canal

HOLLINS GREEN

BLACK SWAN
Manchester Road
⏰12-11 Mon-Sat; 12-10.30 Sun
Tetley Mild, B [H]
Large roadside inn with open-plan interior
furnished with low beams and several seating
areas. No smoking dining area.

HOLMES CHAPEL

GEORGE AND DRAGON
Middlewich Rd
⏰11.30-11 Mon-Sat; 12-4.30, 7-10.30 Sun
Robinsons Hatters Mild Best B [H]
A modern building but with a peaceful and
quiet lounge where you can drink and
converse. Separate pleasant public bar with
pool table. Outside there is a patio with tables
and umbrellas where you can watch the world
go by. Meals 12-2 all week, 7-9 Tue-Sat.
Children are admitted up to 9pm and the pub
has a children's certificate.
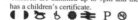

HOLLY LODGE HOTEL
70 London Rd
⏰11-3, 6.30-11 Mon-Sat; 12-3, 7-10.30 Sun
**Ruddles Best Bitter, occasional guest beers
in summer [H]**
Hotel welcoming non-residents to its bar, restaurant, and regular dinner dances. In addition
to the bar meals, it has a restaurant offering
full menus, and a no smoking area. There is a
relaxed atmosphere of the type found in country hotels. Popular for wedding receptions.

RED LION
19 London Rd
(in the exact centre of the village)
⏰11.30-11 Mon-Sat; 12-10.30 Sun
Tetley Bitter, Guest Beer (occasional) [H]
An old pub with beams and wood panelling
inside. One end is very reminiscent of a gentleman's club with the décor and armchairs.
Very relaxing. All over the pub are interesting
pictures and artefacts. The garden is a patio.
Worth a visit just to see the inside.

SWAN HOTEL
Station Rd
⏰APH
Samuel Smiths Old Brewery B [H]
A popular pub that has accommodation, with a
splendid garden reached by driving through an
arch in the middle of the building. A small
public bar is still a separate room, and two
other rooms (without doors) provide snug and
cosy drinking areas. Bar meals are very
popular, and generally eaten in yet another
area. The walls heave with most interesting
artefacts and ancient photographs. A rare
opportunity to drink Sam Smith's in this area.

VICARAGE HOTEL
Knutsford Rd (½ mile from the village centre)
⏰12-2, 6.30-11 Mon-Sat;
12-2, 6.30-10.30 Sun
Worthington Draught Bitter
A small smart hotel where non residents are
welcome to drink, eat bar meals or patronise
the "no smoking restaurant". A family-run
concern that has a calm and snug ambience,
and one in which you can hold a conversation.
There are tables out at the front for a peaceful
pint in the summer months. Popular venue for
wedding receptions.

HOO GREEN

KILTON INN
Warrington Rd (A50 between A556 and High
Legh)
⏰11.30-11 Mon-Sat; 12-10.30 Sun
**Boddingtons B, Greenalls B, Original,
guest beer [H]**
Standard Miller's Kitchen menu in roadside
food-based pub with attached lodge. The
garden includes a play area. Reputed to be
associated with Dick Turpin and claims to be
one of the oldest licensed houses in Britain
but unfortunately now characterless.
Lifted by the presence of a guest beer.

HOOLE

BROMFIELD ARMS
Faulkner Street
⏰11-11 Mon-Sat; 12-3, 7-10.30 Sun
Greenalls Mild, B [H]
Unspoilt public bar and cavernous lounge in
this centre of village local.

FAULKNER
Faulkner Street
⏰11-11 Mon-Sat; 12-3, 7-10.30 Sun
**Draught Bass, Greenalls Mild, B, Original,
Tetley B [H]**
A popular local normally featuring five real
ales and an occasional guest beer. Darts and
pool are taken very seriously here.

HOOLE HALL HOTEL
On the main road
⏰12-3, 5-11 Mon-Sat; 12-3, 7-10.30 Sun
Banks B [H]
Superior hotel on the edge of town. Bar snacks
and restaurant. Real ale is found in Rigby's
Bar, open to non-residents.

PIPER
Pipers Lane (A41)
⏰APH
Boddingtons B. Greenalls Mild, B [H]
A completely undistinguished theme pub. It
has a games room with large screen TV and a
split level lounge. Live music and karaoke.

ROYAL OAK
Faulkner Street
⏰11-11 Mon-Sat; 12-3, 7-10.30 Sun
Banks B, guest beer (occasional) [H]
An unspoilt pub with three distinct drinking
areas off one bar.

HOOTON

THE CHIMNEYS
Hooton Green
(next to Hooton crossroads on the A41)
⏰APH
Draught Bass, Worthington B [H]
Formerly a Gentleman's Club in the
19th Century, it features seventeen chimneys!
Now a pub-restaurant, with a wide choice of
good value food served all day until 9.30.

HOUGH

WHITE HART
Newcastle Road (at A500/Buck Lane junction)
⏰12-3, 6-11 Mon-Fri; 12-11 Sat;
12-10.30 Sun
Banks Mild, Tetley B, guest beer [H]
Welcoming open plan pub with patio and
servery. Has a reputation for good beer and
home-cooked food at reasonable prices.
Meals all day at weekend.

HOUGH GREEN

FOUR TOPPED OAK
2 Hough Green Road
⏰12-11 Mon-Sat; 12-10.30 Sun
Tetley B [H]
Large pleasant and comfy, with real fire.

HAMMER & PINCERS
Liverpool Road
⏰APH
Tetley B; guest beer (occasional) [H]
Large open-plan town pub.

SPORTING FORD
No real ale.

SUNDOWNER
No real ale.

HOUGHTON GREEN
PLOUGH
Mill Lane
⏰11.30-11 Mon-Sat; 12-10.30 Sun
Boddingtons B, Greenalls Mild, B, Original, guest beer [H]
Popular pub, enlarged in the 1990s.
The emphasis is on food. Children's play area.
The guest beer is from the Greenalls list. **GBG**
 P

HUNTINGTON
RAKE & PIKEL
Farndon Road
⏰11-3, 6-11 Mon-Fri; 11-11Sat;
12-3, 7-10.30 Sun
Boddingtons B [H]
A comfortable lounge and basic public bar in a
roadside hostelry, at the centre of its
community. Pool, darts and quiz nights.
● **P**

HUXLEY
FARMERS ARMS
Huxley Lane
⏰11-3, 5-11 Mon-Fri; 11-11 Sat;
12-10.30 Sun
**Boddingtons B, Burtonwood B,
James Forshaws B, Castle Eden Ale [H]**
Friendly 17th century village pub with diverse
clientele. Separate restaurant, and charcoal
grilling at weekend. Real fires in winter.
● **P**

INCE
DUKE OF WELLINGTON
Marsh Lane
⏰APH
Greenalls Mild, B [H]
Friendly, family-run old pub in a historic vil-
lage mentioned in the Domesday Book.
Extensive views from the large well-equipped
garden. Separate restaurant area. Vocalist on
Saturdays. The landlord has won Best Kept
Cellar awards from the brewery.
● **P**

KELSALL
FORESTERS ARMS
Chester Road (at the top end of the village)
⏰5-11 Mon-Fri; 12-11 Sat; 12-10.30 Sun
**Theakstons Mild, Websters Yorkshire B,
guest beer [H]**
A traditional pub with basic public bar and
lounge. Open fires The guest beer is from the
Scottish & Newcastle list. A rare outlet for
the rare and underrated Theakstons Mild.
P

ROYAL OAK
Chester Road (off the A51)
⏰12-11 Mon-Sat; 12-10.30 Sun
**Draught Bass, Mild,
Worthington Draught B [H]**
A large three-roomed pub tastefully
refurbished recently. Sensibly they kept the
cask mild.
● **P**

KELSALL
BOOT
Willington Lane, Boothsdale (south of Kelsall, signposted from Willington Road)
⏰11-3, 6-11 Mon-Thu; 11-11 Fri-Sat; 12-10.30 Sun
Bass Worthington B, Greenalls Mild, B, 2 guest beers [H]
Tucked away down a minor no through road south of the village, this secluded rural gem shelters
under a long, tree-clad ridge known as "Little Switzerland". Deceptively large, the red sandstone
building was in fact systematically converted from half a dozen terraced cottages over the last
hundred years. Originally built the year of the Battle of Waterloo, it was first licensed in 1872.
Despite being knocked through into one, it still has two areas for drinkers that are distinct from the
main, dining section. The end snug is especially atmospheric, with its low-lighting, wooden settles,
black-leaded open-fire grate, dried flowers and side bar. The main bar area has a small, wood-
burning stove, tiled floor and the daily papers. The large, dining area also supports a log fire and
tempting menu served all day at weekends. The exposed timber, brickwork and local sandstone
everywhere adds to the overall rustic charm. As there is no music, there is no impediment to the age
old art of conversation.
There are benches both on the paved area outside the front door and in the garden at the
back. The field by the car park houses friendly donkeys! The guest beers are from independent
brewers, such as Weetwood from nearby Tarporley, and change weekly.
The locality is popular with walkers, and the Frodsham to Whitchurch Sandstone Trail
passes nearby. The Boot is an attractive country pub with good views over surrounding countryside,
and although it can be difficult to find, we think you will be rewarded for your efforts.
● **P**

TH'OUSE AT TOP
Chester Road
(at the top end of the village - obviously!)
⏰12-3, 5.30-11 Mon-Sat;
12-3, 5.30-10.30 Sun
**Draught Bass, Greenalls Mild, B,
Tetley B [H]**
A three-roomed pub with an eating area set to
the back of the lounge. Filled with bric-a-brac.
● **P**

WILLINGTON HALL HOTEL
No real ale.

KETTLESHULME
BULLS HEAD
Macclesfield Road
⏰7-11 Mon-Fri,12-3, 7-11 Sat; 12-3, 5.30-
10.30 Sun
Boddingtons B, Castle Eden Ale [H]
Stone terrace, just inside Peak National Park
village. Separate vault. The car park is a short
distance from the pub.
Superb surrounding countryside.
● **P**

SWAN
Macclesfield Road
⏰5.30-11 Mon-Fri; 12.30-3, 5.30-11 Sat; 12-
3, 5.30-10.30 Sun
Marstons B, Pedigree [H]
Picturesque white-walled 15th century
coaching inn. Classic country pub, with stone
fireplace, horse brasses and coppers. Does not
open on Sunday evenings in winter.
P

KINGSLEY
HORSESHOE INN
Hollow Lane (B5153)
⏰5-11 Mon-Fri; 11-5, 7-11 Sat; 12-5,7-10.30
Sun
Greenalls Mild, B [H]
Two-roomed locals pub. Features a real fire,
pub games and a vault.
● **P**

RED BULL
The Brow
⏰5.45-11 Mon-Fri; 12-3,7-11 Sat; 12-3,7-
10.30 Sun
Greenalls B [H]
Open-plan village local. Beautiful garden at
rear runs down to a stream. Evening meals
Thursday to Sunday, lunches at weekends
only. Real fire.
● **P**

KELSALL

MORRIS DANCER

Chester Road (off the A54)
⊘APH
Greenalls B, 2 guest beers [H]
Greatly extended, but suprisingly homely, the Morris Dancer is a black and white coaching inn. Oak timbers dominate, particularly in the two main drinking areas where rows of keys hang from the beams. These are on the right as you enter from the large landscaped car park, in the older part of the pub. Each has its own open fire, book shelves, large potted plants and bare boards which are liberally covered with rugs. Satellite TV sometimes shows live sport in the corner room.
The windows have small padded seats. The unusual barrelled bar sits centrally, surrounded by a red-tiled floor and tall wooden stools. Nearby is an old butter churn and, a thoughtful touch more pubs could emulate, a shelf containing the daily papers. There are a number of changes of level, but ramps are included. The ghost of a drowned girl is said to stalk the place at night! Outside are two patios, front and rear, decorated with hanging baskets and clothes mangles!
The old stables now form the large, separate and up-market restaurant. This provides an excellent choice of good quality food at a fair price, although you may have to wait. Although it may look like a theme pub from the outside, it is lovely inside, and well worth a visit.
The guest beers are from independent breweries.

KNUTSFORD

ANGEL
(See opposite)

BUILDERS
(See overleaf)

COTTONS
No real ale.

CROSS KEYS HOTEL
King St.
⊘11.30-3, 5.30-11 Mon-Fri;
11.30-3, 7-11 Sat; 12-3, 7-10.30 Sun
Boddingtons B, Taylor Landlord, guest beers [H]
A coaching inn in the 18th century, this is now a friendly and lively town centre pub with modern accommodation. There is both a lounge and vault, separated by an unusual wood and glass partition. Five handpumps are in the former, with two and a pool table in the latter. Food is to be had Tuesday to Saturday, bar meals at lunchtime, restaurant meals 7-9. The quieter restaurant area has been converted from the old cellar, has a no smoking section and allows children. It is advisable to book at weekends. This is the town's only free house, always providing three guest beers, two from the Whitbread lists, the other from an independent brewery. For an excellent pint, try a lunchtime visit, as the pub can fill up in the evening.

FALCON BEARER
No real ale.

FIVE OAKS
No real ale

FREEMASONS ARMS
Silk Mill St. (between Princess St. & King St.)
⊘APH
Draught Bass, Websters Yorkshire B, Wilsons Original B [H]
Large, white, pebble-dashed pub next to marketplace with pay and display car park opposite. Three comfortable, beamed rooms (one being the vault), each with its own open fire, add to the cosy and relaxed atmosphere. Knutsford's hidden gem! After a change of ownership, the excellent Burtonwood beers from have been dropped for run-of-the-mill alternatives, which are nevertheless well-kept.

KING CANUTE
Princess Street
⊘11.30-11 Mon-Sat; 12-10.30 Sun
John Smiths B, Websters Yorkshire B [H]
Features a disco and lightshow and quiz nights. Beware the keg cider on fake handpump. One for dancing rather than drinking.

LEGH ARMS
Brook Street / Chelford Road
(A537 south east of town)
⊘11-3, 5-11 Mon-Thu; 11-11 Fri, Sat;
12-10.30 Sun (winter), APH (summer)
Banks Mild, Marstons B, Pedigree, Head Brewers Choice [H]
Smart pub on the edge of town in 1930s Art Deco style, although the oldest part of this listed building dates from 1734. Note the eagles in the etched windows by the car park. Interesting benches and copper fire canopy at the end of the bar. Bowling green.

LORD ELDON
Tatton Street
⊘APH
Ruddles County, John Smiths B, Tetley B, Webster Yorkshire B [H]
This historic 300 year old pub has a lovely exterior with a sundial and hanging baskets. The cosy, rambling and attractive interior has four rooms plus a bar. Fires, low beams and a riot of brass and pictures provide the background to darts dominoes and a golf society. There is a cheap beer policy possibly due to the proximity of a Holt's house.

RED COW
Princess Street
⊘APH
Martons Pedigree [H]
Very much a young persons' meeting place, with real ale no more than an afterthought. The lone handpump is lost in a forest of keg fonts, and quality cannot be relied upon. Not one we can recommend.

ROSE & CROWN
No real ale.

ROYAL GEORGE
No real ale.

WHITE BEAR
1 Canute Place
⊘11.30-11 Mon-Sat; 12-10.30 Sun
Greenalls Mild, B, guest beer [H]
Attractive thatched 18th century building set prominently on the roundabout by the old market place. Stone-flagged floors, historic photographs and cosy drinking areas add to the charm of this listed building. A patio is planned. The guest beer is often the tasty Cains Traditional Bitter.

WHITE LION
King Street
⊘11.30-11 Mon-Sat; 12-10.30 Sun
Tetley B [H]
Extended sideways from a superbly historical frontage, it has been opened out internally. Relaxing décor with fires, beams, plush seats and pictures of old Knutsford and a former landlady of 32 years. We are told guest beers are to be installed; this will make it a very good pub.

LACH DENNIS
DUKE OF PORTLAND
Holmes Chapel Road (B5082)
⏰ 11.30-3, 6-11 Mon-Sat; 12-10.30 Sun
Marstons B, Pedigree [H]
Basically a themed food pub but has a tiny area for drinkers

LACHE
WESTMINSTER PARK
No real ale.

LANGLEY
LEATHERS SMITHY
(See overleaf)

ST DUNSTAN'S INN
Main Road
⏰Times not provided.
Marstons B, Pedigree [H]
Mid-terrace local on the road leading to the Macclesfield Forest.

KNUTSFORD
ANGEL
96 King Street
⏰APH
Holts Mild, B [H]
A smart and substantial town-centre pub, stunningly refurbished after years of neglect, the Angel stands as a beacon for a generation of slipshod pub architects. Wood panelling, beams and open fires feature in the several separate drinking areas, and there is a separate vault at the rear, with a dartboard. It has a function room available for hire. A popular meeting place for local societies it is set near the top end of the "bottom street", close to the main shopping and eating area.

Handy for Manchester Airport and close to the south gate of Tatton Park, the Angel offers accommodation and the cheapest beer in town, although with a recent change of licensee, we cannot yet comment on the beer quality. Holts is a Manchester brewery, and this is a relatively rare brew for the county, although those who have acquired a taste for the distinctive, uncompromisingly hoppy Bitter swear there is nothing to beat it. The dark Mild can be equally delicious when on form, with a strong roast malt taste, and unusually bitter. **GBG**

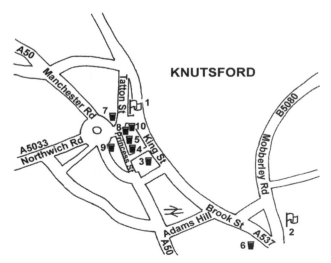

KNUTSFORD

1 - Angel
2 - Builders Arms
3 - Cross Keys
4 - Freemasons
5 - King Canute
6 - Legh Arms
7 - Lord Eldon
8 - Red Cow
9 - White Bear
10 - White Lion

KNUTSFORD

BUILDERS ARMS

Mobberley Road (on one-way street off main Chelford Road, A537)
⌚APH
Banks Mild, Marstons B, Pedigree, Head Brewers Choice [H]
The Builders is a wonderful, unspoilt and incredibly cosy pub perched on the hill on the outskirts of the town, in an attractive row of cottages. It may be approached along the one-way street from Chelford Road near the Legh Arms, or by foot up a cobbled path through the trees from Hollow Lane. Divided into two rooms by the central bar, the public bar to the left and lounge to the right. The former is characterised by "Fisherman's Corner" decorated with a multitude of photographs depicted the ones that didn't get away! The Builders has its own angling club. A dart board is to be found tucked in another corner. The subtly-lit, but sometimes smoky, lounge features wood-panelling, comfortable seating and a collection of toby jugs. The ticking of the wall clock can sometimes be heard during lulls in conversation.

It has featured in 24 consecutive editions of the CAMRA's Good Beer Guide, only missing the first one by an oversight! Marstons have an agreeable and popular policy of producing a regular succession of new beers, termed the Head Brewer's Choice. This provides welcome variety, with a fresh taste every couple of months. **GBG**

LAWTON HEATH

HORSESHOE

Sandbach Road
⌚12-3, 5.30-11 Mon-Sat; 12-3, 7-10.30 Sun
Draught Bass, Worthington Draught B, guest beer [H]
A regular entertainment venue. Jazz on Thursday evenings, open mike Fri-Sun. Fancy a rousing chorus of "I did it my way"?

LEDSHAM

CHESHIRE YEOMAN

Welsh Road (off A550 near A540 junction).
⌚APH
Greenalls B, Tetley B [H]
A pub-restaurant, near the old Ledsham station. A wide range of substantial and good value meals is available all day.

TUDOR ROSE
Chester High Road (Two Mills crossroads, on the Birkenhead-Queensferry road)
⌚APH
Boddingtons B, Cains Traditional B, guest beer (occasional) [H]
Unmistakeable roadhouse with accompanying Travelodge. Meals 12-10 every day. Not your average local, but worth a visit.

LEFTWICH

PILLAR OF SALT
No real ale.

QUINCEYS
No real ale

LITTLE BOLLINGTON

NAGS HEAD
Chester Road (Set back from the A556 near the M56 roundabout)
⌚APH
Boddingtons B, Castle Eden Ale, Flowers Original, Marstons Pedigree [H]
Large food pub with separate drinking areas, and a restaurant. Meals all day. Play area, but traffic noise.

STAMFORD ARMS
Lymm Road (A56)
⌚APH
Boddingtons B, Flowers IPA, Marstons Pedigree, Wadworth 6X [H]
A food-based Whitbread chain pub, the restaurant has a no-smoking area. The range of cask ale has recently expanded from a solitary Boddingtons handpump, but the range is subject to change. The pub was closed for refurbishment as we went to press.

SWAN WITH TWO NICKS
(See after "A Woman's View" article)

YE OLDE No. 3
Lymm Road (A56)
⌚11.30-3, 5.30 -11 Mon-Thu; 11.30-11 Fri, Sat; 12-10.30 Sun
Courage Directors, John Smiths B [H]
Food-based roadhouse, squeezed uncomfortably between the A56 and the Bridgewater Canal.

LITTLE BUDWORTH

CABBAGE HALL
Forest Road (A49)
⌚ 12-3, 6-11 Mon-Sat; 12-3,7-11 Sun
Greenalls B [H]
Plain, but tidy, country pub with a public bar. Pub football pitch adjacent ! Formerly doubled as a tailor's workshop – the cabbages were the remnants of cloth that the tailor used to make his own clothes.

EGERTON ARMS
No real ale.

FOX & BARREL
Forest Road (A49)
⌚ APH
Boddingtons B, Marstons Pedigree, Tetley B, guest beer [H]
Large pub, recently renovated to high standard. Small nature reserve adjacent.

LITTLE LEIGH
HOLLY BUSH
Warrington Road (A49)
⏲APH
Burtonwood B, Tetley B, guest beer [H]
Half-timbered, thatched and over 500 years old, this was formerly one of the last working farm pubs in the area, but is now effectively a country pub "theme park". Nevertheless, it retains the three original rooms, with new dining areas formed from converted outbuildings and extension. A separate servery now opens out into the parlour.
A renovated barn provides accommodation. The gents is also outside and a children's play area is in the former orchard. The cobbled frontage, and stone flagged floors in the bar remain, but those who remember its former historic and down-to-earth character mourn that it has been sacrificed to cater for an almost wholly dining clientele.
◖ ◗ ⛺ ● P ⊗

LANGLEY
LEATHERS SMITHY
Clarke Lane (at edge of Macclesfield Forest by Ridgegate Reservoir)
⏲12-3, 7-11 (Fri from 5.30) Mon-Thu, Sat; 12-3. 5.30-11 Fri; 12-10.30 Sun
Banks Mild, B, Marstons Pedigree, guest beers [H]
An 18th century stone-built, former smithy, as the name suggests, its rather plain exterior belies attractiveness within. It comprises two main areas, both with low ceilings and some original beams, one being stone-flagged (useful for walkers with muddy boots). The carpeted lounge has a real log fire and is often full of diners. The other room contains the unusual, copper-topped bar, another fire and a piano. Vases of fresh flowers are dotted here and there. The landlord is a vintage car enthusiast, hence the multitude of automobile prints, photos and even car fenders (!) on the walls of the two cosy rooms. The extensive menu includes sandwiches and roast dinners. Food is served all day on Sundays. Children under 14 are not allowed in the bars.
There are large gardens and benches on a small green opposite Ridgegate reservoir. It is convenient for the Macclesfield Forest and the Gritstone Trail, and not suprisingly it can be busy during sunny weekends. With such scenic surroundings, it is very popular with visitors to the area. The guest beers are usually from Morrells of Oxford (the only regular outlet we know in Cheshire). *However, beware inferior keg cider misleadingly served via a real handpump.*
◖ ◗ ⛺ ● P

HORNS
Warrington Road (A49)
⏲12-11 Mon-Sat; 12-10.30 Sun
Greenalls Mild, B, Original [H]
A pleasant country pub with several separate areas, including one for dining. Close to canal and River Weaver. Children's play area outside. Accommodation available.
◖ ◗ ● P ⊗

LEIGH ARMS
Warrington Road (A49)
⏲12-11 Mon-Sat; 12-10.30 Sun
Burtonwood B, Buccaneer, seasonal beers [H]
Large black-and-white half-timbered building by swing bridge over Weaver. Now opened out, but retains some interesting features including stained glass. Restaurant and large garden.
◖ ◗ ⛺ ● P

THE FOXCOTE - LITTLE BARROW

LITTLE BARROW
FOXCOTE
Station Lane (B5132 between the A56 and A51)
⏲12-3, 6-11 Mon-Sat; 7-10.30 Sun
Greenalls B, Original, Tetley B [H]
A pleasant rural pub in an isolated spot. The unassuming exterior of this country pub belies the friendly and individual welcome which awaits the visitor. Originating in the mid-Nineteenth century as an ale house called the Railway Inn, after the main Chester to Manchester line which runs close by. It was created 200 years earlier by knocking together two cottages into an alehouse known as the Snig (eel). The present pub benefits from having a sandstone cellar. In the mid eighties it was renamed the Foxcote Manor after a restored steam locomotive on the Llangollen railway in North Wales, and the name was shortened more recently. The beamed interior includes timber sleepers taken from the nearby railway line. Part of the lounge is non-smoking, and offers superb views over the surrounding countryside. This is a popular area for walking. There is a strong emphasis on country cooking, with a European style a la carte influence, which is reflected in the décor. The chef makes his own bread and ice-cream, and specialises in fish and traditional dishes.
◖ ◗ ⛺ ● P

A WOMAN'S VIEW...

I'm a wine drinker and always will be...BUT, I'm now a real ale enthusiast as well.

It all arose from my frustration at trying to get a decent glass of wine in a pub. I was usually offered a choice between "dry white" (cheap French supermarket plonk) or "medium white" (poor quality, thin, German rubbish) or, the ultimate insult, wine on draught which was usually warm. Red wines , if available, were usually undrinkable. I'd usually end up with a tonic water instead.

Over the years I'd tried standard pub lagers but found them too gassy and with an unpleasant, artificial taste. In general, other beers seemed to be too bitter tasting as I'm sure many women find. My "conversion" came on a walking holiday in the Yorkshire Dales with a crowd of friends. After being served yet another awful glass of wine in a pub where we had stopped for lunch, one of our group (who turned out to be a CAMRA member), offered me a sip of his beer as consolation. It was a revelation! Smooth, complex and malty with a marvellous liquorice aroma. Gone was the bitterness that I had always associated with beers. It was **Theakstons *Old Peculier (OP)***. I was hooked.

I soon learnt that I didn't need to travel to Yorkshire to taste beers of this type and quality. There are plenty in Cheshire. There's even outlets for *OP* (the *Boathouse* in Chester and *Ship* in Styal for instance). I also discovered that it wasn't necessary to drink strong beers like *OP* (5.7% ABV) to achieve a full, rounded flavour. Milds, for example, often have similar qualities. Try **Burtonwood *Mild*** (3%) and **Coach House *Gunpowder "Strong" Mild*** (3.8%), both brewed in Cheshire. Also, **Cain's *Dark Mild*** (3.2%) and **Banks'** (3.5%), which is also available in bottles. For a few more, read the "Born to be Mild?!" article at the beginning of Out *Inn* CHESHIRE.

I prefer the taste of predominently "malty", rather than "hoppy" beers, because of the bitterness associated with hops. I suspect that many women are put off beer because they are first offered the hoppy (bitter) type that may suit the male palate better. I've found that, in general, beers from Scottish brewers tend to be on the maltier side. Now, if I go into a pub and I'm not familiar with what is on offer, I ask for a malty beer and even for a taste before I choose! Most landlords appear delighted that I'm showing an interest.

I also enjoy the ever-expanding range of unusually flavoured beers. These are often produced seasonally, such as the honey-flavoured **Coach House *Honeypot*** or all-year-round, like **Vaux *Waggledance*** (named after the bee's knees-up!). Wheat beers, which originated on the continent and are becoming increasingly popular for those warm sunny days, have a clean, refreshing taste (dare I say just as good as gin & tonic!). **Marston's *Summer Wheat Beer*** and ***Dragonfly*** (a raspberry wheat beer from **Salopian** in Shrewsbury) are super. Both are bottled and the former is also available on draught in Marston's pubs serving beers from the Head Brewers Choice range (the *Builders* and *Legh Arms* in Knutsford for example). **Cain's *Victorian Winter Ale*** has a distinct nutmeg and cinnamon taste, with a hint of satsuma. Jilly Goulden eat your heart out! Lastly, new this Easter, is the delicious **Cain's *Chocolate Ale*.** It really smells and tastes like chocolate truffle torte. Pop down to Sainsbury's for a bottle before they sell out!

I'm delighted to see more and more good quality bottled beers in supermarkets (I avoid cans like the plague as they give that horrible metallic taste). Tesco, Booths (of Knutsford and elsewhere "up north") and particularly Oddbins (who are fast gaining a reputation for their stock of beers as well as wines) have an extensive choice. It's just as exciting as choosing good bottles of wine. The labels are, if anything, even more appealing

Many winter-warmers are dark and spicy, reminiscent of mince pies and Christmas pudding. Luckily, several of these are brewed in the North West. Two real gems are the full-bodied, richly-flavoured **Lees' *Moonraker*** (7.5%), available at *the Golden Pheasant* in Plumley and the *Spreadeagle* in Lymm and **Robinson's *Old Tom*** (8.5%), to be found at the *Windmill* in Tabley and elsewhere in the county. **Lees** also brew *Harvest Ale* in autumn, a true <u>strong</u> ale at 11.5%!. You can get all three of these in small bottles, to enjoy by the fireside at home.

Finally, just a few more personal favourites; **Jennings' *Snecklifter*** (from the Lake District), widely available in bottles and sometimes seen at the brewery's only Cheshire pub, the *Red Fox* in Tiverton. **Marston's *Nut Brown Ale*** and the classic *Oyster Stout* (both Head Brewer's Choice beers, the latter to be seen in many supermarkets).

I like my beer in an attractive stemmed glass. If fine wines justify elegant glasses, then why not fine beers? Being offered a choice of glass tells me that the landlord is giving some thought to the wishes of his customers rather than "take it or leave it". It's just good business. Other women I know prefer the ordinary, "straight" or even "handled"glasses. Many are put off by the large volume that beer is usually served in, also that beers are said to be fattening. I only drink half-pints, and contrary to popular belief there isn't much calorific difference between them and glasses of "medium" wine, and cetainly not of lager.

Talking of calories, apart from enjoying drinking bottled beers at home, I like to have some around when I'm cooking. If a recipe calls for beer as an ingredient I find it pays to use a really good one to add depth of flavour. In Delia Smith's Winter Collection there is a lovely recipe for *Beef in Designer Beer*. I use **Black Sheep *Riggwelter*** and it's terrific!

What has amazed me most about my venture into real ale is the vast variety and complexity of taste available. I would never have believed that it was on a par with wine. I've even bought a copy of the Good Beer Guide for the tasting notes at the back.

I'll certainly never again order a glass of wine in a pub.

Come on ladies, educate those taste buds!   WS

LITTLE STANNEY
STANNEY OAKS
A5117 (near the Cheshire Oaks retail outlet)
⏰APH
**Boddingtons B, Castle Eden,
Wadworth 6X [H]**
Recently opened on an old petrol station site, with emphasis on food. Typical Brewer's Fayre, with Charlie Chalk Fun Factory for the kids. Bar meals. One for a meal when shopping, but no more than that.
◖◗ ⛪ ♿ ● P ⊘

OLD HALL FARM
Kinsey Road (at M53 junction 10)
⏰APH
**Banks B, Camerons Strongarm,
Marstons Pedigree [H]**
New roadhouse opposite Sainsburys, created from an old farmhouse. Stone flagged conservatory overlooks the Motorway. Food all day except Sunday. The upstairs restaurant and the playground indicate the intended clientele.
◖◗ ⛪ ♿ ● P ⊘

LITTLE BOLLINGTON
SWAN WITH TWO NICKS
Park Lane

⏰11.30-3, 5.30-11 Mon-Fri (Sat in Winter); 11.30-11 Sat (Summer); 12-10.30 Sun
Boddingtons B, Castle Eden Ale, Coach House Two Nicks, Flowers IPA, Marstons Pedigree, guest beer (occasional) [H]
The Swan is a classic, if somewhat extended, country pub, set on a quiet country lane. It is very handy for Dunham Hall & deer park (National Trust) via the pedestrian entrance near the water mill.

Very popular with diners, the pub has a large restaurant at the rear serving meals all day till 9.30 on Sunday (children are admitted only if they are eating). However, the cosy front rooms of the original building are welcoming to drinkers. Copper-topped tables, beams, horse-brasses and subtle lighting add to the intimate atmosphere, and the back bar boasts a superb black-leaded range. It can be very popular at weekends and Bank holidays, and wooden benches outside cater for overspill on sunny days. It is also a staging post for the local Morris dance troupe (e.g. Boxing Day)! All this, and a house beer from the excellent local brewery, Coach House (served from the rear bar).

The guest beer is often from an interesting microbrewery, such as Cheshire's Weetwood. As we went to press, the licensee was considering dropping the Pedigree in favour of a further guest beer. Variety is the spice of life!
◖◗ P

LITTLE STANNEY
RAKE HALL
Rake Lane
⏰APH
Burtonwood B, Top Hat [H]
Recently refurbished large pub with strong food accent. Meals all day till 10pm. Roaring fire in winter. Function rooms available for hire. Caravan park nearby.
◖◗ ⛪ ♿ ● P

LITTLE BUDWORTH
RED LION
Vicarage Lane (village centre, opposite church)
⏰6-11 Mon; 12-3, 6-11 Tue-Sat; 12-10.30 Sun
Robinsons Hatters Mild, Best B, other Robinsons beers (occasional) [H]
Situated across the road from the red sandstone Norman church, this smart, clean and welcoming ex-coaching inn sits in the heart of an unspoilt rural retreat. Where finer to relax after feeding the ducks on the local pond, watching the narrow boats tackle the infamous "staircase locks" or even a long country ramble?

The comfortable interior is split into a front, no-smoking family room, a central bar room with roaring fire and a large side room frequented by diners. Beamed ceilings, wooden settles and copper-topped tables are in evidence of course. Local farmers, golfers and visitors to Oulton Park chat and mingle casually. Food, including specials, is served all day Sunday, though not Monday. In the summer months, people spill out into the elevated garden, overlooking the bowling green. On a clear day the Pennines can also be seen. The pub celebrated its bicentenary last year - happy anniversary!
◖◗ ⛪ ♿ ● P ⊘

LITTLE SUTTON

BLACK LION
No real ale

BURLEYDAM
No real ale

ELLESMERE ARMS
No real ale

MARQUIS
No real ale

RED LION
307 Station Road (at A41)
☉APH
Boddingtons B, Cains Traditional B, Flowers Original, Fuggles Imperial IPA [H]
Large town pub with one bar serving several areas. Games room, big screen TV and Thursday Quiz.
◀ ♿ ❀ ⇌ P

LITTLE SUTTON

TRAVELLER'S REST
14 Ledsham Road, 100 yards from the A41.
☉APH
Marstons Pedigree,Tetley Walker Mild, B, plus a house beer" [H]
Large two-roomed pub, separate eating area and helpful staff. Special rates for pensioners. Small car park. Rare outlet for the mild.
◀ ♿ ❀ ⇌ P ⊗

LOCKING STUMPS

TURF & FEATHER
Glover Road (next to shops)
☉12-11 Mon-Sat; 12-10.30 Sun
Marstons Pedigree, Tetley B [H]
Featuring large tap room and lounge, with access to garden through conservatory.
◀ ▶ ☡ ❀ P

LITTLE BUDWORTH
SHREWSBURY ARMS

Chester Lane (main A54 road on outskirts of village)
☉11.30-3, 6-11 Mon-Sat; 12-3, 7-10.30 Sun
Robinsons Best B, Frederics [H]
Promised an outer lick of paint by Robinsons, this internally spotless ex-farmhouse is a real find. About 350 years old, it became a beershop in 1841, was purchased by the Earl of Shrewsbury in 1872, and was a working dairy farm 30 years ago, though it retains 25 acres of land and old stables. There are four distinct areas inside, including a cosy snug and a separate dining room, once the farm kitchen. Exposed timbers, cast-iron tables, wooden settles and dried flowers are found throughout. Interesting historical maps and documents are displayed on the walls. Read the account of the legendary brawl between locals and Oulton Park racegoers on the central fireplace! There is no piped music and all the food is freshly prepared. Note that there are no meals on Monday evenings.

As you would expect from an ex-farmhouse, there is an extensive garden. The Frederic's is served under light gas pressure. Opening hours may change/extend on the retirement of current, friendly landlord later this year. We wish him all the best! **GBG**
◀ ▶ ☡ ❀ P

LITTLE NESTON
HARP INN

Quayside (turn off Burton Road to the bottom of Marshlands Road, and left onto Marsh Road)
☉APH
Timothy Taylors Landlord, Whitbread Chesters Mild, Flowers IPA, Trophy B [H]
The Harp is a small and unassuming 19th century inn, in an out-of-the-way waterside location The local colliery is now long gone, but lends the Harp much of its atmosphere. A delightful two-roomed, ex-miners' pub, it has views over the Dee marshes and the distant Welsh hills. It may be difficult to get to, but it is a joy to find. A few tables outside are popular with families and walkers, and there are times when the only sound is birdsong. The wonderfully unspoilt public bar on the left has fascinating historic photographs of the pub and the local mine and in the winter months, provides a warm welcome with a blazing coal fire. The low beams are festooned with horse brasses, miner's lamps and a coal hammer. With its tiled floor and homely atmosphere, it is possible to imagine how it looked a century ago. On the right is a narrow tiled lounge, with wooden wall panelling and a gas fire. Meals finish at 7.30, but are served right through on Sunday afternoons. Situated on the banks of what was the River Dee quayside, it is approached by a dirt track, and high tides can be an occasional hazard, but there could be worse places to be marooned for an hour or two! Regularly in the Good Beer Guide, and awarded the Pub of the Month accolade by Wirral CAMRA in March 1998. It is good to see you can still find Chesters cask mild. **GBG**
◀ ▶ ☡ ❀ P

LOWER PEOVER

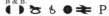

BELLS OF PEOVER

The Cobbles (next to St. Oswald's church, signposted up a cobbled lane from the B5081)

⏱11.30-3, 5.30-11 Mon-Fri; 11.30-11 Sat; 12-10.30 Sun

Boddingtons B, Greenalls B, Original [H]

This is a quintessentially English pub in a superb rural setting. Set directly opposite a beautiful half-timbered 13th century church, you can sit on the patio and watch weddings or listen to the bells being rung. The white-painted exterior is graced by the original inn sign, dating from 1839 and showing the crest of the de Tabley family. It was known originally as the "Warren de Tabley Arms", and later passed to the Bell family, which is the origin of the name, rather than the proximity of the church. Bow windows with leaded lights feature behind the cobbled frontage. If you enter from the patio, passing the hanging baskets and window boxes, you will note the hearts picked out in black on the walls, and the enormous blue Wisteria which almost covers the frontage.

Although it can be very busy, the interior is most attractive, with cameos, bedpans and a barometer adorning the walls. On the right as you enter is a delightful small snug with wooden fireplace and large mirror. This room and the small bar boast a collection of Toby jugs.
The back room has antique wooden furniture, including settles and a lovely sideboard.
The lounge on the left has a blackleaded fireplace, huge brass plates, old county maps and atmospheric lighting provided by brass coach lights. Newspapers and magazines are thoughtfully provided.

The large car park unusually has a fountain in the middle, and visitors will note the Union Jack and the Stars & Stripes flying from the wall. This commemorates the wartime meeting of Generals Patton and Eisenhower here. At the bottom of the attractive rose-strewn gardens flows a small stream, the Peover Eye. This follows the route of a very pleasant six-mile circular walk between the two Peovers, taking in the Whipping Stocks inn and an attractive church in each village. The paths are marked on the O. S. map. This is one of Cheshire's classic country walks and is detailed in several books.

The beers are kept very well, but the perfectionists amongst us would wish for a more interesting choice of beers. With a guest beer policy the Bells could be unsurpassable.

FLAGSHIPS – CHESHIRE'S TOP 100

This book lists, so far as we can, every pub in the county. In addition, we give special prominence to our selection of the top 100, the best pubs in Cheshire. Much lively debate at local CAMRA meetings was involved, although many pubs were obvious candidates.

This excluded the most obviously "themed" pubs and those which suffer from the curse of "McDonaldisation", where some sort of combination creche and burger joint seemingly has a bar tucked on as an afterthought, with an uninspired choice of beers. Do not misunderstand me, I eat and am a parent, but when I go to a pub I look for character and individuality, not for a formula concocted by a marketing drone.

The hostelries we have selected show many variations in age and setting, not all serve food, or have a garden, or admit children, although most do. What they do have in common is that they capture the quintessential nature of the traditional English pub. They serve good, real beer in civilised and enjoyable surroundings. In most cases they have done this for scores, if not hundreds of years. Enjoy them before the brand manager gets his hands on them!

LOSTOCK GRALAM

SLOW & EASY
Manchester Road
⏱APH
Greenalls B [H]
Large, wood-themed roadhouse with a bowling green. Next to Lostock Gralam F.C. Separate vault. Quiz, pool, big screen TV, karaoke. Food to 7 in evenings, not weekends. B & B.

WHARF
216 Manchester Road
⏱12-3, 5.30-11 Mon-Fri; 12-11 Sat; 12-10.30 Sun
Boddingtons B; Tetley B [H]
Converted warehouse on canal, now a split-level pub. Restaurant; evening food Fri-Sun only.

LOWER STRETTON

RING O' BELLS
Northwich Road (near the M56 junction 10)
⏱12-3, 5.30-11 Mon-Fri; 12-11 Sat; 12-10.30 Sun
Greenalls Mild, B, guest beer [H]
Quiet, friendly local with a gorgeous front snug, open fires and oak beams. Converted from three 19th century cottages, with all the character you would expect. A deliberate decision has been made not to go for the food trade, and it remains a rural gem dedicated to good ale. The persistently hungry can have a pie. Unusually, there is a boules pitch with resident team. Guest beers from the Greenalls lists

LOWER WITHINGTON

BLACK SWAN
Trap St
⏱12-3, 7-11 Mon-Sat; 12-3,7-10.30 Sun
Greene King Abbot,
Marstons Head Brewers Choice [H]
A 17th century pub/restaurant taken up market by dedicating the original pub to dining, and adding a new bar. A homely, comfortable and cosy place to eat. The menu is interesting, and considering that the car park usually boasts BMWs and Jags and even Rolls Royce, it is surprisingly affordable. Half of the eating area is non-smoking.

LOWER WITHINGTON
RED LION
Dicklow Cob (centre of the village, just south of the B5392)
⏰12-2.30, 5-11 Mon-Sat;
12-3,7.30-10.30 Sun
Robinsons Dark Best Mild, Best B [H]
Comfortable if a little bland, it is dominated by the attached restaurant. Meals 12-2. Monday-Sunday; 7-9.30 Tuesday-Saturday, 7-9 Sunday. The outside lights make a most welcoming sight if you arrive by night. Good to find Robinson's on hand pump in this area. Handy for Jodrell Bank. A Good Beer Guide entry for many years. A very rare outlet for the Dark Mild, despite the misleading pumpclip for Hatters. **GBG**

LYMM
ANCHOR
Booths Hill Road (A56)
⏰APH
Boddingtons B, Greenalls B [H]
Old, two-roomed, local. Modernised, but still retains its village atmosphere, aided by the retention of a vault and a real fire. Landlord has been in the trade for over 30 years.

BALMORAL LOUNGE
15 Whitbarrow Road
⏰APH
Caledonian Deuchars IPA, 80/- [H]
Scottish-themed lounge bar attached to Lymm Hotel tucked away in older part of village. Food served lunchtimes in bar, evening meals in attached bistro or separate restaurant.
Rooms available in hotel. Adjacent to Trans-Pennine Trail. Unusual to see Scottish beers as standard so far south of the border.

BULLS HEAD
32 The Cross
⏰11.30-3, 5.30-11 Mon-Thu; 11.30-11 Fri-Sat;
12-10.30 Sun
Hydes Mild, B [E]
16th century inn with comfortable lounge and public bar. Frontage now below road level due to subsequent building of the canal (and bridge) in 1765. Sheltered courtyard at rear. Serves one of the three Hydes cask milds.

LOWER PEOVER
CROWN
Crown Lane, Swan Green (B5081)
⏰11.30-3, 5.30-11 Mon-Sat; 12-3, 7-10.30 Sun
Boddingtons B, Chesters Mild, 3 guest beers [H]
The Crown is a homely, 17th century inn which is still part of a working farm and has been in the same hands for 25 years. The pleasant-looking exterior has a cobbled frontage, flower tubs, window boxes and hanging baskets. Inside there is a friendly, almost family atmosphere, with a welcome extended to locals and visitors alike. The walls are adorned with a cornucopia of fixtures and fittings collected during the lifetime of the licensees. Three very homely rooms are centred round the bar. The room you enter from the porch has a wonderful timeless feel with scrubbed, wooden tables, benching and a regularly used darts board. The central room houses copper-topped tables and a cosy snug adorned with china plates of every description. Low ceilings, beams and exposed stonework abound, along with multitudes of prints (some of Peover) and postcards. Horse brasses and horse collar feature by the rear fire. The smart front room is given over mainly to diners. Darts and dominoes are played and there is an annual gooseberry competition on the last Saturday in July!

    This is one of the few remaining outlets for the rare, real (i.e. non-keg) and excellently kept, Chesters Mild. Five real ales are available. Two of the guests are from major breweries, one from an independent such as Cheshire's Weetwood microbrewery.

TIME FOR ONE MORE?

Out *Inn* CHESHIRE lists our selection of the best 100 pubs in the county.
We would like to give you the opportunity of selecting one more flagship pub.

    Using the specimen survey form at the end of the book, feel free to check out your own favourites and see how they compare.

    If you feel that any one pub really does qualify as one of the Cheshire's flagships, let us have the details via your CAMRA branch contact (see page 2 of the guide).

    After 31st December 1998, we will judge the suggestions, and the most suitable additional flagship pub will be chosen. The winner will be presented with a limited edition Out Inn CHESHIRE T-shirt at the nominated pub as a token of our thanks for finding number 101.

LYMM

SPREAD EAGLE
47 Eagle Brow
⏰11.30-11 Mon-Sat; 12-10.30 Sun
Lees GB Mild, B [H] , Moonraker (in Winter) [E]
You are assured a friendly welcome in this three-roomed old pub in the village centre, and not just because of the open fire. Long and rambling, it has been much extended into neighbouring cottages. On the right as you enter by the colonnaded entrance lobby is a classic cosy snug with a real fire and historic photographs of the pub. Beyond this, on the right, is a small, basic vault with a dart board and TV. Ahead is a bar, opening out into a lounge, which has a plate rack all round the walls.
Keeping a watchful eye on proceedings is a stuffed Golden Eagle. Old photographs of Lymm, low ceilings and subdued lighting give a relaxing atmosphere. Beyond is a large dining and function room, and the leaded bow windows are a feature. A wooden staircase leads up to the Ballroom.
The food is good and home cooked, including Sunday lunches. There is however, limited parking. Set near the canal and Lymm cross, the Eagle is an excellent place to visit in combination with a few hours sightseeing in this attractive and historic village. Lees is a comparatively rare brew for the county, and hails from Middleton in Greater Manchester. Their wonderful, strong winter ale, Moonraker, is sold here in winter. **GBG**
◖ P

CHURCH GREEN
Higher Lane (A56)
⏰12-11 Mon-Sat; 12-10.30 Sun
Greenalls B, Original;
Worthington Draught B [H]
Modernised open-plan family pub serving food all day (until 9pm). Large outdoor drinking and childrens play area.
◖ ▮ 🐎 ♿ ● P ⊗

CROWN
15 Booths Hill Road (A56)
⏰APH
Boddingtons B; 2 guest beers [H]
Large, single room, village pub with partitioned and raised areas. Emphasis on diners and families. Food served all day.
◖ ▮ 🐎 ♿ ● P ⊗

FARMERS ARMS
222 Rushgreen Road, Oughtrington
⏰APH
Greenall's Mild, B, Original ; Tetley B [H]
Large recently renovated country pub with central bar and several varying alcoved areas. Emphasis on food and families.
◖ ▮ 🐎 ♿ ● P ⊗

GOLDEN FLEECE
41 The Cross
⏰12-3, 6-11 Mon-Fri; 12-11 Sat; 12-10.30 Sun
Greenalls B, Original [H]
Modernised black & white pub, popular with local students. Wood panelling, exposed brick-work and floor tiling dominate.
◖ ● P

POP INN
No real ale

SADDLERS
No real ale

MACCLESFIELD

108's (formerly Bull and Gate)
70 Waters Green (across from station)
⏰12-11 Mon-Fri; 11-11 Sat; 12-10.30 Sun
Vaux Samson [H]
Smallest of three pubs next door to one another, the name (complete with grocer's apostrophe) is that of the quaint series of Victorian steps rising behind the pub to the back of the church above. Live music some Wednesday nights. No meals but sandwiches served all day. Vaux is rare in Cheshire.

ABORIGINALS
No real ale

BARNFIELD
24 Catherine Street (near Chestergate)
⏰12-3, 5-11 Mon-Fri; 12-11 Sat; 12-10.30 Sun
Robinsons Best [H]
Welcoming, three room local in centre of town. No evening meals at weekends. Quiz night Sunday.
◖ ▮ ●

BATE HALL HOTEL
39 Chestergate
⏰11-11 Mon-Sat; 7-10.30 Sun
Marstons B, Pedigree,
Head Brewers Choice [H]
A grade II listed building on pedestrianised street in town centre. There is a fine Jacobean staircase but much of the rest of the history of this 16th century town house of the Stafford family is hidden beneath a more recent frontage. Busy lunchtimes and evenings.
◖ ⇌ P

BATHS
40 Green Street (off lower end of A537)
⏰12-4.30 (not Mon-Fri), 6.30-11 Mon-Sat; 12-4, 7-10.30 Sun
Banks B, Boddingtons B, Hansons Mild [H]
Small thriving pub just a few minutes' walk uphill from station, on other side of track from entrance (turn right out of forecourt). Traditional games room popular with all ages and both sexes. Cosy lounge. Hansons is an unusual brew for the town. **GBG**
⇌

BEEHIVE
262 Black Road (off Windmill Street)
⏰11.30-11 Mon-Fri; 11.30-4, 6.30-11 Tues-Thur, Sat; 12-3, 7-10.30 Sun
Boddingtons B, Beehive (house beer) [H]
Comfortable pub in Victorian terrace, neatly renovated and backing onto canal, high on the eastern edge of town. Overlooks a playing field at the front, with an ample terraced garden at the back. No meals Sundays. Beehive is a medium strength beer brewed by Tetley for Greenalls.
◖ 🐎 ● P

BLUEBERRY INN
Park Lane (off Mill St)
⏰APH
Banks B [H]
Welcoming, single room local in town centre. Originally the called "Hole I' Th' Wall" and situated opposite the Paradise Silk Mill to slake the thirsts of local workers. Quiz night Tuesday.
⇌

BREWERS ARMS
139 Bridge Street
⏰12-11 Mon-Sat; 12-10.30 Sun
Draught Bass, Walker Best B,
Mansfield Grays B [H]
Basic town local. Built in the 1820's by William Okell who owned an inn in the centre of Macclesfield which boasted a small brewery, possibly the source of this pub's name. Gray's bitter is made by Nottinghamshire's Mansfield brewery.
⇌

BRIDGEWATER ARMS
174 Buxton Road (just below canal)
⏱11-3, 4-11 Mon-Sat; 12-10.30 Sun
John Smiths B, Wilsons B [H]
Former Wilson's local with traditionally
partitioned rooms. Enthusiastic landlord.
Popular with canal trade in season. Beer range
may change soon. Interesting jukebox.

BRITISH FLAG
42 Coare Street
⏱5.30-11 Mon-Fri; 4.30-11 Sat;
12-3, 7-10.30 Sun
Robinsons Hatters Mild, Best B [H]
Old-fashioned, friendly town local with four
comfortable rooms and central bar. Pub games
popular with skittles in one room, darts and
pool in another. Big screen TV.
Wheelchair accessible. **GBG**

BRUCE ARMS
231 Crompton Road (southern end)
⏱5-11 Mon-Fri; 12-11Sat; 12--10.30 Sun
Tetley B, guest beer (occasional) [H]
A surprisingly extensive pub set in a long
street of terraced housing. The vault runs along
the bar at the front, and there are three lounges.
A garden is planned "soon".

BULL
Buxton Road (near the bottom)
⏱APH
Robinsons Hatters Mild, Best B [H]
Built as part of a council flat complex at the
end of the sixties, near what is now a busy
junction at the bottom of Buxton Road.
"Caff" next door.

BULLS HEAD HOTEL
No real ale

CHESTER ROAD TAVERN
Chester Road
⏱11-4, 6-11 Mon-Thurs; 11-11 Fri-Sat;
12-4, 7-10.30 Sun
Greenalls Mild, B, Stones B, guest beers [H]
Thriving, four room pub on the edge of the
town centre. Real fire and horse brasses.
Pool and darts in back room. Guest beers
usually from independent breweries.

CROMPTON ROAD TAVERN
Crompton Road
⏱6.30-11 Mon-Sat; 7-10.30 Sun
Burtonwood B [H]
Bustling multi-room local with beautiful
North Cheshire Brewing Co etched glass entry
door and large whisky jug collection over bar
area. Pool and other pub games popular.

MACCLESFIELD

BOARHOUND
37 Brook Street
⏱APH
Robinson Hatters Mild, Best B [H]
An imposing brick-built local overlooking the busy town section of the Silk Road, a few minutes'
walk from the station and Waters Green. It was formerly a more modest pub called the Commercial.
The notice board is testimony to the Boarhound's popularity as the headquarters to various pub
teams, with crib, Nine Card Don, quiz, dominoes, pool and Sunday football all being featured. The
bar looks into comfortable lounges on the front and away to the side. There is a large function room
upstairs available for meetings. The garden area at the back typifies the trend to utilise back-yards in
these days of global warming! Although there is no car park, there is ample street parking nearby.
The beers are brewed a few miles up the road in Stockport, and have a committed local following.
They are kept so well here that the pub is a regular entry in CAMRA's national Good Beer Guide.
GBG.

CROWN
No real ale.

DOLPHIN
76 Windmill Street
(off southern end of Silk Road)
⏱6-11 Mon-Fri; 4-11 Sat; 12-10.30 Sun
Robinsons Best B [H]
Friendly local overlooking playing field.
Traditional layout. Try a brisk walk up Windmill Street to the pub to work up a thirst!

DURHAM OX
68 Hurdsfield Road
⏱3.30-11 Mon-Thurs; 12-11 Fri, Sat;
12-10.30 Sun
Vaux B, Samson, Wards Best B [H]
Basic town much at the bottom of road to
Whaley Bridge, opposite council flats.
Club room at side for weekend entertainment.

FILIGREE & FIRKIN
85 Mill Street
⏱11.30-11 Mon-Sat; 12-10.30 Sun
**Frilly Knickers, Silkworm, Dog Bolter, one
Firkin guest beer [H]**
Town-centre rendezvous with one large room
housing eaters, drinkers and area for unusual
games. Typical mixture of original and bizarre
breweriana on walls. The beers are brewed by
Firkin brewpubs elsewhere.

FLOWERPOT INN
1 Congleton Road (A536)
⏱11.30-11 Mon-Sat; 12-10.30 Sun
Robinsons Best B [H]
Large, multi-roomed, post-war pub on main
road. Young clientele in the evening.
Thursday is karaoke night!

FLOWER POT INN
110 Hurdsfield Road
⏱12-11 Mon-Sat; 12-10.30 Sun
Greenalls B [H]
Set about halfway out of town centre on
B5470 to Whaley Bridge. Large pub with vault
and divided lounge, on edge of Hurdsfield
estate. Comfortable seating areas, surrounded
by much traditional polished wood.

FOX & GRAPES
No real ale - *despite fake handpumps*

FRANKLIN
27 Steeple Street (close to Hurdsfield Road)
⏱12-3, 5.30-11 Mon-Fri; 12-11 Sat;
12-3, 7-10.30 Sun
Robinsons Best B [H]
Small friendly back street local set in row of
terraced housing. One of the smallest pubs in
the town. The bar lounge is like someone's
sitting room.

MAXWELLS
13 King Edward Street
☺12-11 Mon-Thurs; 12-12.30 Fri; 7-12.30 Sat; closed Sun
Ind Coope Burton Ale,
Marstons Pedigree [H]
Up-market, town-centre, multi-room pub which is occasionally populated by rugby club members. Doors are sometimes closed early and there is a dress code that excludes wearing training shoes, but the good quality beer and over 21 late license make up for it. Try the Burton Ale before it is axed by the brewery.

MIDDLEWOOD
Springwood Way (Tytherington Business Park)
☺APH
Boddingtons B, Wadworth 6X, guest beer [H]
Newly built Brewer's Fayre pub very much orientated to the family food scene, in a new 'business park' complete with motel, etc. Drinkers definitely feel subsidiary to eaters. Lots to entertain children, indoors and out. Meals from 11 am -10 pm.
 P

CASTLE
Churchwallgate (Church Street) (a narrow cobbled street near church, uphill and left from Waters Green)
☺12-3, 7-11 Mon-Sat; 7.30-10.30 Sun
Courage Directors, Theakstons Mild, Best B [H]
An untouched, timeless and now perfect example of an old-fashioned town pub. The quaint exterior belies its inner proportions, which are equally charming. There are leaded lights, moulded plaster ceilings, copper-topped tables, wooden settles, brasses and even a grandmother clock, dotted throughout its warren of little rooms. The piece de resistance, however is the wonderful hatch bar reminiscent of a traditional, bowed, shop window, full of spirit miniatures and old beer bottles. On the right as you enter is a tiny vault, with a narrow lounge on the left. Past the bar is another lounge or snug on the right, and beyond this is a larger, raised area. This part of the pub has something of a conservatory feel, due to the presence of a glass roof. The landlord keeps a Second World War Tommy's helmet and the old key to Macclesfield castle behind the bar! Not unsurprisingly, it is on CAMRA's National Inventory of Heritage Pubs. This is altogether a quiet, relaxing haven from the busy shopping centre and railway station nearby. It's also a rare outlet for one of Theakston's unsung classics, the Mild Ale.

GEORGE HOTEL
No real ale

GEORGE & DRAGON
61 Rainow Road
☺12-3, 7-11 Mon-Fri; 7-11 Sat; 7.30-10.30 Sun
Theakstons Black Bull B, 2 guest beers [H]
Last of half a dozen pubs set along the road out to Whaley Bridge. Guest beers from independents. May open all day Sunday for live TV football. Black Bull is the only Theakstons beer solely brewed in Yorkshire.
P

GEORGE & DRAGON
Sunderland Street
☺11-4, 5.30-11 Mon, Thu; 11-3, 5.30-11 Tue, Wed; 11-11 Fri; 11-5, 7-11 Sat; 12-3, 7-10.30 Sun
Robinsons Hatters Mild, Best B [E]
A basic regulars' pub, handy for the bus and railway stations. Strong pub games following. Sandwiches only. GBG

GOLDEN LION
98 Moss Lane
☺12-11 Mon-Sat; 12-10.30 Sun
Tetley B [H]
Three room local with open fire. A number of bottle conditioned beers are also stocked.
P

IVY HOUSE
118 Park Lane
☺APH
Burtonwood B [H]
Small street-corner local with two rooms at the front and a lounge made to look bigger by two large mirrors.

IVY LEAF
No real ale

JOLLY SAILOR
63 Sunderland Street
☺4-11 Mon-Fri; 11-11 Sat; 12-3, 7-10.30 Sun
Camerons B, Marstons B, Pedigree [H]
Small pub, former supreme Bass outlet, a couple of hundred yards from the station. Monday night entertainment.

LORD BYRON
Chapel Street (corner of St. George's Street)
☺12-3, 5.30-11 Mon-Sat; 12-3, 5.30-10.30 Sun
Robinsons Best B [H]
Recently renovated corner local. The pub games are very popular.

MULBERRY BUSH
Carisbrook Avenue (Hurdsfield)
☺APH
Boddingtons Mild, B [H]
Large two roomed pub (conventional lounge and vault) set in middle of Hurdsfield estate on NE side of town. Rare sighting of Boddies mild in this area. Food is fast (microwaved).
P

NAGS HEAD
60 Waters Green
☺12-11 Mon-Sat; 12-10.30 Sun
Robinsons Best B, Hartleys XB, Frederic's [H]
Basic pub next to the 108 church steps. Live music most Saturdays, jam nights Thursdays. Pool and games room with loud music. Runs annual bed push for charity. Chess club.

NAVIGATION
161 Black Road (near Windmill Street)
☺12-11 Mon-Sat; 12-10.30 Sun
Boddingtons B, Tetley B [H]
A prominent street-corner local high on eastern edge of town, popular with all ages. Built, as the name suggests, at the same time as the nearby canal.

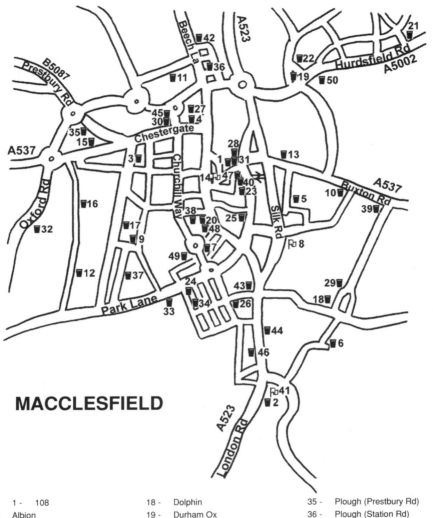

MACCLESFIELD

1 -	108	18 -	Dolphin	35 -	Plough (Prestbury Rd)
2 -	Albion	19 -	Durham Ox	36 -	Plough (Station Rd)
3 -	Barnfield	20 -	Filigree & Firkin	37 -	Prince Albert
4 -	Bate Hall	21 -	Flower Pot	38 -	Prince of Wales
5 -	Baths	22 -	Franklin	39 -	Puss in Boots
6 -	Beehive	23 -	George & Dragon	40 -	Queens Hotel
7 -	Blueberry Inn	24 -	Ivy House	41 -	Railway View
8 -	Boarhound	25 -	Jolly Sailor	42 -	Ship
9 -	Brewers Arms	26 -	Lord Byron	43 -	Sun Inn
10 -	Bridgewater Arms	27 -	Maxwells	44 -	Three Crowns
11 -	British Flag	28 -	Nags Head	45 -	Three Pigeons
12 -	Bruce Arms	29 -	Navigation	46 -	Travelers Rest
13 -	Bull Inn	30 -	Old Kings Head	47 -	Waters Green Tavern
14 -	Castle	31 -	Old Millstone	48 -	White Lion
15 -	Chester Road Tavern	32 -	Ox-Fford	49 -	White Swan
16 -	Crompton Road Tavern	33 -	Park Tavern	50 -	Woodsman
17 -	Crown	34 -	Peel Arms		

OLDE KINGS HEAD
Chestergate
⏰11-3, 5-11 Mon-Fri; 11-3, 7-11 Sat;
12-3, 7-10.30 Sun
Greenalls B [H]
Deceptively large and busy with locals and
shoppers popping in for the popular lunches.
Darts and pool rooms. Despite having no
special facilities, wheelchair customers are
welcome. No food Sunday.
 P

OLD MILLSTONE
Waters Green
⏰12-11 Mon-Sat; 12-10.30 Sun
**Marstons B, Pedigree,
Head Brewers Choice [H]**
Middle one of three adjoining pubs on the
corner of Waters Green opposite the station.
Multi-level interior with several, cosy drinking
areas. Old prints with fascinating historic
views of the pub. Three pool tables in the back
room with a view of the 108 steps up to the
parish church.

OVAL
No real ale

OX-FFORD
73 Oxford Road
⏰12-3, 5-11 Mon-Thu; 11-11 Fri-Sat;
12-10.30 Sun
**Theakstons Best B, Black Bull B, XB,
guest beer [H]**
Free house which is very much a locals' haunt.
Active sports teams. Once the Oxford Hotel,
the reason for the change to the current
spelling seems to have been lost in the mists of
time! However, an interesting story about
some previous landlord is framed on the wall.
The Black Bull Bitter is the only Theakston's
beer still brewed solely at the original brewery
in the Yorkshire Dales town of Masham.

PARK TAVERN
158 Park Lane
⏰12-3, 5-11 Mon-Fri; 12-11 Sat;
12-5.30, 7-10.30 Sun
Robinsons Best B [H]
Lively terraced local popular for TV sport, as
well as entertainment, musical or otherwise, on
small stage on Saturdays.

PEEL ARMS
Peel Street
⏰11-1.30, 4-11 Mon-Fri; 11-11 Sat;
12-3, 6.30-10.30 Sun
**Banks B, Martons Pedigree, guest beer [H]
Addlestones cask cider [H]**
Small, quiet, terraced pub. A rare outlet for
Banks Bitter and cask cider.

PLOUGH
1 Station Road
⏰12-3, 7-11 Mon-Sat; 12-3, 7-10.30 Sun
Marstons B [H]
Corner pub overlooking old railway sidings,
now a brand new by-pass.

PLOUGH
Prestbury Road
⏰11-3, 5.30-11 Mon-Fri;
11-3.30, 6.30-11 Sat; 12-3, 7-10.30 Sun
Greenalls B [H]
Small, brick corner local. Three rooms
including a carpeted public bar. The walls are
covered in country prints (including the
famous Little Moreton Hall), mirrors, brass-
work and even a map of Olde Cheshire. Sports
fans are catered for by a darts area, pool table
and TV! Regular entertainment evenings.
No food at weekends.

PRINCE ALBERT
140 Newton Street (off Park Lane)
⏰12-11 Mon-Sat; 12-10.30 Sun
Tetley Mild, B, guest beers [H]
Small street corner local strong on darts, and
home of a well-known angling club. The guest
beer is usually from the excellent Phoenix
brewery in Heywood.

PRINCE OF WALES
33 Roe Street
⏰11-3, 7-11 Mon-Thu; 11-11 Fri; 12-11 Sat;
12-3, 7-10.30 Sun
Porters Ale, 2 guest beers [H]
A one room, Greenalls "Porters" theme alehouse, opposite the Heritage Centre. Wood-
finished interior with reproduction signs of the
towns old silk industry. Popular with shoppers.
Newspapers provided. Wednesday quiz.
No food Sunday. House ale is made by Tetley
in Burton.

PUSS IN BOOTS
198 Buxton Road (next to canal)
⏰12-11 Mon-Sat; 12-10.30 Sun
Boddingtons B [H]
Solid and tastefully refurbished stone-built pub
set alongside the Macclesfield canal at a
bridge, with interesting views from lounge,
and tables on towpath.

QUEENS HOTEL
1 Albert Place (opposite the station)
⏰APH
Holts Mild, B [H]
Huge pub with a games room on the right,
popular and smoky lounge on the left. Tuesday
Table Skittles team, ladies darts team.
Function room for hire. Public car park
opposite.
Meals comprise Sunday lunch only, 12 till 5.

RIDGEGATE
Princes Way (off B5392)
⏰12-11 Mon-Fri; 11-11 Sat; 12-10.30 Sun
Tetley Dark Mild, B [H]
Two room pub in housing estate off Chester
Road. Pool table and large screen TV.
 P

SHIP
61-63 Beech Lane
⏰APH
**Draught Bass, Worthington Draught B,
guest beers [H]**
Formerly two cottages, converted to a single-
roomed pub in the 1960's. Food available
throughout the day, with occasional
international cuisine evenings.
Gents, note the interesting urinal!
 P

SILKMAN(formerly Brambles)
159 London Road (A523)
(part of football ground)
⏰12-11 Mon-Fri, 12-3, 7-11 Sat,
12-10.30 Sun
Tetley Dark Mild(evenings only),
B (match days only),
Coach House Silkman B(house beer) [H]
Large open-plan pub next to Macclesfield
Town football ground with a
name reflecting the local industrial heritage.
House beer is brewed by the independent
brewer, Coach House of Warrington.
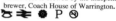 P

STAR INN
173 London Rd
⏰12-3, 6.30-11 Mon-Sat; 12-3, 7-10.30 Sun
Marstons Bitter, Pedigree [H]
Games oriented in winter and also very
convenient for the football ground. Sadly
under threat of demolition, this multi-roomed
pub has real fires and beautiful wood panelling
in the "Tudor Room".
 P

SUN INN
45 Mill Lane (A523)
⏰5-11 Mon-Thurs; 11-11 Fri & Sat;
12-10.30 Sun
**Burtonwood B, Cains Traditional B,
guest beers [H]**
Recently renovated, three room pub stocking
up to four guest beers from independent
breweries. Sandwiches available at lunchtime.
Nice open fire.

THREE CROWNS
Mill Lane (A523)
⏰12-11 Mon-Sat; 12-10.30 Sun
Holts Mild, B [H]
Open plan, Victorian, stone pub just off main
road. Handy for canal.

THREE CROWNS
38 Rainow Road (B5470)
⏰7-11 Mon-Fri; 12-4, 7-11 Sat;
12-4, 7-10.30 Sun
Robinsons Best B [H]
A small friendly stone-built local in a neat row
of terraced cottages. Parking is tricky on narrow road. The garden at back overlooks the
town.

THREE PIGEONS
Little Street (off Chestergate)
⏰12-11 Mon-Sat; 12-10.30 Sun
Greenalls B [H]
Street corner local still retaining small separate rooms. One houses a dartboard and map of old Cheshire - "The County Palatine of Chester", another a pool table. A few reprints of 18th century pub notices adorn the walls.

 P

TRAVELLERS REST
27 Cross Street (corner of London Rd., A523)
⏰11.45-3, 5.30-11 Mon-Sat;
12-3, 7-10.30 Sun
Robinsons Hatters Mild [H] ,
Best B [H] & [E]
Large, two roomed pub built in 1935, to replace an older pub of same name and catering for local custom, with an organist at weekends and a strong emphasis on pub games. There are seven letting bedrooms. Although there are no disabled toilets, wheelchairs are welcome. Value for money oversized, lined glasses used to ensure full beer measures.

WATERS GREEN TAVERN
Waters Green (on square just up from station)
⏰11-3, 5.30-11 Mon-Fri; 11-3, 7-11 Sat;
12-3, 7-10.30 Sun
Mansfield Riding B, 4 guest beers [H]
A centrally located ale house with the best range of independent beers in the town. Slightly opened out with three distinct areas, one of which houses a pool table. The pub has been in the care of the same tenant for 17 years. Men's and women's darts teams. Lunch is served 12 till 2 except Sunday. Street parking is usually available nearby. **GBG**

WEAVER
11 Thornton Sq. (off Thornton Ave off A535)
⏰12-3.30, 4.30-11 Mon-Thurs;
12-11 Fri & Sat; 12-10.30 Sun
Tetley B, Robinsons Best B, guest beers [H]
Modern, two room pub in shopping precinct. Warm and welcoming with a good rotation of guest beers from independent breweries.
 P

WHARF
No real ale.

MACCLESFIELD
RAILWAY VIEW HOTEL
Byrons Lane (off London Road-A523)
⏰6.30-11 Mon-Thu; 11-11 Fri; 11-3, 5-11Sat; 12-3, 6-10.30 Sun
(sometimes open all Saturday when Macc are playing at home!)
Batemans Dark Mild, XXXB, Boddingtons B, Coach House Railway Steam, 2 guest beers [H]
A justifiably popular beer house which has been a frequent Good Beer Guide entry. Deceptively large, it was originally two cottages, built in around 1700, and in its most recent guise, possesses a number of intimate eating and drinking areas. Atmosphere is provided by an open fire and by pub games, including darts, dominoes, bar football and cards. Leaving the main A523 Macclesfield-Stoke road at the traffic lights for the Langley and Wincle road, you cross the West Coast Main Line, and find the pub on your right. Its name is particularly appropriate, given that the patio at the rear overlooks the line, and would provide an idyllic spot for Railway Buffs. Meals are available all the time the pub is open. This is a rare outlet for Batemans XXXB in this area. The 4.2% ABV house beer, Railway Steam, is provided by Cheshire's own Coach House brewery. In addition to the hand pumps, a cask is usually to be found behind the bar, with a further guest, sometimes a winter warmer, and sometimes a real perry. See elsewhere in Out *Inn* CHESHIRE for details of this fascinating drink, which is akin to cider, but made from pears rather than apples. At the time of our survey, cask beer was on offer at £1.20 a pint on Mondays. Not so much a happy hour as Oh Happy Day! **GBG**

WHITE LION
105 Mill Street
⏰11-3, 5.30-11 Mon-Sat; not open Sundays
Boddingtons B [H]
Popular town centre pub next to cinema. Live music venue. Lively lunchtime food trade. Quiet area on Sundays; recuperation time!

WHITE SWAN
7 Rodney Street
⏰3-11 Mon-Thur; 11-11 Fri, Sat;
12-10.30 Sun
Boddingtons B, [H]
Small back-street local, close to the ring road with a high volume of beer sales. Upstairs function room. A skittles table holds its own amid electronic attractions.

WOODMAN
131 Hurdsfield Road
⏰12-3, 5.30-11 Mon-Fri; 12-11 Sat;
12-10.30 Sun
Robinsons Hatters Mild, Best B [E]
Recently reopened with enthusiastic and experienced landlord after a prolonged shutdown. Community pub. Stage and dance area for all kinds of entertainment. Handpumps may return.

MALPAS
CROWN HOTEL
No real ale

OLD VAULTS HOTEL
No real ale.

RED LION
Old Hall Street
⏰APH
Draught Bass, guest beers [H]
Quiet pub with games room in back bar

MARBURY
SWAN
⏰ 12-3, 7-11 Mon-Sat; 12-3, 7-10.30 Sun
Greenalls Original, Tetley B [H]
Food oriented country pub with open fires and well kept garden. Noted for good food and a wide range of specials. No Monday lunch. Late supper licence to 12. The lounge is no-smoking.

DOWN AT THE DOG & DUCK

" ...this house notes the long-established historical traditions which lie behind the ancient names of public houses and appreciates the special role they play in community life; deeply regrets the growing trend towards theme pubs, with contrived names that have no relevance for the local community and which can cause embarrassment, ridicule and a sense of alienation for local people..."

So read an Early Day motion set down in the House of Commons by **Macclesfield MP Nicholas Winterton**. It reflects a problem which continues to grow, with the ever increasing trend to branded theme pubs. Nicholas Winterton followed up his motion with a Private Members Bill, and writes here for CAMRA about his campaign to protect this neglected part of our pub heritage.

"The British pub is a unique institution. It has survived and developed over the centuries so that today it is part of the social fabric not only of the nation, but of each and every local community. There have been changes to pubs in recent years, many of them welcome – an improvement in the quality and diversity of the food available, a wider range of beers and spirits at prices which, as a result of duty reductions have actually begun to fall, and a cleaner, fresher environment which is more welcoming to women and to families.

But other changes have been more unwelcome. I do not deny that the owners of public houses have the right to change their décor and their layout to attract different groups of customers. Whilst I personally have no time for "theme" pubs, thrown together to realise an ad-man's dream of perfection, publicans are perfectly free to do with their property as they wish. But do we really need to change the ancient names of those hostelries which have in some cases been around for centuries and which are firmly established in the collective history of the local area?

The names of public houses frequently record important, if local historical events, and give their names to local areas. It is both wrong that centuries of community heritage can be erased at the stroke of a marketing-man's pen and unfortunate that many local residents feel embarrassed or alienated by the contrived names adopted, particularly by theme pubs.

A classic example was the threat by Allied Domecq to change the name of Macclesfield's ancient coaching inn, "The Bull's Head", to "The Pig and Truffle", and I was delighted by the way in which the local community, our local Borough Council, and many other interested parties cried "foul" and saw off, at least for the time being, this squandering of our heritage.

But this is happening all over the country and in my campaign to call a halt to this decimation of our cultural heritage. I have received letters of support from parish councils, civic societies, historical study groups, academics and individual people from every quarter of the British Isles. The "Bolton Abbey" became "Boom Boom", "The Elgin" became the "Frog & Firkin", and umpteen "Queen's Heads", "King's Arms" and "Coach & Horses" have become fake Irish or other theme pubs going by the name of "Scruffy Murphy's" or "Filthy McNasty's".

I am not one to quit the fight and I am seeking to introduce a Bill into the House of Commons to force a debate on this important subject before it is too late and all these historic names have forever been lost.

What I am proposing is not a ban on changes or excessive regulation, merely an amendment to the existing regulatory regime, namely that the name of a public house should be part of the licence conditions and be changed only after local consultation. It is otherwise a bizarre anomaly that the size, scale and luminosity of a pub sign is regulated, but the name which it displays and which can cause greater offence is not.

We should remember that the free market is our tool, not our master, and that society has every right to control that market to ensure that it conserves from the past that which is worth preserving, and changes that which needs improving.

To me, it would be foolish and reckless to allow these pieces of our living history to be destroyed."

Nicholas R. Winterton

MARSTON
SALT BARGE
Ollershaw Lane
⏱ 11-3,5-11 Mon-Thu; 11.30-11 Fri-Sat;
12.30-10.30 Sun
Burtonwood B, Buccaneer, Top Hat [H]
Large food-orientated pub with quirky décor.
Extended to rear. Handy for Lion Salt Works
museum and canal. Occasional guest beer
from Burtonwood stable.

MARTON (Northwich)
PLOUGH
Beauty Bank
⏱ Not provided
Robinsons Hatters Mild, Best B [H]
Quiet, rural and friendly pub, with separate
vault.

MICKLE TRAFFORD
ROYAL OAK
Warrington Road (A56)
⏱ APH
Draught Bass, guest beer (occasional) [H]
The restaurant includes a carvery, the bar has
big screen TV and billiards. Beer quality has
not always been what it should be.

SHREWSBURY ARMS
Warrington Road (A56)
⏱ APH
**Boddingtons B, Flowers IPA,
Morland Old Speckled Hen, guest beer [H]**
A recently refurbished roadside hostelry with
several drinking areas. Trying hard to be a
'traditional pub', it will appeal to the country
set.

**We originally had a logo for
Morland's Old Speckled Hen
in this position.
However, having taken over
the Ruddles Brewery in
September 1997, Morland's
have now threatened to
close this brewery.
The editors are therefore
unwilling to advertise their
products in this space.**

MARTON (Congleton)
DAVENPORT ARMS
Congleton Road (A34)
⏱ 11.30-3, 6-11 Mon-Thu; 11.30-3, 5.30-11 Fri-Sat; 12-10.30 Sun
Courage Directors, Ruddles Best B, Websters Yorkshire B [H]
Prominently sited on the A34, with a large car park, the Davenport Arms is a popular destination,
especially for diners. Although it could be said to be more of a restaurant than a pub, the large
L-shaped bar has a low-beamed ceiling, wooden settles and a real fire which provide a homely
atmosphere. As you enter through the wooden entrance porch, the bar is found on the right hand
side, and you can even keep an eye on your car with the closed-circuit TV monitor! The separate
dining room has a no smoking area, and serves from an extensive menu, but be aware that no food is
available on Monday evenings. We stop short of referring to it as *well-equipped*, but there is
actually an old well in the restaurant! The family room has a pool table, and there is also a 3½ acre
beer garden, with a play area for the children. A second, smaller garden can be made available for
wedding receptions.

   Very much part of its community, the Davenport has a good local trade and provides the
headquarters for football and darts teams. It hosts the village bonfire and an annual Gooseberry
show (the Guinness Book of Records entry for the largest gooseberry refers to the pub). Marton is an
attractive village, said to have the oldest Oak tree in England, as well as the oldest half-timbered
church in Europe. At one time part of the Capesthorne estate, the Davenport Arms has been a pub
only since the 1950s but has previously had several functions including Court House, Collecting
House and a site for hanging highwaymen. Perhaps the practitioners of Road Rage could be given
similar treatment? It would be good to see the Davenport experiment with a more interesting range
of beers.

MIDDLEWICH
BIG LOCK
Webbs Lane
⏱ APH
Websters Yorkshire B, guest beers [H]
Imposing, red brick canalside pub, recently
refurbished, but the beer range appears
unaltered with guest beers still available.
Might still hold its October beer festival.

BOARS HEAD
Kinderton Street
⏱ 12-11 Mon-Sat; 12-10.30 Sun
Robinsons Best B [H]
Large, tidy Victorian pub with several open
rooms and a separate TV/games room.
Fine tiled floors. Close to canal. Functions
catered for. Accommodation.

CHESHIRE CHEESE
Lewin Street
⏱ 7-11 Mon-Thu; 12-3,7-11 Fri-Sat;
12-10.30 Sun
Draught Bass [H]
Pleasant two-roomed traditional local,
featuring live music. Due for refurbishment in
early 1998 and cask beer range due to be
expanded. Food expected after refurbishment.
Limited parking.
● P

GOLDEN LION
Chester Road
⏱ 12-11 Mon-Sat; 12-10.30 Sun
**Greenalls Mild, B, Original,
Worthington Draught B [H]**
Traditional town-centre local.
Accommodation.

KINDERTON ARMS
Booth Lane (A533)
⏱ 12-11 Mon-Sat (summer);
12-3,7-11 Mon-Sat (winter); 12-10.30 Sun
Tetleys B, Theakstons Best B [H]
Traditional pub on outskirts of town, close to
canal.

KINDERTON HOUSE HOTEL
(MAYO BAR)
Kinderton Street
⏱ 12-2, 7-11 Mon-Sat; 12-10.30 Sun
**Morland Old Speckled Hen, Tetley B,
guest beer (monthly) [H]**
Pleasant, friendly and comfortable privately-
run hotel bar. Attached no smoking restaurant.
Outside area in summer. Guest beer changes
monthly.

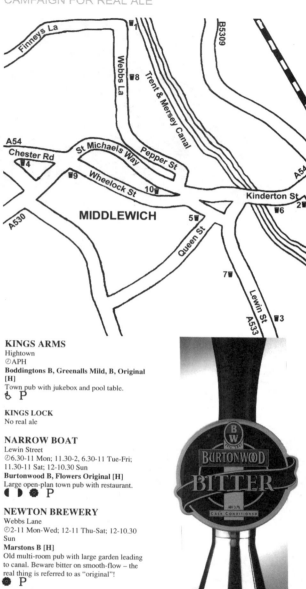

Map labels: Finneys La, B5309, Webbs La, Trent & Mersey Canal, Pepper St, A54, Chester Rd, St Michaels Way, Wheelock St, A54, A530, MIDDLEWICH, Kinderton St, Queen St, Lewin St, A533

1 - Big Lock
2 - Boars Head
3 - Cheshire Cheese
4 - Golden Lion
5 - Kings Arms
6 - Kinderton Hotel
7 - Narrow Boat
8 - Newton Brewey
9 - Tut n Shive
10 - White Bear

KINGS ARMS
Hightown
⏲APH
Boddingtons B, Greenalls Mild, B, Original [H]
Town pub with jukebox and pool table.
🚻 P

KINGS LOCK
No real ale

NARROW BOAT
Lewin Street
⏲6.30-11 Mon; 11.30-2, 6.30-11 Tue-Fri;
11.30-11 Sat; 12-10.30 Sun
Burtonwood B, Flowers Original [H]
Large open-plan town pub with restaurant.
◖◗ ● P

NEWTON BREWERY
Webbs Lane
⏲2-11 Mon-Wed; 12-11 Thu-Sat; 12-10.30 Sun
Marstons B [H]
Old multi-room pub with large garden leading to canal. Beware bitter on smooth-flow – the real thing is referred to as "original"!
● P

TURNPIKE
No real ale

TUT 'N' SHIVE
Wheelock Street
⏲5-11 Mon-Thu; 12-11 Fri-Sat; 12-10.30 Sun
Worthington Draught B [H]
Large open-plan pub with bare-board "ale-house" décor, but disappointing beer choice.
● P

VAULTS
No real ale.

WHITE BEAR HOTEL
Wheelock Street
⏲12-11 Mon-Sat; !2-10.30 Sun
Wilsons B [H]
Large, noisy pub, popular with youngsters.
Lone handpull amongst myriad keg fonts.

MOBBERLEY

CHAPEL HOUSE INN
Pepper Street
⏲3.45-11 Mon; 12-11 Tue-Sat; 12-10.30 Sun
Tetleys B [H]
Small and attractive, white-washed, brick inn decorated with hanging baskets and flower tubs. Through the porch is the lounge, with a lovely old clock ticking over the open fire.
At the rear, with its own entrance, is a tiny vault where darts and dominoes are played. The benches on the cobbled frontage are very popular during warm weather. No lunches Monday.
◖➤ P

CHURCH INN
Church Lane (off B5085)
⏲11-3, 5-11 Mon-Fri; 11-11 Sat;
12-10.30 Sun
Boddingtons B, Greenalls B, Tetley B, Greenalls Original or Marstons Pedigree [H]
An 18th century, grade III-listed, brick building, unsurprisingly positioned opposite the parish church. Tastefully refurbished very recently, with wooden panelling, comfy chairs and settles and retaining the individual rooms that give it quite a homely atmosphere. In fact, Peter Greenall (a.k.a. Lord Daresbury) unveiled the new look - a good example of what the company can do when it puts its mind to it. Homemade food, cooked to order. Two gardens. Childrens play area and bowling green.
◖◗ 🏇 🚻 ● P

PLOUGH AND FLAIL
Paddockhill Lane (no through road off Knutsford Road at Lindow End junction)
⏲11.30-3, 6-11 Mon-Fri; 11.30-11 Sat;
12-10.30 Sun
Boddingtons B, Marstons Pedigree, Tetley B, guest beer [H]
Hard-to-find establishment in peaceful location, once a row of four cottages. Originally serving home-brewed beer to local farm workers (hence the name). Now with an emphasis on food. Quite extensive and open-plan, featuring old beams and newer brickwork. The focus is a lovely inglenook fireplace with side seating. Benches and childs' playground outside on grassed area by car park. Separate restaurant. Food all day Sunday. Guest beer from major brewery.
◖◗ ● 🏇 P

RAILWAY
Station Road
(next to station house, near level crossing)
⏰12-11 Mon-Sat; 12-10.30 Sun
Boddingtons B, Greenalls Mild, B, Original [H]

A converted mill house, which became a pub when the railway arrived. In fact, a full-sized semaphore signal stands right outside. A more recent addition in 1985 was the bowling green, and there is a cabinet full of bowling trophies and a number of photos of its previous incarnations. Dominoes are the winter alternative. The open-plan lounge has two real fires and a separate restaurant to the rear.

The piece de resistance however is the gorgeous vault, with wood panelling, polished copper door plates and red leather seating. There is a pets corner for children with sheep, pigs and a goat. Home grown vegetables are used in the home cooked meals, which are available all weekend. Bowling green at side.

◀ ▶ ⛄ ✿ ⇌ P

ROEBUCK
(See overleaf)

ABV 5%

MOLLINGTON
CRABWALL MANOR HOTEL
Parkgate Road
⏰APH
One beer from Weetwood Brewery, plus occasional guest beer [H]

A former manor house, whose history can be traced back to Saxon times, it was converted ten years ago into a high class 48 room hotel. It is approached along a long drive from the A540, opposite the southern junction to Mollington village. The A La Carte restaurant will set you back £40 a head. It is encouraging to see support for one of Cheshire's own micro-breweries.

◀ ▶ ⛄ ♿ ✿ P ⊗

MOLLINGTON
BANASTRE HOTEL
No real ale.

MOBBERLEY
BIRD IN HAND
Knutsford Road (B5085, Knolls Green)
⏰APH
Samuel Smiths Old Brewery B [H]

This is a recently and sympathetically redecorated 18th century roadside pub (though some parts are considerably older). Sited on a bend on a country road, it presents an inviting aspect to passing motorists. It has numerous cosy drinking areas separated by arches and wooden panelling. The low ceilings, beams and wooden settles add to the intimate atmosphere. The walls are adorned with lots of small prints depicting birds, flowers, fishing and hunting and, in the restaurant area, a map of Olde Cheshire. There are no less than five open fires scattered throughout the building! Football is sometimes watched unobtrusively on a television in the rear room. Dominoes and cribbage are played. You can recline on sunlit bench seating at the front. Food is available all day on Sundays. Wheelchair friendly, although there are no special facilities. All this and it sells one of the cheapest and best beers around!

◀ ▶ ⛄ P ⊗

BULLS HEAD
Town Lane, off Alderley Road(B5085)
⏰APH
Boddingtons B, Coach House Hedgehopper, Tetley B, guest beer [H]

This excellent country local is thought to date from the 17th century. The cobbled frontage and overgrown exterior are a promise of the delights within. You will not be disappointed by the interior with its exposed beams and two open fires, one of them a 'through fireplace'. The layout provides a number of cosy spots, and bar and walls are decorated with original framed photographs of the area and a fine collection of jugs. Behind the small car park, you will find a bowling green, and there can be few better spots to spend a warm summer's evening.

"Happy Hour" is from 5-7 during the week and a music workshop on Tuesday evenings. One interesting feature is the provision of a minibus service for customers, at half taxi rates. Given the expected changes in the drink-driving law, this can only be applauded. The inner man (and woman) is catered for every lunchtime and evening. The house beer is brewed by Coach House in Warrington. **GBG**

◀ ▶ ⛄ ✿ ⇌ P ⊗

MOBBERLEY
ROEBUCK

Town Lane (off Alderley Road, B5085)
⏰APH
Hydes B, five guest beers [H]

Set almost opposite the Bulls Head, down a quiet by-passed lane, the Roebuck also has a cobbled frontage and impressive foliage-strewn walls. Catering well for the food trade, especially in the quieter library area, this large pub serves meals on Sundays from noon to 8.30, as well as lunch and evenings on the other days. We are told that half the meals are home cooked. Subdued lighting and dark wallpaper help create a relaxing atmosphere and there is a hunting-theme decor, while a posy of fresh flowers on each table is a nice touch. The games room may not be immediately apparent, as it is in a barn across the car park. The staff is friendly.

With a music quiz on Monday, and an exotic bird sanctuary next door, there is no shortage of reasons to go to the Roebuck. The licensee previously ran a Hydes house and liked the beer so much he brought it with him! In addition, the quality and variety of the independent guest ales has been outstanding, making this one of the best venues for beer lovers for miles around.

MOORE
RED LION

Runcorn Road
⏰ 11.30-11 Mon- Sat; 12-10.30 Sun
Greenalls Mild, B, Original; Tetley B, guest beer [H]

A popular village pub with cobbled frontage, thought to date back to the 17th Century. Originally built as a farmhouse, it was extended in Georgian times at the front to become a pub. The older part of the pub can be distinguished in the lounge by the lower ceiling. The stables at the back were built at the same time, to accommodate horses used on the nearby Bridgewater Canal, and until 1966, a blacksmith operated there. The waterway connection is now provided by diners and drinkers using the canal for leisure pursuits. The nearby riding school occupies the site of a WWII gun battery which was commanded by Edward Heath.

MOTTRAM ST. ANDREW
BULLS HEAD

Wilmslow Road
(A538 Prestbury to Wimslow road)
⏰11.30-11 Mon-Sat; 12-10.30 Sun

Boddingtons B, Flowers Original, Marstons Pedigree, guest beer (occasional) [H]

Open plan with lots of nooks and crannies. Low ceilings and lighting. A Beefeater inn with a no smoking area in the large restaurant and a kitchen open until late. The Pedigree and Flowers are occasionally replaced by a more adventurous guest beer.

MOULTON
LION

74 Main Road
⏰7-11 Mon-Fri; 12-5,7-11 Sat;
12-3,7-10.30 Sun

Boddingtons B, Tetley B [H]

Large red-brick Victorian cosy local in quiet village.

TRAVELLERS REST

1 Whitlow Lane
⏰APH

Boddingtons B, Chesters Mild, Whitbread Trophy [H]

Good community local. Large open plan but retains many separate areas. Accommodation. Rare outlet for Chesters cask mild.

MOUNT PLEASANT
CROWN

No real ale.

The Red Lion was refurbished in "country inn" style in January 1998. The comfortable lounge is given more atmosphere by the low ceiling and the hop decorations. Historic local photographs and a good selection of bric-a-brac provide more character. Of particular note is the illustrated mirror over the fireplace on the right as you enter. A separate vault is to be found at the rear for drinkers and games enthusiasts. The children's play area outside is due to be joined by a new beer garden early in 1998. The pub participates in the music and beer festival each August, and the music theme is continued by the presence of a piano and the occasional appearance of a troop of Morris Men. Nature lovers will appreciate the proximity to Moore Nature Reserve with its extensive woodland and two large meres.

Food is clearly important to rural pubs in these times, and the Red Lion is clearly making an effort. Most of the food is home-cooked, and is very good. The specialities of the house are curries and tikkas. Specially priced menus for children and senior citizens are thoughtfully featured.

The guest beers are from the Greenalls list, and change weekly. They are available during the warmer 9 months of the year. *The unwary drinker should note that the fake Scrumpy Jack handpump dispenses keg cider and not the genuine article.*

Gawsworth – Harrington Arms

Over Peover – Dog Inn

Goostrey – Red Lion

Lower Peover – Bells

Great Warford – Stags Head

Scholar Green

Knutsford

Childer Thornton

Lower Withington

Walker Barn – Setter Dog

Higher Burwardsley – Pheasant

Barthomley – White Lion

Lower Peover – Crown

Burleydam – Combermere Arms

Bottom of the Oven – Stanley Arms

Nantwich – Red Cow

Chester – Mill Hotel

Hatton – Hatton Arms

Ashton – Golden Lion

Warrington – London Bridge

Tarporley – Rising Sun

Frodsham – Netherton Hall

Audlem – Shroppie Fly

Penketh – Ferry Tavern

Sutton Lane Ends – Hanging Gate

Out *Inn* CHESHIRE

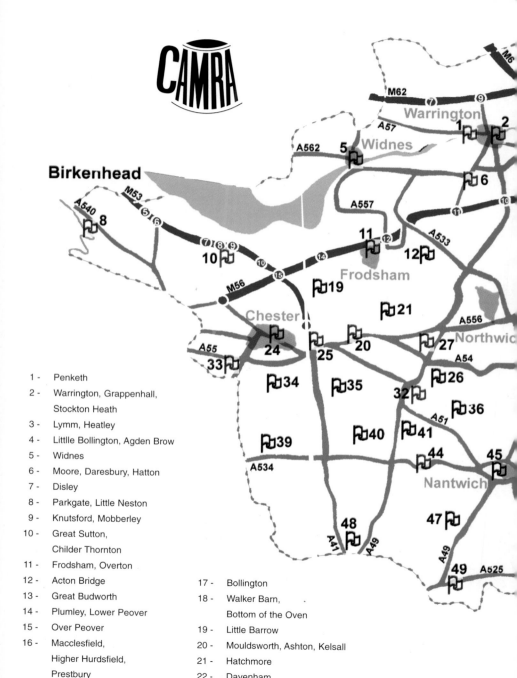

1 - Penketh
2 - Warrington, Grappenhall, Stockton Heath
3 - Lymm, Heatley
4 - Littlle Bollington, Agden Brow
5 - Widnes
6 - Moore, Daresbury, Hatton
7 - Disley
8 - Parkgate, Little Neston
9 - Knutsford, Mobberley
10 - Great Sutton, Childer Thornton
11 - Frodsham, Overton
12 - Acton Bridge
13 - Great Budworth
14 - Plumley, Lower Peover
15 - Over Peover
16 - Macclesfield, Higher Hurdsfield, Prestbury
17 - Bollington
18 - Walker Barn, Bottom of the Oven
19 - Little Barrow
20 - Mouldsworth, Ashton, Kelsall
21 - Hatchmore
22 - Davenham

County Map

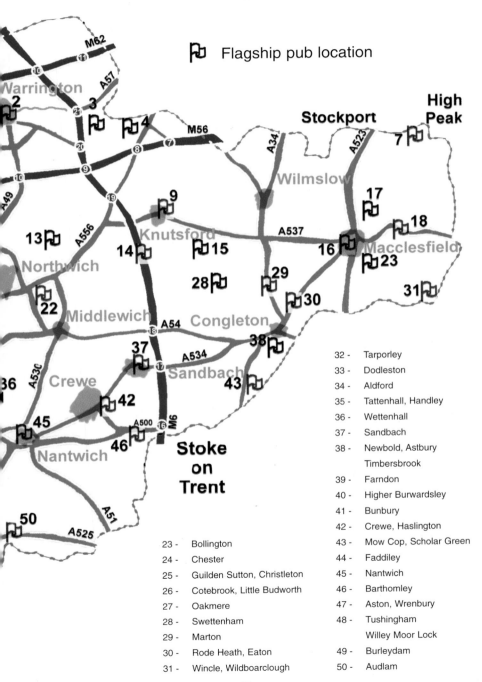

🏴 Flagship pub location

M62

Warrington

M56

M34

Stockport

M523

High Peak

M57

Wilmslow

A537

Macclesfield

Knutsford

Northwich

Middlewich

A54

Congleton

Crewe

Sandbach

Nantwich

Stoke on Trent

Guilden Sutton

Mobberley

Tattenhall

Little Neston

Barthomley – White Lion

Barbridge – Barbridge Inn

Gawsworth – Harrington Arms

Lymm – Spread Eagle

Higher Burwardsley – Pheasant

Aston – Bhurtpore Inn

Penketh – Ferry Tavern

Rainow – Highwayman

Dodleston – Red Lion

Great Sutton – White Swan

Little Bollington – Swan With Two Nicks

Ashley – Greyhound

Bunbury – Dysart Arms

Lymm – Spread Eagle

Plumley – Golden Pheasant

Lower Stretton – Ring O' Bells

Farndon – Farndon Arms

Prestbury – Admiral Rodney

Christleton – Plough

Overton – Ring O' Bells

Aston – Bhurtpore Inn

Great Budworth – Cock O' Budworth

Plumley – Golden Pheasant

Swettenham – Swettenham Arms

NANTWICH

BLACK LION
Welsh Row
⏰APH
Weetwood Best Cask B, Old Dog [H]
Reputedly the oldest pub in town. Open fire in
winter. Seating in veranda-covered garden in
summer. Public car park across the road. This
is one of the few regular outlets for beer from
one of Cheshire's own microbreweries.

WEETWOOD ALES BEST CASK BITTER
WA
ABV 3.8%

BOOT & SHOE
Hospital Street
⏰12-3, 5.30-11 Mon-Thu; 11-11 Fri-Sat;
12-10.30 Sun
Boddingtons B, Tetley B, guest beer [H]
Timbered pub with open fire.
Large supermarket car park at rear.

BOWLING GREEN
The Gullet
⏰11-3, 7-11 Mon-Sat; 12-3, 7-10.30 Sun
Courage Directors,
Websters Yorkshire B [H]
A snug timbered interior. Family room and
outside play area provided for children.
Public car park alongside.

CHESHIRE CHEESE
Crewe Road
⏰6-11 Mon-Fri; 11-11 Sat; 12-10.30 Sun
Greenalls B [H]
A community local on the main road out to
Crewe

CROWN
High Street
⏰APH
Boddingtons B, Flowers Original [H]
An Elizabethan timbered coaching inn,
retaining its Long Gallery upstairs, built to
enable guests to exercise in inclement weather.
Much knocked about and now only one room,
but most of the timberwork is still to be seen.
The Crown is one of the few buildings to
survive the Great Fire of Nantwich in 1583.
Children are admitted at lunchtime only.
Lunches are served in bar and restaurant,
evening meals in restaurant only. Food is
available all day at weekends. Accommodation
includes four poster beds in some rooms.

MOULDSWORTH

GOSHAWK
Station Road (B5395, opposite station)
⏰12-3, 5.30-11 Tue-Sat; 12-10.30 Sun
Greenalls Mild, B, 2 guest beers [H]
This huge brick hilltop former coach house, dating from 1869, has two stylish lounges, a public bar
and a restaurant and has plush carpeting throughout. The stone fireplace with its stout wooden lintel
is a most attractive feature. There is also a games room and floodlit bowling green used by two local
teams. Near the front door there is bench seating under a veranda. At the rear a children's play area
is provided, along with a few seats with a commanding view of the surrounding countryside.
　　　The highly regarded meals and bar snacks are good value and served all day Sunday.
At least one of the guest beers is from an independent (often Cheshire's Weetwood microbrewery).
Conveniently located opposite Mouldsworth railway station, it is easy to reach and is consequently a
popular spot for walkers in the Delamere Forest and on the Sandstone Trail and users of the
Cheshire Cycleway. The Mouldsworth Motor Museum is nearby. Note however that the pub is
closed on Mondays.

FROG & FERRET
4 Oatmarket
⏰12-11 Mon-Fri; 11-11 Sat;
12-3.30, 7-10.30 Sun
Banks B, Banks Frog Beamheath,
Camerons Strongarm, 2 guest beers [H]
Popular, open-plan, student-oriented pub.
Main venue for town's jazz and folk festivals.
DJ sometimes in residence. Busy weekends.
Ample seating on forecourt. Guest beers from
independents. **GBG**

GLOBE
Audlem Road (A529, on Stapeley border)
⏰11-3, 6.30-11 Mon-Fri; 11-11 Sat;
12-10.30 Sun
Greenalls B, 2 guest beers [H]
Comfy and clean two-room brick pub with
etched windows and hanging baskets. Popular
for food, child and pensioners specials,
monthly theme nights. Wheelchair access.
At least one guest beer is from an independent
brewery. Beware keg cider on real handpump.

1 - Black Lion

2 - Boot & Shoe

3 - Bowling Green

4 - Cheshire Cheese

5 - Crown

6 - Frog & Ferret

7 - Lamb Hotel

8 - Leopard

9 - Malbank Hotel

10 - Millfields

11 - Oddfellows Arms

12 - Old Vaults

13 - Railway

14 - Red Cow

15 - Red Lion

16 - Rifleman

17 - Three Pigeons

18 - Union

19 - Vine

20 - White Horse

21 - White Swan

22 - Wickstead Arms

23 - Wilbraham Arms

MOW COP

CHESHIRE VIEW

Top Station Road

⏲12-2.30 Tue-Sat; 7-11 Mon-Sat; 12-3.30, 7-10.30 Sun

Marstons B, Pedigree, Head Brewers Choice [H]

This is a stone-built, former station house on an astonishingly steep road close to the summit of Mow Cop, nestling below the folly. As you would expect, there are excellent views over the Cheshire countryside; on a clear day the vista is remarkably extensive. Inside you will find a photographic display of Mow Cop past and present, including pictures of railway wagons being hauled up the hill in front of the pub to the now disused quarry. Given the local topography, the gardens are also at an alarming incline.

Ask for a demonstration of their working pianola; this is played most evenings. There is a separate dining room and children are admitted to the pub at lunchtimes. The Cheshire View is handy for walkers finishing the Mow Cop Trail (and foolhardy learner drivers wishing to practise hill starts!) It is good to see a brewer producing a changing range of beers; the Head Brewer's Choice range has produced some classics, notably the wonderfully dry Oyster Stout, which has now become a regular brew, available widely in bottle-conditioned form.

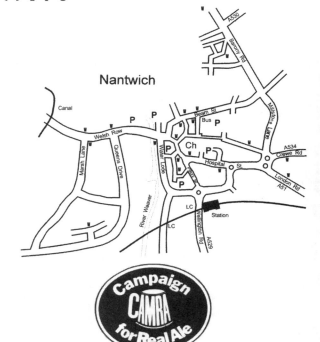

A CYCLING TOUR OF CHESHIRE

Cheshire is an excellent county for the cyclist. The gently rolling countryside, long straight Roman roads and the plethora of quiet lanes provide are an open invitation for casual two-wheelers and serious racers alike. The county also boasts a range of "pit-stops" to suit everyone, be they families, cycling clubs or those of a more solitary disposition. Indeed, with the increased availability of real ales, you need never be far from a decent, refreshing pint. Another boon has been the recent extension of Sunday licensing hours, which has lessened the need to hurry in order to get to the pub before it closes for the afternoon.

A good way to discover or reacquaint yourself with the diverse Cheshire countryside by bike, is to travel the route of the official **CHESHIRE CYCLEWAY**. This route covers a total of **135 miles** and forms a huge circle, wending round the county. Preferably, it can be explored bit by bit on a series of day-long outings from home, or over a few days or long weekends staying overnight in accommodation along the way. The details of the route can be found in the Cheshire Cycleway leaflet available from the county's main Tourist Information Centres and libraries. It describes a signed route along by-ways "rarely discovered by car" (hah!), through a cross-section of Cheshire's varied scenery, ranging from the undulating countryside of the Cheshire Plain with its myriad lanes, to the steep-sided hills and valleys of the Peak District moorlands. To quote the publication's admirably prioritised list; the Cycleway is an opportunity to discover country pubs, picturesque canals, historic churches and many other attractions including castles, craft workshops and beautiful gardens.

Although the directions in the leaflet are brief and clear, with 'Care!' to indicate the tricky junctions or crossings, it is advisable to take a copy of the two Ordnance Survey Landranger maps (Nos. 117 & 118) on which the rough course of the route is shown. The Cheshire Street Atlas is also an asset, as the route takes many minor diversions, often after only 1 or 2 miles on any one road. As well as places of interest, the leaflet gives the locations of camp and picnic sites, tourist information centres, shops (including those for cycle repair!), railway stations, and some cafes and pubs. Details are also provided on cycle hire and arrangements for bikes on trains. There are four InterCity stations: Chester, Crewe, Macclesfield and Wilmslow. It is worth remembering that cycles can be taken free of charge inside the Greater Manchester and Mersey Rail areas.

As regards pubs on the Cycleway, Out *Inn* CHESHIRE will obviously be your guide to success. The route passes directly or close by more than a dozen of the "flagship" pubs in this guide, as well as others in CAMRA's Good Beer Guide.

Starting at Chester, in the manner of the leaflet, we pass near to the *Foxcote* in **Little Barrow** after only a few miles. Next, the route (but not necessarily the follower!) passes the front door of the *Goshawk* at **Mouldsworth**. Further along is a convenient picnic site (and toilets!) in the Delamere Forest. The *Carriers*, beside the lake in **Hatchmere**, is the another potential refreshment stop, as is the later *Hazel Pear* at **Acton Bridge**. Passing the *Holly Bush* at **Little Leigh** we come to the picturesque village of **Great Budworth**. Here we find two differing types of flagship pub. The first involves a very short detour of about half a mile up the A559 towards Warrington, but is well worth it for the bitterest and cheapest bitter around, in the *Cock o'Budworth*. In the centre, just off the A559 and opposite the impressive red sandstone church stands the *George & Dragon*. Before crossing the busy A556 you could do worse than pop in

at the *Windmill* in **Tabley**. The attractive market town of **Knutsford** is well worth exploring for its shops and Heritage Centre, in addition to its many excellent inns, including the *Angel*, *Cross Keys*, *Builders* and *Legh Arms*. After several more miles, the *Stags Head* in **Great Warford** is reached. Continuing, we eventually pass Hare Hill Gardens before entering **Prestbury** and the welcoming *Admiral Rodney*. **Bollington** thankfully has a disproportionately high number of pubs (all real ale at the last check) including the *Church House* and *Poachers*. The going, or at least the gradient, now gets tougher.

The route to the east of Macclesfield in the Peak District is through impressive switchback countryside and will be thirsty work. Allow more time and check out the roadside options: the excellent *Setter Dog* in the tiny hamlet of **Walker Barn** (near Tegg's Nose Country Park), the *Stanley Arms* at **Bottom of the Oven** (next to the Macclesfield Forest), the *Crag Inn* in **Wildboarclough**, set on an attractive stretch of road alongside the brook in the valley below the Shutlingsloe peak, a prominent local landmark at over 500 m. After climbing the crest of the hills, the route passes **Sutton's** *Hanging Gate Inn*. This affords panoramic views to the west past Jodrell Bank and the power stations towards the Wirral on a clear day, and serves superb ale to boot!

Soon after dropping down to Sutton, the road becomes easier again as it doubles back south of Macclesfield. Another pleasant slight diversion here might be a detour past **Gawsworth** Hall and lakes, and the timeless *Harrington Arms*. After crossing the A34, the route proper meanders towards Congleton passing close to the *Davenport Arms* at **Marton** , skirting it to the west, but passing two nice Robinsons pubs the *Egerton Arms* at **Astbury** and the *Horseshoe Inn* at **Newbold**. The Cycleway bypasses Alsager and after a little while we come to the magnificent *White Lion* at **Barthomley** (as pictured on the cover of Out *Inn* CHESHIRE). Next, the route goes south of Crewe and Nantwich to its southernmost town, **Audlem** and another flagship - the *Shroppie Fly*. Several miles after we cross the A530, and pass the excellent *Bhurtpore Inn* at **Aston**, and the lovely, canalside *Dusty Miller* at **Wrenbury**. Between Marbury and Malpas, the road crosses two A-roads a couple of miles apart - the A49 (a mile north of the *Willey Moor Lock Tavern*) and the A41. At the junction with the second it is well worth a minor diversion south for about 1½ miles to the *Blue Bell* at **Tushingham**.

The route then takes the Roman road through Tilston on a scenic looping diversion to Stretton Mill before heading off north-west towards the two castles, Peckforton and Beeston, passing east of both. Not far away over the hill is **Higher Burwardsley**, and the *Pheasant*, an oasis amongst a desert of rather ordinary pubs. Later, in **Tiverton**, is the *Shady Oak* sitting on the bank on the Shropshire Union Canal. The final run-in to Chester more or less follows the canal, and the last port of call is nearby *Plough* at **Christleton**. Finally, you can celebrate your completion of this fascinating journey, and rest your weary limbs, in one of Chester's flagship hostelries.

OLD VAULTS
High Street
⏲APH
Tetley B [H]
Recently renovated and refurbished, with bare
boards etc. Loud music often played in
evenings. Children admitted at lunchtime only.
◖⚞

PEACOCK
Crewe Road
(at the A534 junction with the A500 by-pass)
⏲11.30-11 Mon-Sat; 12-10.30 Sun
Greenalls B, Original, guest beer [H]
Typical family, food and accommodation-
focused theme pub at the edge of town, with a
garden playground and no-smoking area.
Meals all day.
◖◗ ⚞ ⚲ ✿ P ⊗

NANTWICH
RED COW

Beam Street
⏲11-3, 5-11 Mon-Thu; 11-11 Fri-Sat; 12-3, 7-10.30 Sun
Robinsons Best B, Frederics, other Robinsons beers (occasional) [H]
This beautiful 15th century grade I listed former farmhouse has deservedly achieved a number of
awards for its restoration. Originally built in wattle & daub, it still displays a section of this for the
curious. Thought to be the oldest building in Nantwich, it is a delight to enter, consisting of a
number of rooms, one of which has a warming open fire in winter. Another is a no-smoking room.
At the rear is a bar room with lower beer prices, pool and darts. At the back there is a children's area
in the garden, with a variety of "adventure playground" apparatus to keep them happy. It would be a
cliché to describe the Cow as a country pub in the town, but it is well worth a visit. Particularly
convenient is the Bus station opposite. The town itself owes its origins to local brine springs which
led to the establishment of a salt works, before the discovery of rock salt elsewhere led to its decline.
The pub was one of the few buildings to survive the Great Fire of Nantwich in 1583. Beam Street is
named after timbers which were hauled from Delamere forest during the reconstruction of the town.

  Although the Cow is still very much a pub, the food is excellent, rating a fulsome entry in
the Good Pub Food Guide from CAMRA. A speciality of the house is vegetarian cuisine, the
landlady herself being a vegetarian. However, meals for carnivores are also delicious.
◖◗ ⚞ ✿ ⚞ P ⊗

LAMB HOTEL
Hospital Street
⏲APH
Flowers Original, Theakston Best B [H]
Built in 1551, it features the traditional
atmosphere of a country-town hotel.
Rooms available for conferences or
accommodation Separate restaurant.
◖◗ ⚞ ✿ ⚞ P ⊗

LEOPARD
London Road
⏲APH
Marstons Pedigree, Tetley B [H]
Large pub popular with families.
Food available all day.
◖◗ ⚞ ✿ ⚞ P

MALBANK HOTEL
Beam Street
⏲APH
Tetley B, guest beer [H]
Accommodation is available as the name
suggests. Live music on Sunday and Thursday.
There is no garden, but there are tables in the
yard. Meals available from mid-day till 9pm.
◖◗ ⚞ ⊗

MILLFIELDS
14 Blagg Avenue
⏲7-11 Mon-Fri; 12-3, 7-11 Sat;
12-4, 7-10.30 Sun
Bass Worthington B [H]
1970s pub in middle of a housing estate.
Close to canal. Food Sunday lunch only. Hours
and mealtimes may be longer in summer.
◖ ✿ P

ODDFELLOWS ARMS
Welsh Row
⏲11-3.30, 5.30-11 Mon-Sat;
12-3.30, 7-10.30 Sun
**Burtonwood B, James Forshaws B,
seasonal beers (occasional) [H]**
Lovely, small, timbered single-roomed building with beams, low ceiling and two open fires
ablaze in winter. The large garden to the rear
hosts barbecues in summer. Open folk evening
on Wednesdays. Good range of well-kept
Burtonwood ales. **GBG**
◖◗ ✿ ⚞ ⚞

RAILWAY
Pillory Street
⏲APH
Greenalls Mild, B [H]
Food served all day from noon. Separate
dining room available. Occasional live music.
Bed & breakfast.
◖◗ ⚞ ✿ ⚞ P

RED LION
Barony Road
⏲APH
Greenalls B [H]
Large pub on edge of town. Live music Sat
night. Food in separate restaurant.
Accomodation available.
◖◗ ✿ P

RIFLEMAN
James Hall Street
⏲11-11 Mon, Fri, Sat; 2-11 Tue-Thu;
12-10.30 Sun
Robinsons Hatters Mild, Best B [E]
This community local occasionally enjoys
karaoke and other functions. Bar snacks can be
had Friday to Monday.
⚞ ✿ ⚞ P ⊗

SHAKESPEARE
No real ale.

SWAN WITH TWO NECKS
No real ale

THREE PIGEONS
Welsh Row
⌚APH
Greenalls Mild, B, Tetley B [H]
Community pub near town centre. Public car park at rear.

UNION
High Street
⌚11-3, 7-11 Mon-Fri; 11-11 Sat; 12-10.30 Sun
Marstons B, Pedigree, guest beer [H]
Situated in town centre, looking down street to river. No food Sun and Mon or evening meals Friday and Saturday.

VINE
Hospital Street
⌚12-2 Tue-Fri, 5.30-11 Mon-Fri; 12-11 Sat; 12-2, 7-10.30 Sun
Draught Bass, Worthington Draught B, guest beer [H]
17th century building with its floor below street level. The no-smoking dining room is available to non-diners also. No food Monday, or Tuesday and Sunday evenings.

WHITE HORSE
Pillory Street
⌚11.30-11 Mon-Sat; 12-10.30 Sun
Boddingtons B, Greenalls B [H]
Recently refurbished pub on one of the town's most picturesque streets. Food served until 6pm daily. Children admitted until 8pm. Loud music evenings. Public car park at rear.

WHITE SWAN
15 Pillory Street
⌚11-3, 7-11 Mon-Fri; 11-11 Sat; 12-10.30 Sun
Bass Worthington B [H]
Friendly town centre local.

WICKSTEAD ARMS
Mill Street
⌚ 11-11 Mon-Sat; 12-3, 7.30-10.30 Sun
Boddingtons B, guest beer [H]
A back street pub near the centre of Nantwich.

WILBRAHAM ARMS
Welsh Row
⌚APH
Theakstons Best B, guest beers [H] occasional cask cider.
A dignified Georgian frontage to this former coach-house, leads into an open-plan interior with many square pillars. The place has retained a friendly atmosphere and has a strong local following. Live music Fri and Sat nights. Bed & breakfast. **GBG**

NESS
WHEATSHEAF
Neston Road (close to Ness Gardens)
⌚12-11 Mon-Sat; 12-10.30 Sun
Thwaites B [H]
This large pub occupies a prominent position on a quiet road. It is very friendly, with a clientele of mixed ages.

NESTON
BREWERS ARMS
1 Park Street
(off A540 Liverpool Road, near village centre)
⌚11-11 Mon-Sat; 12-3, 7-10.30 Sun
Boddingtons B, Castle Eden Ale, Flowers IPA, Marstons Pedigree, guest beer [H]
This is a traditional village pub dating back to the 1640's. The single bar serves three areas in an open plan lounge. The comfortable cottage interior is in keeping with the age of the building.. Jazz is played every Monday, with Country music on Sunday evenings. This is a Good Food Awards pub, well worth visiting.

BROWN HORSE
2 The Cross (in the centre of town)
⌚APH
Tetley Dark Mild, B [H]
A lively, open-plan community local.

COACH & HORSES
No real ale

GREENLAND FISHERY
Parkgate Road (50 yards from Neston Cross)
⌚APH
Greenalls B [H]
This 17th Century pub, reputedly haunted, was combined with the adjoining Black Bull in 1892. Live entertainment Saturdays. Lunch daily, evening meals Wed-Fri only

HINDERTON ARMS
Hinderton Road (from Chester High Road, at crossroads signed for Neston)
⌚APH
Greenalls B, Original, Tetley B, Theakston Best B [H]
This busy ex-Whitbread pub is described by our surveyor as having 'everything going for it'. It has a superb beer garden with a children's play area. Food all day Sundays.

LADY HAMILTON
Henley Road
(½ mile from Neston Cross toward Chester, first right under the railway bridge)
⌚12-11 Mon-Sat; 12-10.30 Sun
Boddingtons Mild, B, John Smiths B [H]
A Higsons pub, which in the perverse logic of these times, does not sell Higsons beer. It does have a good mix of customers, and surprisingly, a tennis court at the rear. A relatively rare outlet for Boddies cask mild.

LODE STAR
20-24 Brook Street
(50 yds from Neston Cross)
⌚APH
Cains Dark Mild, Traditional B, Courage Directors B, Theakston Best B, guest beers [H] Westons Cider [H]
A Wetherspoons outlet, with typical open-plan bar with split levels. Pleasant decor and relaxing atmosphere. Suits all ages, although children are not admitted. Traditional pub food served all day, with concessionary prices early evening. Holds occasional Beer Festivals with unusual guest ales. A regular outlet for cask cider, and a rare Cheshire outlet for the superb Cains Dark Mild.

MALT SHOVEL
Liverpool Road (close to village centre)
⌚APH
John Smiths B [H]
This two-roomed town centre local boasts a friendly welcome. The only catering is the provision of sandwiches. It uses lined, oversize glasses to ensure you get a full pint.

NO MANS HEATH
WHEATSHEAF
A41 (5 miles north of Whitchurch)
⌚11.30-3, 6-11 Mon-Sat; 12-3, 7-10.30 Sun
Ruddles Best B [H]
Quiet village pub. With the impending closure of the Ruddles brewery, the beer range is expected to change.

NORLEY
TIGER'S HEAD
Pytchleys Hollow
⌚5-11 Mon; 12-11 Tue-Sat; 12-10.30 Sun
Burtonwood Mild, B, Top Hat, seasonal beer [H]
17th C two roomed pub (one with jukebox and pool table) with a bowling green, in a small village west of Cuddington. Open views over north Cheshire. No food served on Mondays. Good range of Burtonwood beers.

NORTH RODE
CHAIN AND GATE
Just off A536 Congleton to Macclesfield road, in secluded lay-by to West (not in village)
⌚12-3; 5.30-11 Mon-Fri; 11-11 Sat; 12-10.30 Sun
Marstons B, Pedigree, guest beer [H]
This is a small, cosy and very hospitable 200 year old former coaching house. A little hard to find, on a by-passed road, it has an exceptionally remote and peaceful atmosphere. The front door has the old form of the pub name, 'Cheyney Gate', but the origin is lost in the mists of time. One theory concerns a form of toll gate. The main room is split into a lounge area on your left with a real fire and comfortable settees, and a more basic, but pleasant area laid out like an old-style public bar. The walls are festooned with bric-a-brac, all of which is for sale! Food is available at almost any time on request. There is no smoking in the separate dining room to the right of the bar. Wheelchair access for Gents is possible. One room is available as overnight accommodation. Since a recent change of licensee, guest beers have become available.

Out *Inn* CHESHIRE

NEWBOLD ASTBURY

HORSESHOE
Force Lane (off the A34 through Astbury village, turning right after the canal bridge)
⏰12-3, 5.30-11 Mon-Sat; 12-3, 7-10.30 Sun
Robinsons Hatters Mild, Best B [E] Frederics [H] (summer only)
This former farmhouse frequented by locals and visitors alike is a fine example of an isolated real country pub, of which there are so few left. It has been kept up to date over the years, but has lost none of its atmosphere, and one can imagine stepping back many years in time. While it serves bar meals all week, it is very much a pub rather than a food-house with a bar, and it is still possible to have a "pie and a pint". The Horseshoe has received a certificate from CAMRA for ten continuous years in the Good Beer Guide. Wheelchair access may be possible. There is an excellent children's play area. Overall, the Horseshoe amply rewards the effort to find it. **GBG**
◖❱ ⚲ ● P

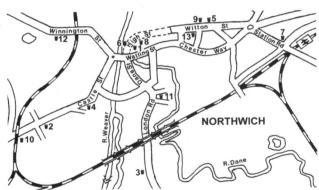

1 -	Beehive
2 -	Blue Barrel
3 -	Bowling Green
4 -	Freemasons
5 -	Green Dragon
6 -	Lavins Wine Bar
7 -	Lion & Railway
8 -	Old Crown
9 -	Roebuck
10 -	Thatched Tavern
11 -	Volunteer
12 -	Winnington Lodge
13 -	Witton Chimes

NORTHWICH

BEEHIVE
High Street
⏰ 11-11 Mon-Fri; 11-5,7-11 Sat; 12-3,7-10.30 Sun
Boddingtons B, Greenalls Mild, B, Original [H]
Attractive small traditional town-centre pub with several rooms. Fine terracotta exterior.
◖

BLUE BARREL
Chester Road
⏰3-11 Mon-Fri; 12-11 Sat; 12-10.30 Sun
Websters B, guest beer [H]
Large pub popular with locals. Separate bar with pool table. Accommodation.
≇

BOWLING GREEN
164 London Road
⏰11.30-11 Mon-Sat; 12-10.30 Sun
Boddingtons B, Greenalls Mild, B [H]
up to 3 guest beers [P]
Multi-roomed "Country Ale House" with guest beers served via fake barrel-ends behind the bar. Listed building (1650) still retaining many original features.
Close to the Salt Museum. Beer availability variable due to limited supplies. The guests are from the Greenalls list.
◖❱ ⚲ ● P

COCK
No real ale.

FREEMASONS
Chester Road, Castle
⏰APH
Wilsons Mild, B; guest beer [H]
Popular local with friendly landlord and locals. Separate area with dart board. Guest beer usually available at weekends.

GREENBANK
No real ale

GREEN DRAGON
169 Witton Street
⏰11.30-4.30, 7-11 Mon-Thu; 11-11 Fri-Sat; 12-4.30, 7-10.30 Sun
Greenalls B [H]
Pleasant open-plan pub near town centre.

LAVINS WINE BAR
High Street
⏰11.30-11 Mon-Sat; 12-3, 7-10.30 Sun
Boddingtons B,
Morland Old Speckled Hen,
Wadworths 6X, guest beer [H]
Lively town-centre bar with regular events such as quiz nights and "jam" sessions. Bar snacks available all day. The guest beer is from the Whitbread list. Good to see so many real ales in a wine bar.
◖❱

LION & RAILWAY
Station Road
⏰APH
Greenalls B [H]
Street corner local opposite the station, close to Tesco. Separate public bar. Small car park.
≇ P

OLD CROWN
High Street
⏰11-11 Mon-Fri; 11-5,7-11 Sun; 7-10.30 Sun
Greenalls B; Tetley B [H]
Open-plan town pub.
◖ ●

ROEBUCK
157 Witton Street
⏰11.30-11 Mon-Sat; 12-10.30 Sun
Boddingtons B, Greenalls Mild, B; 'Porters Ale', guest beer [H]
2 roomed "Porters Ale House". Porters Ale is believed to be Davenports Traditional Bitter. The guest is from Greenalls list.
◖❱ ⚲ ● P

SIDINGS
No real ale

87

THATCHED TAVERN
Chester Road, Castle
⏰12-3, 5-11 Mon-Thu; 11-11 Fri-Sat;
12-10.30 Sun
Greenalls Mild, B [H]
Large single room pub with pool area.

VOLUNTEER
London Road
⏰11-3, 7-11 Mon-Sat; 12-3,7-10.30 Sun
Tetley Dark Mild, B [H]
Single story timber-frame and red brick
building housing a single large room.

WINNINGTON LODGE
Winnington Street
⏰APH
**Boddingtons B; Castle Eden Ale;
guest beer [H]**
Large and lively "Millers Kitchen" with large
restaurant. Guest beer from Greenall's list.

WITTON CHIMES
Witton Street
⏰APH
Holts B [H]
Characterless but lively open plan pub on edge
of town centre. Constructed from red brick
with a timber frame to avoid the effects of
subsidence which is common in the area due to
old salt workings.

OAKGROVE
FOOLS NOOK
London Road (A523 Leek to Macclesfield
road, 1 1/2 miles North of A54 junction)
⏰11.45-3/3.30, 6-11 Mon-Sat; 12-3/3.30, 6-
10.30 Sun
Boddingtons B [H]
Built in 1829, this clean, well-presented
family-run pub is renowned for its food.
Unusually a separate snug complements the
lounge. The pleasant, sunken patio garden is
an abundance of colours and flowers in
summer. Children under parental control
welcome. Very close to a drawbridge over the
Macclesfield Canal, this is a good spot to
watch the narrow boats.

OLLERTON
DUN COW
Chelford Road
⏰11.30-3, 5.30-11 Mon-Sat;
12-3, 7-10.30 Sun
**Boddingtons B, Greenalls B, Original,
guest beer [H]**
Historically a coaching inn, this gorgeous rural
pub was recently "McDonaldised" by
Greenalls. Once a haunt of Knutsford's
famous Highwayman Higgins and judges for
the Bucklow Hundreds Court. They
undoubtedly would not recognise it today, as it
retains little of its original character.
Very much a food-and-family-oriented
establishment. Attractive, brick open fire in
bar area. Benches in front in summer.

FESTIVE FUN

One of the most enjoyable things CAMRA does is run
Beer Festivals. These are not like the popular vision of the
Bavarian binges, with Oompah bands, sheep's knuckles and
buckets of lager. Instead, they are a celebration of the art of
British Brewers. You can expect to find dozens of rare real ales,
ciders & perries, served at pub prices, by keen and knowledgeable
CAMRA volunteers. This is a great chance for a sampling session.
The atmosphere is invariably good, and you can usually find food,
music and CAMRA products. Details are available from Branch
contacts (see page 2 of Out *Inn* CHESHIRE), and festivals are
usually advertised locally.

Some festivals are run by charitable organisations, such as the
local Round Table, with CAMRA assistance. The most popular
month for festivals in Cheshire is May, with events in **Chester,
Frodsham, Macclesfield** and **Stockport**. There are also regional
festivals in **Northwich, Stoke** and **Birkenhead** later in the year.
CAMRA also holds beer & cider festivals all over the UK
throughout the year. The showpiece event is the...

Great British Beer Festival in London,

"the biggest pub in the world!".

OAKMERE

FOREST VIEW

Gallowsclough Lane junction with Cheese Hill Lane (off Chester Road, A556)

⏰12-3, 6-11 Mon-Sat; 12-3, 7-10.30 Sun

Greenalls Mild, B, Original [H]

Named for its view northward over Delamere Forest, this comfortable country pub has an attractive interior and a big food interest. It is a rather unprepossessing brick building sitting on a hill near Delamere Forest. It is quite cosy inside with a logs burning in a large brick fireplace at one end. Some original timbers remain intact and there are various plates and prints depicting British birds and freshwater fish. Some tropical examples are also displayed in large aquarium. Popular with weekend diners (the menu that is!). There is bench seating, a child's play area and a duck pond in the rear garden. It is a shame the forest views are mainly blocked by the caravan site. The pub is a Vale Royal Tourist Centre, with leaflets available in the porch

◖ ▶ 🏇 ❀ P

OVERTON

BELLE MONTE

Bellemonte Road

⏰12-3, 6-11 Mon-Sat; 12-3, 7-10.30 Sun

Sam Smiths Old Brewery B [H]

Locals' pub at top of village with views over Mersey Valley. Unremarkable, but quirky. Public bar.

P

OVERTON

BULLS HEAD

Bellemonte Road

⏰12-4, 7-11 Mon-Sat; 12-4,7-10.30 Sun

Greenalls B; guest beer [H]

Large pseudo-rustic village pub with thriving locals bar. Lounge bar is eclectic mix of periods. The guest beer is from the Greenalls list.

◖ P

OVER PEOVER

WHIPPING STOCKS

Stocks Lane

(junction of A50 Holmes Chapel Road)

⏰11.30-3, 5-11 Mon-Fri; 11.30-3, 6-11 Sat; 12-10.30 Sun

Samuel Smiths Old Brewery B [H]

Imposing, historical Cheshire-brick pub, once a courthouse as evidenced by the name and paintings of judges inside, but now sadly lacking the stocks in the car park. There are four smart, wood-panelled, heavily-beamed rooms, the central of which houses the bar and impressive brick fireplace. In one room there are fascinating pictures depicting extracts from the 17th and 18th century diaries of the local Mainwaring family.

There is also a ghostly maiden believed to have been ill-treated by a landlord in the 16th century, who thankfully only makes herself known to other tenants! More recently, General Patton paid visits while encamped nearby with his troops during the last war. Also popular with besuited workers from nearby Radbrooke Hall.

No food Monday evenings.

◖ ▶ 🏇 ❀ P ⊗

YE OLDE PARK GATE INN

(See overleaf)

OVER PEOVER

DOG

Well Bank Lane

(take Peover Lane from Chelford roundabout, over the railway bridge and across at next junction)

⏰11.30-3, 5.30-11 Mon-Sat; 12-3, 5.30-10.30 Sun

Boddingtons B, Flowers IPA, Tetley B, Weetwood Old Dog [H] Addlestones Cider [H]

The Dog is a large, comfortable, rambling building, part of a long row of 18th century cottages. Converted to the New Inn early this century as can be seen from the photograph in the front room, later renamed the Gay Dog and finally simply The Dog as a result of the modern slant on the former nomenclature! There are three main sections; the tap-room (with pool table and darts board) popular with younger clientele, the lounge bar and an extensive eating area. In fact the demand for food has necessitated two evening "sittings" at weekends, so that booking is advisable. There are old beams and dried flowers throughout, some wonderful photos of old village life, and a real fire. Outside the front are wooden benches nestling amongst the justifiably famous array of flower tubs and hanging baskets.

There is a daily one hour supper licence extension on the bar. The dining areas are non- smoking. Accommodation is available, as readers of CAMRA's Room at the Inn guide will know. Another CAMRA publication in which the Dog features is the Good Pub Food Guide. Weetwood Old Dog is now served to support local brewery (the food also made from locally grown produce) and incidentally reflects the pub name - CAMRA applauds this new venture!

◖ ▶ 🏇 ♿ ❀ P ⊗

OVER PEOVER

PARK GATE INN
Stocks Lane
⏰ 11-11 Mon-Sat; 12-3, 7-10.30 Sun
Samuel Smiths Old Brewery B [H]

This is a picturesque, ivy-clad gem. Wood panelling and lots of bric-a-brac feature in some of the five rooms, and there are lots of cosy corners.
Beams, settles and open fires are complemented by fresh flowers and collections of plates and old prints, making for a civilised and relaxing atmosphere.
The meals which are served every lunch and evening have a good reputation locally. The vault is to the rear, with a separate entrance, and there is a
dining room/lounge on the left. In addition to the non-smoking room on the extreme right, there are two bars. The locals say the pub was created by
knocking together three or four cottages, and the Parkgate has the ambience you would expect. There is no garden as such, but tables are set out in front
on a quiet roadside.

One local tradition is the Gooseberry Show, held each year in late October. Another is an occasional visit from the local Morris Dancers.
The opening hours may be longer in the summer. Although there is only one cask beer available from this brewery, it is kept exceptionally well, and sells
at a very low price for the area. Leaflets on the bar celebrate the range of bottled beers from Sam Smiths. These are a sign of great potential for a wider
range of draught beers, and you should be aware that they are not bottle-conditioned. **GBG**

◖ ◗ 🐦 ♿ P

PARKGATE

BOAT HOUSE
The Parade.(northern end)
⏰APH
**Cains Traditional B, Greenalls B,
Tetley B [H]**
A half-timbered pub on the Dee Estuary, with
views of the Welsh hills. There is good pub
food, and a more exotic choice in the
restaurant. Jazz nights are a feature.
◖ ◗ 🐦 ♿ ❀ P

OLD QUAY
Station Road (at the southern end of
The Parade, next to the cricket club)
⏰APH
Morlands Old Speckled Hen [H]
This large food-oriented Brewer's Fayre outlet
serves meals all day, has a Charlie Chalk Fun
Factory and is close to the Promenade.
◖ ◗ 🐦 ♿ ❀ P ⊘

PARKGATE HOTEL
Boat House Lane
(off the A54, near the Parade)
⏰APH
Bass Worthington B [H]
A large hotel with comfortable lounge,
restaurant and function rooms. Situated close
to Parkgate Promenade. Pub meals served all
day, except Sunday, on which there is a break
between lunch and the evening.
◖ ◗ 🐦 ♿ P ⊘

RED LION
(See overleaf)

SHIP
The Parade
⏰APH
**Theakstons Best B, XB,
Websters Yorkshire B [H]**
Promenade pub and hotel with trendy and
more sedate contrasting lounges.
◖ ◗ P

OVERTON

RING O' BELLS
Bellemonte Road
⏰ 11.30-3, 5.30-11 Mon-Thu; 11-11 Fri; 11.30-4, 6-11 Sat; 12-3, 7-11 Sun
Greenalls B;1 or 2 guest beers [H]
Named for the church opposite, the Ring o' Bells is an attractive, long, low cottage-style inn dating back to the 15th century, and originally built in wattle & daub. The pleasant frontage is cobbled and graced by foliage. The low ceilings, beams and an interesting collection of varied areas give it plenty of charm. It has five small rooms and many of its original features. On the left as you enter is a "newsroom" behind an ancient etched glass screen with brass rails. This leads through to a small room with a dart board and scrubbed tables. To the rear, on the left is a lounge with a roaring open fire, a sewing machine, a collection of wine bottles, wooden settles and a seat nestling under the stairs. Continuing clockwise, you find another, oddly-shaped room, and then the cosy public bar, with more settles and the collection of handpumps, one offering a guest beer. The bar itself is noteworthy for its collection of small bells, a gentle visual pun on the pub's name.

It is set opposite the parish church in this higher suburb of Frodsham, and there are sweeping views over the Mersey estuary from just outside. The guest beers are from the Greenalls list, but are proving popular with the locals. The mild, unfortunately is keg.

◖ P

PENKETH

CROWN & CUSHION
Farnworth Road
⏰ 11.30-11 Mon-Sat; 12-10.30 Sun
Greenalls B, Original, Stones B [H]
Victorian pub with standard Greenall's refurbishment.
P

FERRY TAVERN
(See overleaf)

RED LION
Warrington Road
⏰ 12-11 Mon-Sat; 12-10.30 Sun
Tetley B, Imperial, Marston Pedigree [H]
Big Steak Pub and Wacky Warehouse.
Ho-hum.
◖▮ ㋴ ❀ P

SPORTSMAN
Warrington Road
⏰ APH
Burtonwood Top Hat, seasonal beer [H]
Recently refurbished cosy community local.
Beware of the keg bitter on smoothflow.
◖▮ ㋴ P

PICKMERE

ELMS
Park Lane
⏰ 11.30-11 Mon-Sat; 12-10.30 Sun
Burtonwood B, Tetley Dark Mild, B [H]
Popular village pub with pool table.
Evening food Thursday to Saturday only.
◖▮ ㋴ ❀ P

RED LION
Park Lane
⏰ 12-3, 5-11 Mon-Fri; 12-11 Sat;
12-10.30 Sun
Tetley Dark Mild, B, guest beer [H]
Large pub with a vault with TV and a lounge split into several areas for drinking or dining. Friendly service. No food Sunday evenings.
◖▮ ㋴ ❀ P

VILLAGE INN
Mere Lane
⏰ 12-11 Mon-Sat; 12-10.30 Sun
Boddingtons B [H]
Basically a bar attached to the adjacent Chinese restaurant.
◖▮ ❀ P

POYNTON

BOARS HEAD
2 Shrigley Road North
⏰11.30-3.30, 6-11 Mon-Fri; 11.30-11 Sat;
12-10.30 Sun
Boddingtons B, Marstons Pedigree [H]
Red brick and attractive with impressive
chimney stacks, gables and windows.
Equally pleasing inside. Next to the old
station, and handy for Middlewood Way
walkers and Macclesfield canal boaters.

BULLS HEAD
115 London Road North
⏰APH 11.30-3, 6-11 Mon-Sat;
12-3, 7-10.30 Sun
Boddingtons B, [H]
Lively and busy, but still a comfortable local,
suitable for all age groups. Particularly good
traditional vault.

FARMERS ARMS
90 Park Lane
⏰APH
Robinsons Best B [H]
Open plan young person's pub. Games area
and alcoves help limit agoraphobia.

KINGFISHER
No real ale

VERNON ARMS
London Road South
⏰APH
**Boddingtons B, Cains Traditional B,
Morland Old Speckled Hen [H]**
Brewer's Fayre, to be congratulated on the
imaginative choice of Cains Bitter.
Comfortable inside, play area outside.

PARKGATE

RED LION
The Parade (on Parkgate front)
⏰12-2.30, 5-11 Mon-Thu; 12-11 Fri, Sat; 12-10.30 Sun
Marstons Pedigree, Tetley B, Ind Coope Burton Ale, Walker Mild, B [H]
Situated on Parkgate's promenade and believed to have been a pub since around 1620, the Red Lion
overlooks the Dee marshes where once a thriving port lay, before tide and silt took their toll. It has a
varied clientele, with a host of boisterous regulars supplemented by a busy trade from visitors out to
sample the fresh air, take in views of the Welsh hills, spot the local bird life or try Parkgate's
famous home-made ice cream.
     It has a traditional lounge and bar which extends into a pool room and is decorated with
photographs of old Parkgate. During the daytime, Nelson, a blue and yellow parrot entertains bar
customers. Good food is served at lunchtime. Thanks to the enthusiasm of the licensees and the high
standards maintained, the Red Lion achieved a Wirral CAMRA Pub of the Year award in 1996.
There are four real ales on offer, including an occasional guest from the Tetley list. Try the Burton
Ale before it disappears; the brewery is rumoured to be "rationalising" its range shortly. **GBG**

PRESTBURY

LEGH ARMS / BLACK BOY
Bollin Grove (near the Methodist church)
⏰APH
Robinsons Best B, Frederics [H]
Deceptively large, comfortable, quiet, open-
plan pub, dating from the 14th century. This
Grade II-listed building gained its second
name in 1719 when an incorrect sign was
erected! The Black Boy is the adjoining restaurant, and this is where the emphasis lies;
beer quality can suffer as a result. Bar snacks
can be had, but not cheaply. Function room.
Summer barbecues.

PRESTBURY
ADMIRAL RODNEY
(See after Plumley flagship entries)

PRESTON BROOK
PRESTON BROOK
Chester Road (A56)
🕐APH
**Boddingtons B; Flowers Original;
guest beer [H]**
Identikit Whitbread Brewers Fayre and
Travel Inn. Food and family oriented, and aimed
at shoppers from the nearby Cheshire Oaks outlet
centre. Guest beer from Whitbread list.
◖ ◗ ☲ ♿ ● P ⊛

RED LION
Chester Road (A56)
🕐 APH
Greenalls Mild, B, Original [H]
Large, opened-out pub. Refurbishment planned
for 1998. *Beware keg cider on handpull.*
◖ ◗ ☲ ● P

PUDDINGTON
THE TUDOR ROSE
Two Mills, Parkgate Road (A540)
🕐12-11 Mon-Sat; 12-10.30 Sun
Boddingtons B, guest beer [H]
Modern smart functional pub serving an
excellent selection of good value and above-
standard pub chain food.
Popular with after-work drinkers.
◖ ◗ ☲ ♿ ● P ⊛

PULFORD
GROSVENOR-PULFORD HOTEL
Wrexham Road
(B5445 old Chester- Wrexham road)
🕐11-3, 6-11 Mon-Fri; 11-11 Sat; 12-10.30 Sun
Marstons Pedigree, Tetley B, guest beer [H]
Large village hotel, now bypassed by the main
road. The accommodation is shortly to be
extended. Formerly known as the Talbot, it used
to incorporate the local post office. The sizeable
restaurant serves during all opening hours until
10pm.
◖ ◗ ☲ ♿ ● P ⊛

PENKETH
FERRY TAVERN
Station Road
🕐 12-3,5.30-11 Mon-Fri; 12-11 Sat; 12-10.30 Sun (winter) APH in summer.
**Courage Directors, Moorhouse Pendle Witches Brew, Ruddles County,
Websters Yorkshire B, plus two guest beers [H]**
Close to Fiddler's Ferry yacht marina, the Ferry Tavern is popular with those involved in the pursuit
of leisure, and can be very crowded in summer, while in winter it is a real haven of peace. Set on the
banks of the River Mersey it is prone to flooding, and plaques on the bar and a series of photographs
show the level reached by the tides in past years. The name is of course derived from the location at
the site of an ancient ferry crossing. Fiddler may have been the nickname of the owner of the Manor
of Penketh in 1160 who first had the right to run a ferry. His house would be used to supply
refreshment to travellers. One historic use of the boat was to carry spectators to bare knuckle fights
on the far bank near Moore, safe from the Peelers. There are open views across the estuary toward
the Runcorn bridges, and to the eight huge cooling towers of Fiddler's Ferry power station.
On a sunny and preferably non-windswept day, the garden provides a very pleasant spot to enjoy
some real fresh air, as long as the donkeys leave you alone!
    The brick floored bar area is very attractive, with wood, brass and maps of the inland
waterways. To your right is a very cosy lounge /dining room with a roaring fire in season, and a
beautiful old print of the inn above the fireplace. To the extreme left of the pub is a small games
room, now used for darts and table football, but once in use as a mortuary for bodies fished from the
Mersey. One of the pub ghosts, Charlie, is thought to be a local ferryman. The upstairs restaurant is
non-smoking, where one of the tables is discreetly tucked away in a corner. Above the stairs is an
amusing historic tableau featuring an old salt in a period room with shelves full of bottles and
books.
    The menu is imaginative, with fish, steak and Mexican specialities as well as a Sunday
roast. The chef has a number of varieties of sausage specially made in Grange over Sands.
The portions are very satisfying, and all the meals are made from fresh ingredients, mostly bought
locally. Note, there is no food on Sunday or Monday evenings. Behind the bar is a range of over 150
malt whiskies. There is also an ever-changing range of at least two guest beers from regionals and
micro-breweries, as well as the classic Moorhouses brew made in the shadow of Pendle Hill in
Blackburn. As the pub is separated from the car park by the railway line and the Sankey Canal, you
are guaranteed at least some exercise in these car-borne times.
◖ ◗ ☲ ● P

PLUMLEY

GOLDEN PHEASANT

Plumley Moor Road (off A556, close to Plumley station)
⏰11-3, 5.30-11 Mon-Sat; 12-10.30 Sun
Lees GB Mild, B, Moonraker, seasonal beers [H]
This is a substantial hotel pub in the heart of the Cheshire countryside, easily recognisable by its large inn sign, which is surmounted by a well-painted Golden Pheasant. Golden and common pheasants are often seen in the area, likely escapees from the Tabley estate. The frontage is given elegance by the bow windows with their window boxes. As you enter through a wood and glass panelled entrance corridor, the bar is before you. To the right is a comfortable lounge area with a real fire in a listed Victorian tiled and mirrored surround, adorned with brass pheasants and Staffordshire Dogs. To the left are several discrete dining or drinking areas variously characterised by plentiful plate racks full of porcelain, a massive copper hood over the fire, an impressive grandfather clock and a glass case with stuffed examples of local wildlife. The walls are a riot of copper and brass, with a collection of farm implements, and many prints of British wildlife. To the extreme left is the separate restaurant and the entrance to the accommodation, which comprises eight en suite rooms. The extreme right of the building houses the public bar, with a separate entrance. This is the base for the Dominoes team, pool and darts.

The Golden Pheasant was formerly known as the Station Hotel, for its close proximity to the main Chester to Manchester line. It has a large car park, a bowling green, and a garden with a children's play area.

◖◗ 🐕 ♿ ● ⇌ P

RAINOW

HIGHWAYMAN (See overleaf)

RISING SUN
Hawkins Lane (B5470)
⏰11.45-3, 5.30-11 Mon-Sat; 12-10.30 Sun
Marstons B, Pedigree [H]
Small, comfortable and within easy reach of Macclesfield. Kerridge Ridge right behind. Pleasant pool room. Excellent menu.
◖◗ 🐕 ● P

ROBIN HOOD
Church Lane
⏰12-3, 5.30-11 Mon-Fri; 11-11 Sat; 12-3, 7-10.30 Sun
Greenalls B, guest beers [H]
Primarily serving the needs of this quiet, rural community. Situated on a steep and winding road.
◖◗ P

RAVENSMOOR

FARMER'S ARMS
Marsh Lane (in the middle of the village)
⏰12-3, 6-11 Mon-Sat; 12-3, 6-10.30 Sun
Greenalls B [H]
A comfortable country pub, serving meals at all times, with a good range of specials.
◖◗ 🐕 ● P

RISLEY

NOGGIN
Warrington Road (A574)
⏰11.30-11 Mon-Sat; 12-10.30 Sun
Boddintons B, Cains TraditionalB, Greenalls B [H]
Heavily food-oriented pub, though retaining a lounge area for drinkers. Meals all day Sunday. Handy for Risley Moss Country Park.
◖◗ 🐕 ● P

RODE HEATH

BROUGHTON ARMS
Sandbach Road
⏰ 12-3.30, 5-11 Mon-Fri, 12-11 Sat; 12-3, 7-10.30 Sun
Marstons B, Pedigree [H]
A much altered canalside pub. Evening meals until 8.45 daily.
◖◗ 🐕 ● P

ROYAL OAK (See after Runcorn)

ROWTON

ROWTON HALL HOTEL
No real ale.

RUDHEATH

FARMERS ARMS
Middlewich Road
⏰ 2-11 Mon-Sat; 12-10.30 Sun
Greenalls B [H]
Modern estate pub with large bar and lounge.
P

OLD BROKEN CROSS
Middlewich Road
⏰APH
Greenalls Mild, B [H], guest beers [E]
Canalside pub formed from a row of cottages. Moorings are available Refurbished recently as a "Country Alehouse", with fake barrel dispense.
◖◗ 🐕 ● P

RUNCORN

BANK CHAMBERS
No real ale.

BARGE
No real ale.

BARLEY MOW
Church Street, Old Town
⏰ APH
Tetley Walker B [H]
Smart, red brick frontage with stained glass windows. However, the interior is a bit of a let-down consisting of 2 large rooms.

BEECHWOOD

Beechwood Avenue
⏰ 5-11 Mon-Thu; 3-11 Fri; 2-11 Sat; 12-10.30 Sun
Thwaites B [H]
Recently refurbished estate pub. Games room and large lounge. Thwaites is relatively rare in Cheshire.
⚬ ● P

DANIEL THWAITES BREWERY

BLARNEY STONE
No real ale.

BURMA STAR
No real ale

CANAL SIDE
Canal St
⏰5-11 Mon-Thu; 12-11 Fri-Sat; 12-10.30 Sun
Draught Bass [H]
Three bars, restaurant and function room close to the football ground. Evening food and Sunday lunch.
❚ ⚰ ⚬ ● P

PLUMLEY

SMOKER
Manchester Road (A556)
⏰11-3, 6-11 Mon-Sat; 12-10.30 Sun
Robinsons Hatters Mild, Best B [H]
An attractive and characterful Elizabethan coaching house on the very busy A556, half way between Chester and Manchester. The cobbled frontage and old mounting block give a clue to the antiquity of the Smoker, as does the thatched roof. It is named after a white champion racehorse ridden by the late Lord de Tabley, whose nearby Estate at Tabley House has an impressive art collection, open to the public in summer. Both the Windmill and the Spinner & Bergamot in the vicinity are similarly named after horses owned by the said gentleman. A depiction of his Lordship and Smoker is to be found reproduced both on the menu and on the wall in the snug.

The interior is most attractive, with hop-bedecked beams and a huge collection of jugs and brassware, copper kettles and bed warming pans. A corner cabinet houses porcelain and the furnishings include some attractive wooden settles. As well as hunting matters, the many prints on the walls illustrate Napoleonic infantrymen and cavalrymen, perhaps linking to the Cheshire Yeomanry, which was raised nearby and quartered on the Tabley estate. You will also find a collection of superb old photographs of the pub, opposite the bar, and a map of Olde Cheshire.

On your left as you enter the low beamed lobby is a cosy non-smoking snug, with one of the open fires. To the right is one of the lounges, while the bar is ahead of you, past the interesting phone-box cubby hole. The pub has been extended into outbuildings, and a separate restaurant stretches for some way to the rear. The Cuisine is highly regarded, with a full range of meals from sandwiches up, and vegetarians and children specifically catered for.
❚ ❙ ⚰ ● ⚰ P ⊛

GUINNESS IS NOT ALL IT'S CRAIC' ED UP TO BE!

Don't be taken in by the Blarney; the Guinness you can buy here is brewed in London, not Dublin.

The style of the beer is that it is a Stout. This style is a variation of Porter which was developed on the mainland in the 18th century. The brewer is not particularly Irish any more; it is a multi-national conglomerate with interests in sprits and pizza, and a presence in most countries on the planet.

The 1998 Good Beer Guide lists well over a hundred stouts (and their close relatives, Porters) **brewed traditionally as Real Ale** in the UK. *Guinness is not Real Ale, it is a dead, keg beer.* Real Ale, well-kept has infinitely more character than the keg substitute.

Guinness is an excessively overpriced stout, both as a result of its near-monopoly of the style, and the extensive, expensive advertising campaigns so often needed to promote second-rate products. Real Ale sells on its merits.

The cost of production is not that different. When you pay £2.00 for a pint of Guinness instead of £1.40 for Real Ale , you are giving a very generous tip to the fat cats and the advertising executives. *WHY?*

PRESTBURY

ADMIRAL RODNEY

New Road (opposite St Peter's church).
⏰11-3, 5.30-11 Mon-Thu; 11-11 Fri-Sat; 12-3, 7-10.30 Sun
Robinsons Hatters Mild, Best B [H]
Part of an attractive white-washed, brick terrace, this smart Grade II listed building is decorated with hanging baskets and flower tubs for most of the year. Interestingly, the original entrance became the back door when the new village main road was constructed. Throughout its rambling interior the low ceilings, beams and cosy drinking areas exude a friendly and relaxing atmosphere, popular with all including the "Cheshire Set" contingent. The comfortable furnishings include wooden-panelled seats as well as tables and chairs made from old beer barrels. An open fire warms drinkers on winter evenings and the daily papers are also provided. Children are admitted on Sundays only. A regular entry in CAMRA's national Good Beer Guide.
The Admiral Rodney is named after a famous British naval officer who would have held a much higher profile in British history had he not been a contemporary of Horatio Nelson, whose deeds tended to overshadow him. Interestingly, in the centre of Macclesfield is evidence of their joint fame; two adjacent terraced streets built about two hundred years ago are called Nelson Street and Rodney Street. The nautical theme is reflected in the decor, with numerous sailing vessel prints and even a replica of a ship's wheel! GBG

CASTLE INN
Castle Road, Halton Village
⏰12-3, 5.30-11 Mon-Sat; 12-3, 7-10.30 Sun
Greenalls B [H]
Built in early 18th century as a courthouse; the present day cellar was the dungeon. Ruins of Halton Castle to rear. Function room with regular Wednesday folk night.
No food Saturday.

CHERRY TREE
No real ale.

CLARENDON
101 Church Street, Old Town
⏰11.30-4, 7-11 Mon-Fri; 11.30-11 Sat; 12-5,7-10.30 Sun
Greenalls B [H]
Named after a tug -boat, the once-busy Manchester Ship Canal basin is nearby, this is a cosy town local. Good view of the bridges. Accommodation is available.

CREST HOTEL
Wood Lane, Beechwood
⏰APH
Draught Bass [H]
Typical hotel bar.

CROFT
No real ale.

DOCKSIDE INN
No real ale.

DRAY
Mullion Close, Brookvale
⏰12-11 Mon-Sat; 12-10.30 Sun
Boddingtons B [H]
Large open-plan estate pub.

DUKE OF WELLINGTON
No real ale.

DUKESFIELD
32 Ashridge Street, Old Town
⏰12-3, 7-11 Mon-Tue; 11-11 Wed-Sat; 12-10.30 Sun
Greenalls Mild, B [H]
Formally called the Devonshire and still known as the "Dev", the pub is dominated by the rail and road bridges over the Mersey. Rooms available.

EGERTON ARMS
2 Bridge Street
⏰4-11 Mon-Thu; 2-11 Fri; 12-11 Sat; 12-10.30 Sun
Greenalls Mild, B, [H]
Multi-room pub with emphasis on pub games – close to the football ground. Snacks available.

FIDDLERS THREE
No real ale.

GRAPES
82 Halton Road, Old Town
⏰12-3, 7-11 Mon-Thu; 12-11 Fri,Sat; 12-10.30 Sun
Greenalls Mild, B [H]
Situated opposite the Bridgewater Canal, with a well-kept bowling green to the rear. Emphasis on pub games.

HALFWAY HOUSE
Halton Road, Old Town
⏰12-11 Mon-Sat; 12-10.30 Sun
Greenalls Mild, B [H]
A very friendly large pub with genuine public bar. Twelve games teams! Live music Saturday.

HALLWOOD RAVEN
No real ale.

HALTON ARMS
No real ale.

JOLLY BREWER
No real ale.

LION
Greenway Road
⏰12-3, 5.30-11 Mon-Fri; 12-11 Sat; 12-4.30, 7- 10.30 Sun
Greenall B [H]
Street corner pub with restaurant. Evening food Wednesday, Friday and Saturday only.

MASONIC
Devonshire Square, Old Town
⏰11.30-11 Mon-Sat; 12-10.30 Sun
Cains Dark Mild, Traditional B, Boddingtons B [H]
Known locally as the "Long Pull", it was formerly a Masonic Lodge. Large bar area and comfortable lounge. This is a good range of beer for the town.
A rare outlet for the excellent Cains Mild.

MR BUMBLES
No real ale.

NAVIGATION
No real ale.

NORTON ARMS
Main Street, Halton Village
⏰11.30-3.30 6-11.30 Mon-Fri;
12-11 Sat, Sun 12-10.30
Greenalls Mild, B, guest beer [H]
Built in 1758 and situated at the foot of Halton
Castle. Friendly pub with 2 drinking areas and
upstairs pool room. Well-kept bowling green.
 P

OLD BRIDGE INN
High Street, Old Town
⏰ not provided
Greenalls Mild, B [H]
Uninteresting two-room pub.
● P

OLD TRANSPORTER
Tanhouse, The Brow
⏰1-11 Mon-Fri; 12-11 Sat; 12-10.30 Sun
Tetley B [H]
Modern estate pub with large lounge and bar/
games room.
● P

PROSPECT
70 Weston Road, Weston
⏰12-3, 7-11 Mon-Fri; 11-11 Sat;
12-3, 7-10.30 Sun
Greenalls Mild, B, Original [H]
Two room pub with good views over Mersey
estuary. No food served at weekends.
● P

RAILWAY
Lowlands Road
⏰ APH
Greenalls Mild, B, Original [H]
Multi-roomed pub with attached conservatory.
No evening meals on Sunday.
 P

RED ADMIRAL
Boston Avenue
⏰12-11 Mon-Sat; 12-10.30 Sun
Tetley M, B; guest beer [H]
Large estate pub, named after the butterfly.
Separate vault. Guest beers from Tetley list.
● P

ROUNDHOUSE
No real ale.

ROYAL
No real ale.

ROYAL OAK
Heath Road South, Weston Point
⏰5-11 Mon-Wed; 12-11 Thu-Sat;
12-10.30 Sun
Marstons B, Pedigree [H]
Well supported local with bar, lounge and
games room.
●

SOUTHBANK
No real ale.

STRAW HAT
No real ale.

TANNERS
No real ale.

RAINOW
HIGHWAYMAN
Whaley Bridge Road (B5470, on outskirts of village towards Kettleshulme.)
⏰11-3, 7-10 Mon-Sat; 12-3, 7-10.30 Sun
Thwaites B [H]
The Highwayman must have one of the county's most appealing pub interiors. A very attractive,
remote and windswept moorland inn, with breathtaking views from the front door. It was known as
the Blacksmith's Arms until 1949 and locally as "The Patch". Within, there is a maze of connecting
rooms with a small tap room at the far corner. Very low ceilings and genuine old beams are
complemented by scrubbed wooden tables and numerous settles, with a particularly fine, carved
example in the back room, next to a wall-mounted iron shield. The room to the right of the hall is
reached through a latched, barn-style door and has a separate bar hewn from a single timber.
The front snug is named after a local, historical rogue, Tom King.
The Highwayman is blessed by 18 inch thick walls and no fewer than three blazing open
fires in the winter months. Given the exposed situation, this can be a bleak spot when the snows
come, but there could be worse places to be cut off! Good bar food is to be had. We are told that
darts players in the back room have great difficulty in hitting 'double top', due to the combination of
low ceiling and wooden beams. This is one of the very few pubs serving Thwaites beer in Cheshire.
The benches in front garden have wonderful view over the rolling hills around, and the
Highwayman really is a classic, unspoilt rural gem. **GBG**
● P

TRAVELLERS REST
Highlands Road
⏰12-11 Mon-Sat; 12-10.30 Sun
**Cains Traditional B, Greenalls Mild, B,
Youngs Special, guest beer [H]**
Large friendly single-roomed pub on top of
Runcorn Hill in old part of town. Excellent
beer range for the area. Extension is planned.
Front patio. Food served 12-8 daily.
Beware of keg cider on a fake handpump.
 P

TRICORN
No real ale.

UNION TAVERN
Union Street, Old Town
⏰12-3,7-11 Mon-Thu; 12-11 Fri-Sat;
12-3,7-10.30 Sun
Greenalls Mild, B [H]
Street-corner local which has recently
undergone a tasteful refurbishment.
Separate drinking areas and a cosy bar.
 P

WATERLOO
High Street, Old Town
⏰APH
Greenalls Mild, B, guest beer [H]
Large red brick pub across the road from the
Bridgewater Canal. Public bar and smart
lounge. Very large games room. The guest
beers come from the Greenalls list.
Accommodation.
● P

WEAVER HOTEL
No real ale.

WINDMILL
Local Centre, Windmill Hill
⏰11.30-11 Mon-Sat; 12-10.30 Sun
Hydes Mild, B, Light [E]
Situated in an elevated position at the edge of
the New Town with good views over the
Mersey plain. Family and games rooms. Hydes
is a relatively rare brew for Cheshire. It is good
to see the windmill stocking two of the three
milds from this popular Manchester brewer.
Oversized, lined glasses for a full measure.
● P

RODE HEATH

ROYAL OAK
41 Sandbach Road (A533, near Alsager)
⏰5.30-11 Mon; 12-3, 5.30-11 Tue-Fri; 12-11 Sat; 12-10.30 Sun
Ansells Mild, Draught Bass, Greene King Abbot, Tetley B, Titanic Premium, guest beer [H]
The Royal Oak is a smart and cosy local enlivened by an exposed brick fireplace and beams.
There is a bay-windowed lounge decorated with china plates, old ink bottles and an interesting collection of pictures of the locality, including the canal and a third village pub which disappeared due to subsidence! Also to be found are a separate vault and a games room. We understand that there is no food on Sunday evenings or Mondays. It is situated conveniently close to the Trent & Mersey canal. The associated walks are the South Cheshire Way and the Cheshire Ring Walk.
　　A good range of beers includes those from the Ansells and Titanic breweries, both of which are unusual in the county. The beer quality is consistently good enough to have earned the pub an entry in CAMRA's national Good Beer Guide. **GBG**
◖ ◗ ⅊ ● P

SALTNEY

BREWERY ARMS
No real ale.

CITY ARMS
56 Chester Road (A5104)
⏰APH
Greenalls B, Tetley B[H]
First (and last) pub in England. Large, friendly one-roomed suburban local. Vestiges of the multi-room layout are mockingly evident.
◖ ⅊

SANDBACH

BLACK BEAR
High St.
⏰APH
Marstons Pedigree, Tetley B [H]
Tudor hostelry on cobbled market square. Good range of lunchtime special meals.
◖ ⅊ ●

CRICKETERS ARMS
54 Crewe Rd. (opposite Sandbach school)
⏰12-3, 6-11 Mon-Thu; 12-11 Fri & Sat; 12-4, 7-10.30 Sun
Burtonwood Mild, B [H]
Sports-oriented local on main road. Good to see cask mild sold.

CROWN
10 Market Square
⏰12-3, 7-11 Mon-Sat; 12-3, 7-10.30 Sun
Robinsons Hatters Mild, Best B, another from Robinsons range [H]
Old town pub, opposite the Saxon crosses. Wide range of lunchtime special meals.
◖ ⅊

GEORGE HOTEL
39 High St.
⏰12-11 Mon-Sat; 12-10.30 Sun
Websters Yorkshire B (occasional) [H]
Lively, youth-oriented pub.
⅊ ♿

IRON GREY
Middlewich Road (on main road in centre)
⏰11-3, 5.30-11 Mon-Thu; 11-4.30, 5.30-11 Fri; 11-5.30, 7-11 Sat; 12-4, 7-10.30 Sun
Robinsons Best B [H]
Two-roomed local, with much of its character lost by refurbishment. No food Sun lunchtime.
⅊

LIMES
3 Sweet Tooth Lane
⏰11-11 Mon-Sat; 12-10.30 Sun
Marstons Pedigree, Robinsons Best B, Tetley B, guest beer [H]
Large pub on housing estate, with bowling green. Recently refurbished, now with restaurant area. Excellent choice of food.
◖ ◗ ⅊ ●

LION
No real ale

LOWER CHEQUER (See overleaf)

MARKET TAVERN
The Square
⏰11-3, 7-11 Mon-Fri; 11-11 Sat; 12-3, 7-10.30 Sun
Robinsons Hatters Mild, Best B [E]
Old-fashioned pub, with several separate drinking areas.
◖ ⅊ ● P

THE TITANIC BREWERY

BEST BITTER	3.5% (ABV)	**WHITE STAR**	4.8%
LIFEBOAT	3.9%	**CAPTAIN SMITH**	5.2%
PREMIUM	4.1%	**WRECKAGE**	7.8%
STOUT	4.5%		

SHUGBOROUGH BEERS ALSO AVAILABLE

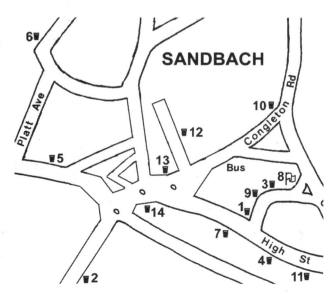

Out *Inn* CHESHIRE

MILITARY ARMS
Congleton Rd. (town centre opposite market)
⏲APH
Stones B, Greenalls B, Original [H]
Comfortable, open-plan pub. Popular on
market day (Thu). Carvery Wed-Fri lunch.
◖ ● P ⊗

OLD HALL HOTEL
High Street (below Sandbach church)
⏲6.30-11 Mon-Sat; 6.30-10.30 Sun
Boddingtons B, Ruddles B [H]
Cosy bar in historic black & white hotel.
● P

RING OF BELLS
17 Wells Street
⏲12-11 Mon-Sat; 12-10.30 Sun
Burtonwood B [H]
Loud street corner local.
⊗

SANDPIPER
The Hill (A533 to Alsager)
⏲12-3, 5.30-11 Mon-Fri; 12-3, 7-11 Sat;
12-3, 7-10.30 Sun
Robinsons Hatters Mild, Best B [E]
Comfortable, two-roomed local
P

SWAN & CHEQUERS
16 Hightown
(opposite Town Hall on mini-roundabout)
⏲11-3, 6.30-11 Mon-Wed; 11-11 Thu; 11-4,
6.30-11 Fri; 11-11 Sat; 12-3, 7-10.30 Sun
Robinsons Hatters Mild, Best B [H]
Large, wood-panelled, town-centre pub.
Built in 1894, it was formerly a corn exchange.
Food on Thursday lunchtime only.
P

SYMPHONY WINE BAR
No real ale.

WHEATSHEAF HOTEL
1 Hightown (in centre by Natwest bank)
⏲11.30-3, 6-11 Mon-Wed; 11.30-11 Thu-Sat;
12-10.30 Sun
Banks B, Marstons B, Pedigree [H]
Large, historic pub, attracting younger crowd
at weekends. Several meetings rooms upstairs
are used by a wide range of societies.
◖ P

1 - Black Bear
2 - Cricketers
3 - Crown
4 - George Hotel
5 - Iron Grey
6 - Limes
7 - Lion
8 - Lower Chequers
9 - Market Tavern
10 - Military Arms
11 - Old Hall Hotel
12 - Ring o'Bells
13 - Swan & Chequers
14 - Wheatsheaf

SANDBACH
LOWER CHEQUER INN

Crown Bank (just off The Square)
⏱5-11 Mon; 12-3, 5-11 Tue, Wed; 12-11 Thu-Sat; 12-10.30 Sun
Hancocks HB, Theakstons Best B, 2 guest beers [H]
In a striking setting on a cobbled street, opposite the churchyard, the half-timbered Lower Chequer is the oldest building in town dating from 1570. One of the many highlights of a Conservation Area, it is close to the old Saxon Crosses, which were first erected in 653AD, and are amongst the oldest Christian monuments in the country. The name comes from the historic use of a chequer board to help uneducated customers count their money at this former money-changing house. The mounting block enabled travellers to dismount from horses or coaches, while underneath the bar, the cellar is exactly as it was when it was used for stabling horses when the pub was one of Cheshire's best known coaching inns, on the main road from Manchester to London. The striking beamed frontage is complemented by the hanging baskets, flower tubs and leaded windows. The building looks wonderful by day or night.

On the right as you enter is a small vault with historic local photographs and a real fire. The Chequer enjoys a good local trade, with a lively social scene encompassing a Golf Society and a Punters' Club for horse racing. Sport is occasionally watched on the TV. The lunchtime meals are of good quality, and include a Sunday Roast. The pub ghost is said to be an erstwhile stable lad, known as "You". His name originates from most of the comments aimed at him in his former life; "You, do this" and "You, do that". Visitors to this historic town will want to know that market day is Thursday, that there is street parking nearby, and outside seating on a patio for those sunny days. The guest beers are a highlight. The Hancocks is a rather ordinary regional brand from Bass.

SANDIWAY
BLUE CAP HOTEL
Chester Road (A556)
⏱11.30-11 Mon-Sat; 12-3,7-10.30 Sun
Courage Directors, Theakstons Best B, Websters Yorkshire B [H]
Attractive roadhouse is let down by interior, full of bric-a-brac and loud music. "Steak and Ale" food menu. Accommodation.

SAUGHALL
EGERTON ARMS
No real ale

GREYHOUND INN
Seahill Road
⏱11-3, 5-11 Mon-Fri; 11-11 Sat; 12-3, 7-10.30 Sun
Boddingtons B, Castle Eden Ale, guest beer [H]
Popular multi-area local, with a quiz night and a Curry and Pint night. No food Sunday evening. **GBG**

SCHOLAR GREEN
BLEEDING WOLF
121 Congleton Road North
⏱11.30-11 Mon-Sat; 12-10.30 Sun
Robinsons Hatters Mild, Hartleys XB, Best B [H]
Large, thatched roadhouse built 1938. The name derives from a legend, in which King John was saved from a wolf by a local keeper. The man's reward was all the land he could walk over in a week! Good value food including a carvery, served from noon till 8pm on Sunday.

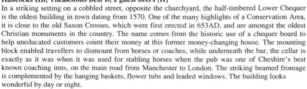

GLOBE
Drumber Lane
⏱7-11 Mon-Fri; 12-11 Sat; 12-10.30 Sun
Marstons B, Pedigree [H]
Unspoilt local with three small rooms. Parking can be difficult.

THREE HORSESHOES
Cinder Hill Lane
⏱12-3, 7-11 Mon-Sat; 12-3, 7-10.30 Sun
Courage Directors, Theakstons Best B [H]
An open plan village local.

TRAVELLERS REST
Congleton Road North (A34)
⏱ 11-3, 7-11 Mon-Sat; 12-3, 7-10.30 Sun
Batemans Mild, Marstons B, Pedigree, guest beer [H]
Single roomed pub with food available

SHAVINGTON
ELEPHANT & CASTLE
289 Newcastle Road (at A500 junction)
⏱12-3, 6-11 Mon-Fri; 12-11 Sat; 12-10.30 Sun
Boddingtons B, Tetley Mild, B [H]
Open plan, lively and friendly. Tuesday Disco, Thursday Karaoke. Evening meals only at weekend.

VINE
Rope Lane (100 yards from Shavington end)
⏱12-11 Mon-Sat; 12-10.30 Sun
Burtonwood B [H]
Open plan village pub. The open fire contributes to the welcome. Large function room available. Wednesday quiz.. Bar snacks.

SHOCKLACH
BULL INN
⏱12-3, 7-11 Mon-Sat (closed Mon lunch) 12-3, 7-10.30 Sun
Burtonwood B [H]
Thriving pub in a fairly isolated village, popular for good value food. Extended to accommodate diners, but the bar area remains.

SMALLWOOD
BLUE BELL
Spen Green
(off Congleton Road, east of Smallwood)
⏱12-3, 6-11 Mon-Sat; 12-3, 7-10.30 Sun
Greenalls B, Original [H]
Attractive 300 year old local in a rural setting. Distinctive bowed frontage added in 1948. Real fires, low beams, tiled floors and high backed wooden settles in a quiet atmosphere with no music. Once part of a farm, it has been in the same hands for 26 years.

BULLS HEAD
Newcastle Road (on the A50)
⏱12-3, 6-11 Mon-Sat; 12-3, 7-10.30 Sun
Marstons Pedigree, Tetley B, guest beer [H]
A typical comfortable country pub, one end given over to eating, and a family conservatory at the other. In between is 'pub' area. Roadside country pub with conservatory. The very attractive garden includes a play area.

LEGS OF MAN
Newcastle Road (A50, ½mile south of A534)
🕐11.30-3, 6-11 Mon-Sat; 12-3, 7-10,30 Sun
Robinsons Hatters Mild, Best B,
Frederics [H]
An inter-war country pub of the kind built so
well by Robinsons. It houses a separate restau-
rant behind its partial mock-Tudor exterior.
The bar menu is extensive, interesting and em-
phasises fish dishes. Large beer garden.

SALAMANCA
No real ale

SPROSTON
FOX & HOUNDS
Holmes Chapel Road,
A54 (3/4 mile W of M6 jct 18)
🕐12-3, 5-11 Mon-Sat; 12-3, 7-10.30 Sun
Greenalls B, Original, Tetley B [H]
This attractive and well-maintained pub with
beams and stone floor features a wide choice
of good food, freshly prepared on the premises,
and a friendly atmosphere. Two separate
eating areas to rear, overlooking bowling
green. No food on Mondays.
Beware keg cider on hand pump.

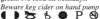

SPURSTOW
YEW TREE
Long Lane
(southern route into Bunbury off A49)
🕐11-3, 5.30-11 Mon-Sat; 12-10.30 Sun
Burtonwood B, Greenall B, Tetley B [H]
A locals' pub on the outskirts of Bunbury.
Originally known as the Crewe Arms, as it
was owned by the Earl of Crewe.

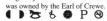

STATHAM
STAR
Star Lane, Statham
🕐3-11 Mon-Thu; 12-11 Fri-Sat; 12-10.30 Sun
Boddingtons B, Greenalls Mild, B,
Worthington Draught B, guest beer [H]
A warm & welcoming community local close
to Bridgewater canal and Trans-Pennine trail.
Well worth a visit. Worthington and
Boddingtons alternate. Snacks available.

STOAK
BUNBURY ARMS
Little Stanney Lane (off A5117 at jct. 10 M53)
🕐12-3, 5.30-11 Mon-Thu; 12-11 Fri-Sat;
12-3, 7-10.30 Sun (all day in summer)
Boddingtons B, Cains Traditional B,
Greenalls B, Original [H]
Within the plain brick exterior there is bare-
timber, traditional wooden seating and the sort
of unfussy decor one wishes for in a small
country pub. In recent times it has become
something of a food house, boasting meals all
day from a varied menu. However, in the
evening the pub often reverts to a convivial
village local. Visitors should note the small,
but highly attractive public bar. There is a no
smoking area in a small bookshelf-lined
alcove. Outdoor seating on the patio. Handy
for Shropshire Union Canal, Cheshire Oaks
outlet village, Chester Zoo and Rake Hall.
GBG

SCHOLAR GREEN
RISING SUN
112 Station Road (off the A34 on the road to Mow Cop)
🕐12-3, 7-11 Mon-Sat; 12-3, 7-10.30 Sun
Marstons B, Pedigree, Head Brewers Choice [H]
The Rising Sun is a comfortable three-roomed hostelry on the edge of Scholar Green and close to
the Macclesfield Canal in attractive countryside. A Victorian brick-built pub, it was enlarged in
1939, being built around the original building. There is a bar decorated with brasses and sporting
prints, and a smaller lounge. Traditional pub games are played here, and an open fire warms the
cockles of your heart after a brisk winter walk along the Cheshire Ring Canal towpath. Mow Cop is
1100 feet above sea level, and is the site of a National Trust owned mock castle ruin. The views
from the top are remarkable.
      The pub features a separate dining room, serving highly recommended food freshly
prepared on the premises. The prices are reasonable, but intending diners should be aware that
during the low season from January to March, neither the pub nor the restaurant is open at
lunchtimes. Evening meals are available on Wednesday to Sunday evenings.

STOCKTON HEATH
MULBERRY TREE HOTEL
Grappenhall Road (village centre)
🕐APH
Boddingtons B, Greenalls Mild, B,
Original [H]
Cavernous pub, much altered in recent years,
catering for younger clientele in the evenings.
Building now listed. Separate vaults.

RED LION
(See overleaf)

STOCKTON HEATH WINE BAR
No real ale.

STRETTON
CAT & LION
Tarporley Road
🕐APH
Greenalls Mild, B, Original;
Boddingtons B; guest beer [H]
Once a multi-roomed inn of character, the pub
is now opened-out and is now a "Miller's
Kitchen". Attractive sandstone exterior.
Attached lodge. Guest beer from Greenalls list.

HOLLOW TREE
Off A49 (close to M56 junction 10)
🕐11-3, 5-11 Mon-Fri; 11-11 Sat;
12-10.30 Sun
Theakston Best B, Old Peculier; guest beer
[H]
Large ex country house with open plan and
separate drinking areas. Separate restaurant.
Children's play area.
Rare outlet for Old Peculier in Cheshire.
Guest beer from Scottish Courage.

THE RED LION - STOCKTON HEATH.

STOCKTON HEATH

RED LION

London Road (A49, close to junction with A56)

⏰APH

Greenalls Mild, B, Original [H]

The Red Lion is a two hundred year old Georgian coaching inn with many rooms, very popular in evenings. It is the proud possessor of a floodlit bowling green to the rear. Set close to the traffic lights in the centre of Stockton Heath, it is very handy for shoppers. It is a true local, popular with older regulars, whilst catering for all. It is the home of many sports teams, is half a mile from the Bridgewater Canal, and is virtually in the suburbs of Warrington. The Red Lion is considered sufficiently attractive and architecturally important to have been added to CAMRA's National Inventory of Heritage Pub Interiors. Go and find out why.

RING O' BELLS

Northwich Road
(A559, just south east of Junction 10 M56)
⏰12-3,5.30-11 Mon-Fri; 12-3, 7-11 Sat;
12-4,7-10.30 Sun
Greenalls Mild, B; guest beer [H]

Once part of a row of cottages, today has one main room with two side rooms. Friendly and comfortable country pub, with an open fire, in an area dominated by knocked-through eateries. A rare example of a rural pub which gets things right and does not need to rely on food. Boules played.

 P

STRETTON FOX

Spark Hall Close (off A49/M56 junction 10)
⏰11.30-11 Mon-Sat; 12-10.30 Sun
Draught Bass; Worthington Draught B, guest beer [H]

Newly converted farm house. 7 separate dining areas. Emphasis on food. Guest beer from Bass list.

 P

STYAL

SHIP INN

Altrincham Road (off B5166)
⏰12-11 Mon-Sat; 12-10.30 Sun
Courage Directors, Theakstons Best B, Old Peculier, Websters B, [H]

Welcoming country pub off the road to Manchester Airport. Open fire and separate dining room. Charming snug with model ship and grandfather clock. Conveniently located close to Quarry Bank Mill (National Trust). A rare outlet in this area for Old Peculier.

 P

SUTTON LANE ENDS

CHURCH HOUSE

By the church.
⏰12-3, 7-11 Mon-Sat; 12-3, 7-10.30 Sun
Boddingtons B, Greenalls B, Robinsons Best B, guest beer [H]

Welcoming, small, single bar pub dating from 1872. Popular with locals, but still with lots of passing trade. The combination of Boddingtons and Robinsons may now be unique. Darts, crib and dominoes played. Extensive bar snack menu. Large outdoor play area and food available in children's portions.

P

LAMB

Hollin Lane.
⏰6.30-11 Mon; 12-3, 6.30-11 Tues-Fri;
12-4, 6.30-11 Sat; 12-4, 6.30-10.30 Sun
Boddingtons B, Tetley B [H]

A small, friendly, old-fashioned, single room pub. Built in 1938 on site of earlier pub and named after Lady Caroline Lamb, one-time consort of Lord Byron. Low ceiling and real open fire. Very reasonably priced, home cooked food (except Mondays).
Children's play area in garden.

P

RYLES ARMS

Hollin Lane
(lower road from Sutton to Wincle, north of A54)
⏰11.30-3, 7-11 Mon-Sat; 12-3, 7-10.30 Sun
Courage Directors, Marston Pedigree [H]

Named after John Ryles, the first banker in Macclesfield. Started life as a mint in 1741. Good food dominates this quiet, popular old pub which always extends a friendly welcome. Situated on the Gritstone Trail. Beers usually alternate, sometimes both.

P

SUTTON HALL HOTEL
(See overleaf)

TABLEY
WINDMILL
Chester Road
(A556, just off M6 jct 19, toward Chester)
⏰12-3, 5.30-11 Mon-Fri; 12-11 Sat;
12-3, 5.30-10.30 Sun
Robinsons Hatters Mild, Best B,
Frederics, Old Tom [H]
A good example of a rural roadside inn, despite
its busy location. This 16th century listed
building remains largely unspoilt with low,
beamed ceilings, lots of cosy rooms and an
open fire. Brassware and prints adorn the walls
and there is a pool room to the rear. The name
derives from a racehorse owned by Lord de
Tabley. They serve an imaginative range of
food in both the bar and non-smoking
restaurant (all day Saturday). One of the few
outlets for the legendary Old Tom ale on
draught all year round. B&B available.
◖◗ ⌂ P

TARPORLEY
CROWN
78 High Street
Boddingtons B, Tetley B [H]
Characterless open-plan pub. Intrusive music.
Views of Peckforton Hills. Accommodation.
◖◗ ⌂ P

FORESTERS
High Street
Greenalls Mild, B, guest beer [H]
 Friendly local with a distinct dining area and
occasional live music. Accommodation.
◖◗ ● P

SUTTON LANE ENDS
HANGING GATE
Meg Lane (Take Ridge Hill road from village centre for 1½ miles, after double bend pub is on right)
⏰12-3, 7-11 Mon-Thu; 12-11 Fri-Sat; 12-10.30 Sun
Cains Traditional B, Formidable Ale, Marstons Pedigree, guest beers [H]
The Hanging Gate is a fascinating pub, dating from 1621 and its name is believed to be a
combination of the Scandinavian "gata", meaning pathway, and the fact that Royal Macclesfield
Forest poachers were hanged here. Earlier this century it was also called "Tom Steels" after a one-
armed landlord!
     Bare stonework peeps through the whitewash all over the pub, adding to its historical
charm. It is a superbly refurbished hillside building, with four small rooms on several levels as you
progress down the hillside. You enter into through a porch into a tiny hall, with an intimate snug
containing a lovely, open fire and main bar ahead. To the right is the first of a number of stepped
rooms, clinging onto the hillside. This contains a small bar, an old wood-burning stove with
surrounding coach lights and a rack with the daily papers. Travelling down the stone steps we pass
a cosy side room containing dried flowers and watercolours by a local artist. The lower room also
houses a fire adorned with a replica Civil War breastplate and a large bay window with ample
seating and a wonderful panorama of the surrounding countryside. Low ceilings and beams afford
a trap for the unwary tall amongst us. There is a witches circle in the top room, whilst the bottom
room commands a magnificent panoramic view over the Cheshire plain and Welsh hills, which
reputedly includes the Liver Building (probably the beer helps!). Aptly, this is known as the
"View Room", and is the only area where children are admitted. In addition to the areas on either
side of the bar, there is a welcome no-smoking room.
     The pub ghost is either a sheep rustler hung outside, or an early landlord, according to
choice. The cellar is built into the rock and is always 10°C (50-51°F in old money) - ideal for beer!
The inner man and woman are catered for by simple home-made pub food, much of it locally
produced, which is served every lunch and evening. The friendly, new tenants pride themselves on
their fresh, home-cooked food, but are nevertheless keen to keep the Gate as a community local.
Walkers are welcome, and this is good walking country. The guest beers are nominated by the
locals. Their excellent choice of beers includes two from Cains of Liverpool and a guest from an
independent brewery. The Gate is a good example of a successful pub renovation which neither
destroys the pub nor its character. Greenalls and other pub chains should take note.
◖◗ ⌂ ● P ⊘

THE TIMES THEY ARE A'CHANGING.

Since the previous Cheshire Pub Guide was produced, eleven years ago, there
have been sweeping changes to the inn scene in the county. The old guide, for
understandable reasons, listed only pubs selling real ale, and these numbered
only 670 - so many pubs were selling *keg* (the so-called tank or bright beer).
We are fortunate in that the huge majority of pubs now sell the genuine article
[874 out of 1064]. There are a few black holes - see Ellesmere Port for
example.

The news is mixed, as pub losses overall continue, urban redevelopment being
one culprit. The expected changes to the 'drink driving' law is likely to result in
the closure of many of the quieter rural pubs. Another worrying trend has been
the recent rise in *'smoothflow'* or *'nitrokeg'* beers - with real ale being displaced
from the bar in a distressingly large number of pubs. This threat is no different
from the *keg tide* of the sixties - which is where CAMRA came in...

Do your tastebuds a FAvour!

SWETTENHAM
SWETTENHAM ARMS
Swettenham Road (village centre, behind church)
⏲APH

Greenalls Original, Jennings B, Tetley B, Beartown Bearskinful [H] Addlestones Cider [H]

Nestling peacefully in the Dane valley, this large yet cosy pre-17th century country pub sits in an area rich in history. The building itself was once a nunnery and was an overnight resting point for funeral parties before they took the bodies through a (now blocked) passage to the church. Suitably, there are legends of ghosts. The countryside around was the site of much prehistoric activity. The Swettenham Arms is made even more attractive by the profusion of flowers in summer, and is well-illuminated by night.

        The pub itself is heavily timbered, with a long single bar and several areas in an open-plan style. There are wooden settles, heavy iron tables, a sofa, piano and a real fire in a large stone, copper-hooded fireplace surrounded by interesting copper and brass contraptions (guesses on a postcard...)! There is a separate restaurant, and occasional popular quiz nights. Live music is featured on Wednesdays. Plenty of outside seating is available on the front patio (overlooking the enormous car park) and in the garden during sunny weather. The "Quinta" arboretum, two minutes walk away, is well worth a visit too. This is a rare local outlet for beers from Jennings brewery of Cumbria. As we went to press, Beartown beers from Congleton had made a welcome appearance. We are very pleased to see support like this for a local independent brewer.

 P

TARPORLEY
RISING SUN
SWAN
(See overleaf)

TARVIN
GEORGE & DRAGON
High Street
⏲APH 12-3, 7-11 Mon-Fri; 11-11 Sat; 12-3, 7-10.30 Sun
Banks B [H]
Village pub with comfortable lounge, and a public bar with pool and darts.

RED LION
Church Street at High Street corner.
⏲APH
Greenalls B [H]
Cosy three room local, HQ of the bowls team. Of special note are the old windows commemorating Chester Northgate Brewery.

 P

STAMFORD BRIDGE
Tarvin Road, Great Barrow. (Off A51)
⏲11.30-11 Mon-Sat; 12-10.30 Sun
Boddingtons B, Greenalls Original [H]
Large two-roomer in a rural setting. One room is especially for families. Popular in summer, it boasts a large beer garden.

VILLAGE TAVERN
Bypass Road, A54
⏲7-11 Mon; 12-3, 6.30-11 Tu- Thu; 11-11 Fri-Sat; 12-10.30 Sun
Greenalls B. Tetley B [H]
Food oriented, with two large rooms. What is described as "Traditional Fayre" is served all day Friday to Sunday in addition to lunch and evenings on the other days.

TATTENHALL
BEAR & RAGGED STAFF
High Street (in the village centre)
⏲APH
Greenalls Mild, B [H]
Traditional village local, on a site occupied by an alehouse since the 15th century. The current incarnation dates from the late 19th century and is reputedly haunted. Bar snacks and Sunday roast.

TATTENHALL

LETTERS INN
High Street
⏰11.30-11 Mon-Sat; 12-10.30 Sun
**Boddingtons B, Cains Traditional B,
guest beer [H]**
17th century former sorting office. Attractive
unspoilt interior with log fire. A friendly local
with a small no-smoking restaurant area.

POACHERS POCKET
Tattenhall Road
⏰12-2.30, 5.30-11 Mon-Sat; 12-10.30 Sun
Banks B, Camerons Strongarm [H]
A 'Poachers' themed restaurant renowned for
large portions. Meals all day on Sunday.
Skittles are available and there is a play area.

SPORTSMANS
(See overleaf)

THELWALL

LITTLE MANOR
Bell Lane
⏰APH
**Boddingtons B, Cains Dark Mild,
Greenalls B, Original [H]**
Large Henry's Table set back from road in its
own grounds. Conservatory and restaurant.
Good to see the superb dark mild on sale.

PICKERING ARMS
Bell Lane
⏰12-3, 4.30-11 Mon-Thu; 12-11 Fri-Sat;
12-10.30 Sun
Greenalls Mild, B, Original [H]
Picturesque, open-plan,,timber-framed village
local. Refurbishment due in early 1998.
Fingers crossed they don't ruin it.

THREAPWOOD

QUEENS HEAD
Barn Road (Off B5069 in Sarn)
⏰12-3, 5-11 Mon-Sat; 12-3, 7-10.30 Sun
Marstons B [H]
Comfortable and small. Cheshire/Clwyd
boundary is marked by garden stream.
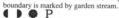

TILSTON

CARDEN ARMS
⏰11.30-3, 5-11 Mon-Sat; 12-3, 7-10.30 Sun
Greenalls B [H]
Lively village local, popular with bikers.

FOX & HOUNDS
No real ale

TARPORLEY

RISING SUN
38 High Street
⏰11-3, 5.30-11 Mon-Fri; 11.30-11 Sat; 12-10.30 Sun
Robinson Hatters Mild, Best B [H]
The Rising Sun is very much the hub of the village. With its many rooms with exposed beams and
low ceilings, and liberally decorated with brasses, it is undoubtedly a classic. Look out for the
black-leaded range in the lovely snug by the front door. There are two bar areas, one further back on
the right, and a lounge and restaurant to the left.
     The menu is extensive, and has to be written in small letters to fit it all on the blackboard!
CAMRA's prestige Good Pub Food Guide includes the Rising Sun. In fact is so renowned that it is
advisable to book a table in advance, particularly at weekends. Although food is clearly an
important part of the business, one bar is reserved for drinkers. The Sun was recently presented with
an award by the local branch of CAMRA for a rare achievement; being the only pub in Cheshire to
have appeared in the Good Beer Guide for 25 consecutive years. This is a major feather in the cap
for both the licensees and Robinson's Brewery. Clearly the beer is top notch. Set on the high street
of a particularly attractive market town, and convenient for the Sandstone Trail, this is a pub with a
lot going for it. **GBG**

BLANDIFICATION

Unfeeling and reckless pub-owning chains are intent on removing
all trace of genuine and original character from many of our pubs,
and replacing them with identikit "theme experiences".
Once gone, they are lost forever.

We already have an excellent example of a theme pub.
It's called the British pub, and has infinite character and variety.
It has evolved over the centuries to be what the customer wants.
Now some smartypants designers think they know better and ruin
perfectly good pubs (for ever) in order to produce a fake
"experience" which rapidly runs out of steam, and needs another
expensive refit after two years.

These fads have to be paid for - by you.

We suggest you avoid such fake pubs, and pick from these pages
the best of British pubs.

TIVERTON
RED FOX
Four Lane Ends (A49/A51 junction)
⊘11-3, 5.30-11 Mon-Fri; 11-11 Sat;
12-10.30 Sun
Jennings B, Cumberland Ale [H]
A large multi-roomed country-themed pub
laying emphasis on value-for-money good
food, with diners in main bar room or the
non-smoking conservatory. Exposed beams in
"barn" roof. Daily papers. Stuffed fox and
farm implements (on wall). Locals sometimes
watch Sky sport in side room. A Jennings tied
house, unique for the county, serving excellent
Cumbrian ales.
◀ ▶ ⅏ ● P ⊗

TYTHERINGTON
BROCKLEHURST ARMS
40 Manchester Road, Tytherington
(take any of 3 marked exits off Silk Road)
⊘APH
**Courage Directors, Theakston Best B,
guest beer [H]**
Typical extensive theme pub geared to families
and food, offering snacks and meals until late,
and now having to compete with other similar
places nearby. Drinkers meanwhile compete
with (or for) large and small screen TVs for
sport in two rooms. Large pleasant garden.
The guest beer is often from the Scottish &
Newcastle stable, but is sometimes a true
guest.
◀ ▶ ⅏ ⅃ ● P ⊗

MIDDLEWOOD
Tytherington Lane
(in business park, just off London Road A523)
⊘APH
**Boddingtons B, Castle Eden Ale,
Marstons Pedigree [H]**
New pub rolled off a production line lacking
in imagination, character, or individuality.
Could be anywhere. Brewer's Fayre. Extensive
children's facilities, but adults can do better
elsewhere.
◀ ▶ ⅏ ⅃ ● P ⊗

TYTHERINGTON
GOLF & COUNTRY CLUB
Dorchester Way
⊘APH
Beer varies [H]
Only the bar is open to the public. Availability
of traditional beer tends to be erratic, but we
are told that Flowers and Wadworths will be
available in 1998, with a guest beer.
◀ ▶ ⅏ ⅃ ● ⇌ P

TARPORLEY
SWAN
50 High Street
⊘11-3,6-11 Mon-Fri; 11-11 Sat; 12-3,7-10.30 Sun
Beer range varies (usually 4-5 beers) [H]
The Swan is an elegant, family-owned hotel with an impressive frontage, dating back to the
18th Century. It stands on the charming high street of a picturesque county town, at the halfway
point on the Sandstone Trail. Two oak-beamed and panelled bars are warmed by open fires,
including a through fireplace. On the left is a comfortable lounge next to the bar, with subdued
lighting and plush armchairs. Moulded cornicework is noteworthy around the ceilings, while the
lobby has some attractive leaded glass. To the rear you will find a second bar, an atrium and several
small, intimate drinking areas.
      A free house, some of the beers are from the Scottish-Courage guest list, and other regular
guests are Morland's Old Speckled Hen, Ruddles Best Bitter and Timothy Taylor's Landlord, plus
beers from independent breweries. You should check the blackboard to see what beers are available,
as two of the hand pumps are in the back bar. Accommodation is of course available, and there is a
separate restaurant. **GBG**
◀ ▶ ⅊ P

TATTENHALL

SPORTSMANS ARMS

High Street (village centre)

⏲APH

Thwaites Best Mild, B [H]

This popular local can be found in a village only eight miles from Chester. A white-painted terrace, it is graced by an attractive cobbled frontage, bedecked with flowers in spring and summer. The front steps lead you into a deceptively large interior of low, beamed ceilings, scrubbed oak tables and central bar with three sides for serving. The decor includes shelves of interesting old bottles, china plates, fresh and dried flowers and jugs hanging from the timbers everywhere! There is a nice, leaded grate in the left front room surrounded by old photos of the village and locality. To the right is a real gem of a snug, with wooden settles and its own fireplace.

Passing the ornate spiral staircase and piano is a large rear room for diners. The traditional interior is comfortable and relaxing, except during busy times, which are encouragingly frequent. Although it has been converted to open plan, the Sportsmans retains a village atmosphere. Darts and pool have their own room. A bowling green sits behind the pub and a nearby swing is provided for children.

The Sportsmans is a pub which has changed little over the years, and has never lost its charm; it is one of those few rural pubs which is not totally dominated by its food trade. Local trade alone would make it busy, but custom flocks from other villages and from Chester. It is an ideal stop for visitors to the region intent on taking in what the Cheshire countryside has to offer. This includes the Cheshire Ice Cream Farm and the Cheshire Candle Workshop. Very good value meals are served in a large dining area which opens onto a patio. The beer, from Blackburn's Thwaites, is relatively rare in the county, and you should use this as an opportunity to try it.

UPTON

BACHE

76 Liverpool Road

⏲11.30-11 Mon-Sat; 12-10.30 Sun

Greenalls B, guest beers [H]

Large open plan formula pub with accommodation and all day catering. *Beware of the keg mild.*

BEARS PAW

Dixons Drive

⏲APH

Wadworth 6X, Whitbread Trophy [H]

Large comfortable estate pub. Children are allowed on the covered patio. Quiz nights, pool & darts.

FROG

164 Liverpool Road

⏲ APH

Boddingtons B, Cains Traditional B, Castle Eden Ale, 2 guest beers [H]

Open plan roadside pub with a large screen TV which can be intrusive if you want a quiet drink and some conversation. Half panelled walls and pillars. Food through the day at weekends. Pool & darts.

WHEATSHEAF

Heath Road (off A41 at Long Lane lights)

⏲APH

Boddingtons B, Castle Eden Ale, Flowers IPA [H]

Large out of town pub with a chain restaurant. Dedicated to food, families and TV.

VICARS CROSS

CENTURION

Oldfield Drive (near A41/A51 junction)

⏲11.30-11 Mon-Fri; 11-11Sat; 12-10.30 Sun

Jennings B, Marstons Pedigree, Robinsons Best B, Tetley Dark Mild, B, guest beer [H]

Big family-type estate pub featuring pub games and Sunday quiz. A half hour walk along the canal from the station. The guest beer is from the Tetley list. Jennings, a nice malty brew from Cumbria, is rare in Cheshire.

TIMBERSBROOK

COACH & HORSES
Under Rainow Road. (A537 Biddulph road from Congleton, left at the traffic lights in Mossley.)
⏲APH

Robinsons Best B [E]

This is a snug country pub nestling under a hill just outside Congleton, close to the Neolithic Bridestones Burial Chamber and The Cloud, one of Cheshires few peaks with outstanding views over the plain. Well worth the struggle up! The pub itself dates from 1825, and replaces an earlier building which traded as the Fairhouse. An extract from the Congleton Chronicle hanging on the wall speculates as to the meaning of the former name and the reason for the change. The interior is typical for a country pub, with exposed beams, and walls decorated with maps, artefacts and pictures, some of which feature aircraft. In the small room there is a coal range, though unlike its counterpart in the kitchen, it is seldom used.

In addition to the food, a further attraction of the Coach is the splendid outlook over open countryside from the beer garden at the rear. Across the road is a safe children's play area, hedged from the road, and equipped with swings and a play tree.

Although you will not see the familiar handpump on the bar, we can assure you that the excellent Robinson's Best bitter is indeed real ale. The pumps are electric, but unlike keg beer dispensers, do not fill the ale with gas.

◖◗ ☏ ● P

WALGHERTON

BOARS HEAD
London Road (A51 between Woore and Nantwich at crossroads opposite petrol station)
⏲11.30-11 Mon-Sat; 12-10.30 Sun
Boddingtons B, Greenalls B, Original [H]
Large pub/restaurant, serving food all day.
◖◗ ☏ ♿ ● P ⊘

WALTON

SHIP
No real ale.

STAG
Ellesmere Road, Lower Walton
⏲11.30-11 Mon-Sat; 12-10.30 Sun
Greenalls Mild, B, Original [H]
Large, well-appointed, open-plan pub. Raised dining area. Bowling green to rear. No food Sunday evening.
◖◗ ♿ ● P

WALTON ARMS
Old Chester Road, Higher Walton
⏲APH
Greenalls B, Original, 2 guest beers [H]
Much altered village pub. Now a theme pub concentrating on food and families. Close by Bridgewater Canal and Walton Gardens. Guest beers are from the Greenalls list.
◖◗ ☏ ♿ ● P

WARDLE

JOLLY TAR
Nantwich Road,
(A51, opposite the canal junction).
⏲12-3, 7-11 Mon-Fri; 11-11 Sat;
12-10.30 Sun
Draught Bass (summer), Greenalls B [H]
A modern pub set opposite the junction of the Middlewich branch of the Shropshire Union canal. The open, light, spacious interior is aimed at families. Food all day at weekend, and a children's menu.
◖◗ ☏ ● P ⊘

WARMINGHAM

BEARS PAW
School Lane (opposite the church).
⏲11-3, 6-11 Mon-Sat; 12-10.30 Sun
Boddingtons B, Flowers IPA, Marstons Pedigree [H]
Large village pub catering mainly for diners.
◖◗ ☏ ● P

KING ARTHURS TAVERN
Warmingham Grange
⏲12-3, 6.30-11 Mon-Sat;
12-4, 6.30-10.30 Sun
Worthington Draught B, guest beer (occasional) [H]
Plush bar, part of the Warmingham Grange complex. Cabaret and late opening Sundays. Attractive garden with long sun terrace.
◖◗

TUSHINGHAM

BLUE BELL
Bradley Farm Lane (signposted off A41, 4 miles north of Whitchurch)
⏱12-3, 6-11 Mon-Sat; 12-3, 7-10.30 Sun
Hanby Drawwell B, Treacleminer, guest beers [H]
The Blue Bell is an ancient timbered building, full of character. A delightful, award-winning pub, presided over by a great dane and an eccentric American licensee, making this an essential stop. The date above the door is 1667, but parts of this black and white coaching inn date back to the 14th century. Passing the mounting block on the cobbled frontage, you enter by a magnificent oak door into a tiled hallway. There are three heavily-beamed rooms, adorned with many horse brasses and other artefacts. The bar itself is tucked into an inglenook. A glass case holds a number of unusual finds, including a Cavalier's hat from around 1600. Visitors should be prepared to join in lively discourse in the main bar, but there is plenty of opportunity to enjoy a quiet pint with the complementary Sunday newspapers by the fire or sequestered in the back rooms
    A good range of home-cooked food is served in generous portions. The superb Hanby beers, rarely seen in Cheshire, are brewed in Wem, North Shropshire. The guest beers are often from this brewery too. The quality of cellarmanship has made the Blue Bell a regular entry in CAMRA's national Good Beer Guide. **GBG**
◀ ▶ ☕ ● P

New Brewery
Aston Park, Soulton Road
Wem, Shropshire
Tel: 01939 232432

WARRINGTON

ADELPHI VAULTS
No real ale.

ALBERTS
No real ale.

ALBION
No real ale.

BARLEY MOW
Golden Square, Town Centre
⏱APH
Firkin beers [H]
Historic 15th century half-timbered building in centre of modern shopping development. Long running battle against alterations has come to a conclusion and the pub is due to become one of the "Firkin" chain.

BAR TEMPO
No real ale.

BAR YEL
No real ale.

BIG BAR
No real ale.

BLACK BEAR
Knutsford Road
⏰APH
Boddingtons B, Greenalls Mild, B [H]
Now opened out, but a sympathetic renovation with some wooden panelling. Adjacent to former Lachford Union Canal (aka Black Bear canal). Childrens play barn.
◖ ☎ ● P

BLACK HORSE
No real ale.

BLACKBURNE ARMS
Orford Green (Orford)
⏰11.30-11 Mon-Sat; 12-10.30 Sun
Greenalls Mild, B [H]
Large pub on a double-bend. Lounge recently redecorated and full of wood panelling and large mirrors. Food Monday to Friday.
◖ ₺ ● P

BLUEBELL
Horsemarket Street
⏰APH
Greenalls B, Stones B, Tetleys B [H]
Busy, town centre, open plan pub.
◖ ▷ ₺ ⇌

BOWLING GREEN
47 Liverpool Road, Bank Quay
⏰12-11, Mon-Sat; 12-10.30 Sun
**Cains Traditional B,
Greenalls Mild, B [H]**
Welcoming Edwardian style pub with red brick and stone exterior. Restaurant, function room and accommodation.
◖ ▷ ⇌ P

BRICKMAKERS
No real ale.

BROOKLANDS
No real ale.

BUZZ
No real ale.

WALKER BARN
SETTER DOG
New Buxton Road (A537, 3 miles from Macclesfield)
⏰5.30-11 Mon,11-3, 5.30-11 Tu-Sat; 12-10.30 Sun
Draught Bass, Taylors Landlord, guest beer [H]
Built in 1740 as part of a thriving farming and quarrying community, the Setter Dog probably began life as a coaching house, and is reputed to have been the last combined pub and post office in England. An old post collection box remains hidden in the corner of the main room. Some original outbuildings still survive on the other side of the road, by the car park. The name has been corrupted over the years, and refers to a 'setting' dog, (i.e. one which has been set on to fetch or follow game). The Dog is intimate and beamed, with a wood-panelled snug, and a second small room which doubles as the dining room. The walls are decorated by many photographs, many showing the pub marooned in deep snow! The stuffed badger and fox seem to fascinate the young, who are welcome until 7.30. Very much a pub for talking in, it has no juke box, games or machines; only quiet background music. Occasionally there is a live folk music night. The open fire in winter offers a warm welcome to Gritstone Trail walkers, and with the low winter sun slanting in through the window, there are few spots more congenial.
This roadside pub, nestled in the hills, is half a mile or so from Tegg's Nose Country Park, and can be busy at weekends, especially in summer. Winter visitors are more likely to use 4 Wheel drive, sledges or skis, but the pub is rarely cut off nowadays. Benches and a large grass area adjoin the car park. Excellent meals are served all day on Sunday, and there are weekday special offers, but note that booking is advisable and the pub is closed on Monday lunchtimes. There are tasting notes for the Timothy Taylors range of beers by the bar, and it is common to see some of the more unusual Taylors beers on tap.Guest beers often include offerings from popular local microbreweries such as Beartown of Congleton.
◖ ▷ ☎ ⇌ ⊗

PLEA

CAMRA, The Campaign for Real Ale, is a volunteer organisation. In Cheshire, it is stretched, with few active members covering a large number of pubs in a wide geographical area. The surveying for this guide has been a major undertaking, and as any football manager would say; "They done good, they gave 110%".

However as editors, we have two comments to make:

1) **We need more help**. If you care about beer or pubs, join CAMRA. If you are a member, come out and meet the local branch - they certainly have a good time!

2) We are not perfect. Some pubs may have been missed, and inevitably some details will have changed, given the state of flux of the trade. **We ask all our readers to let us know of any corrections or updates**. These can be passed to your local branch contact, or to the editorial address.

WARRINGTON

1 - Barley Mow
2 - Blue Bell
3 - Bulls Head
4 - Feathers
5 - Friars Tavern
6 - Golden Lion
7 - Hawthorne
8 - Hop Pole
9 - Lord Rodney Hotel
10 - Lower Angel
11 - Manx Arms
12 - Mersey
13 - Old Town House
14 - Porters
15 - Red Lion
16 - Royal Oak Branch
17 - Theatre
18 - Three Pigeons
19 - Village
20 - Waterside
21 - Wheatsheaf
22 - White Hart
23 - Yates Wine Bar

CAUSEWAY
Wilderspool Causeway
⏰12-11 Mon-Sat; 12-10.30 Sun
Greenalls Mild, B, Original [H]
Large Victorian pub with several rooms
including bar and games rooms.
Large function room available.

CHESHIRE CHEESE
654 Knutsford Road, Latchford
⏰11.30-11 Mon-Sat; 12-10.30 Sun
Greenalls B [H]
Old cottage-style pub now opened out.
Oldest pub in Latchford and reputedly third
oldest in Warrington. Due for refurbishment
in April 1998.

CHEVVIES
No real ale.

CHURCHILLS
No real ale.

COACH & HORSES
No real ale.

COACH HOUSE
No real ale.

DOG & PARTRIDGE
Manchester Road
⏰APH
Greenalls Mild, B, Original, Tetley B [H]
Large pub set back from road, with lounge
and family dining area. Bar with pool table.

EDISONS
No real ale.

FAMOUS KING & QUEEN
147 Padgate Lane (Padgate)
⏰APH
**Boddingtons B, Greenalls Mild, B,
guest beer [H]**
Recently redecorated and renamed (though its
not really clear why they had to add
'Famous'!). Bowling green to rear.

FARMERS ARMS
Fearnhead Lane, Fearnhead
⏰12-3, 4.30-11 Mon-Fri; 12-11 Sat;
12-10.30 Sun
**Greenalls Mild, B, Original,
guest beer [H]**
Comfortable pub with large lounge. Bowling
green. No food Saturdays.

FEATHERS
Bridge Street
⏰APH
Greenalls B, Tetley B [H]
Town pub with inside-out décor resembling a
courtyard surrounded by shops.

FRIARS GATE TAVERN
Rylands Street
⏰12-11 Mon-Tue; 12-12 Wed-Sat;
7-10.30 Sun
Boddingtons B, Theakstons Best B [H]
Large town centre pub with courtyard hidden
off the street. Targets shoppers at lunchtime
and youngsters at night.

GAFFERS
No real ale.

GOLDEN LION
Knutsford Road
⏰12-11 Mon-Sat; 12-10.30 Sun
Greenalls B [H]
Large bar with TV and cosy lounge.
Golden lion on bar rail.

GREENWOOD
No real ale.

BULLS HEAD
33 Church Street
⏰12-11 Mon-Sat;12-10.30 Sun

Cains Traditional B, Draught Bass, Flowers Original, Greenalls Mild, B, guest beer (from Greenalls list) [H]

The Bull is a rambling 17th Century converted row of cottages, now serving very much as a community pub. The modest frontage conceals not only a warren of rooms but also a bowling green and a function room to the rear. Leaded lights and low beams provide a sense of history. Ahead as you enter is the bar, opening out on the left into a lounge, beyond which is a games room with a pool table. On the right is a comfortable small lounge with button-back seating and walls generously hung with prints, including watercolours of old Warrington. Behind the bar is a lovely snug bedecked with book-shelves.

The bar itself is ornately carved, and is festooned with a large number of pump clips, witness to the encouraging guest beer policy. This is an understandably popular pub which sets a standard for other pubs owned by Greenalls.

HARTLEYS CAFÉ BAR
No real ale.

HAWTHORNE
Orford Lane
⏰11-11 Mon-Thu; 12-5, 7-11 Fri-Sat;
12-10.30 Sun
Greenalls B [H]
Victorian two-roomed local.

HIGHWAYMAN
No real ale.

HOOP & MALLET
Callands Road, Callands
⏰11.30-11 Mon-Fri; 12-3, 7-10.30 Sun
Hydes B; 4X Strong (winter) [P]
Newish estate pub. Oversized, Lined glasses to ensure a full pint. Try the wonderful rich 4X in season.

HOP POLE
Horsemarket Street
⏰APH
Boddingtons B, Greenalls B, Original [H]
Open-plan town centre pub. Pizzas
(including takeaway) all day.

HOWLEY
46 Parr Street
⏰11.30-3,5.30-11 Mon-Sat;
12-3.30,7-10.30 Sun
Greenalls B [H]
Street corner pub in area of terraced housing. Historically interesting but otherwise run down. Childrens play area adjacent to road. Public bar. Bar snacks.

IMPERIAL
No real ale.

JASMINE
No real ale.

JOLLY FALSTAFF
Blackbrook Square, Blackbrook
⏰12-11 Mon-Sat; 12-10.30 Sun
Tetley Dark Mild, B [H]
Modern estate pub. 'Feasting Fox' menu!

JOLLY TANNER
No real ale.

KINGS HEAD
No real ale.

LION HOTEL
No real ale.

LORD RODNEY
67 Winwick Road
⏰APH
Cains Traditional B, Marstons Pedigree, Tetley B; 5 guest beers [H]
A well-refurbished Victorian style ale house with bare boards, leaded lights and brass-work, over the road from the site of the former Walker's brewery. Regular changing guest beers and occasional beer festivals produce the best beer choice in town. Real mild is usually available. There are two gorgeous engraved mirrors in the rear bar. Live music Friday & Saturday, quiz Tuesday.

LOWER ANGEL
27 Buttermarket Street
⏰11-4,7-11 Mon-Sat; 12-3,7-10.30 Sun
**Ind Coope Burton Ale, Walker Mild, B,
guest beer [H]**
Classic two-room town centre local.
Collection of beer bottles in bar and resident
ghost in the lounge.
Good to see the rare Walker mild.

Mc CAULEYS
No real ale.

MAD HATTER
No real ale.

MALTINGS
Old Hall Road, Old Hall
⏰APH
**Boddingtons B, Greenalls Mild, B, [H],
guest beers [E]**
Converted farmhouse, formerly Bewsey
Farm. Recent refurbishment as an alehouse,
with up to three guest beers. These are served
by electric pump from fake barrels and are
from the Greenalls list (see article opposite).
◖ ▶ ᵬ ● P

MANX ARMS
31 School Brow
⏰APH
Vaux Mild, Samson, guest beer [H]
A rarity for the town centre, a traditional
local ! Small, well hidden back street corner
pub near to Sainsburys. Bar and separate
lounge. Entertainment Saturday and quiz on
Sunday. Possibly the only Cheshire outlet for
Vaux mild.

MARQUIS OF GRANBY
No real ale.

MEMPHIS BELLE
Gemini Retail Park, Westbrook
⏰APH
Boddingtons B, guest beers [H]
New and very large theme pub handy for
large retail outlets (e.g. IKEA). Family and
food orientated, however real ale drinkers are
also catered for by the provision of two or
more guest beers from the Whitbread stable.
◖ ▶ ᵬ ● P

MERSEY HOTEL
Mersey Street
⏰APH
Vaux Samson, guest beer [H]
Modern, busy and basic pub alongside inner
ring road. Separate bar. Accommodation.
Guest beer on six-week cycle. Bar food
always available, including hot-pot.
Very small car park.
◖ ▶ ⯬ P

WARRINGTON
LONDON BRIDGE
London Road (A49, by the canal bridge in Appleton)
⏰12-11 Mon-Sat; 12-10.30 Sun
Greenalls Mild, B, Boddingtons B [H] plus up to 3 guest [E]
The London Bridge is a newly extended "Country Ale House" set next to Bridgewater Canal.
It features wooden beams and flag floors, several separate dining or drinking areas and a games
room. One of the fireplaces boasts a real log fire. As theme pubs go, this is perfectly acceptable.
There is an annual boat rally on the adjacent canal, and the watery proceedings can be
followed from the patio which overlooks the towpath and the old steps. The canal was dug to carry
coal from the Duke of Bridgewater's mines at Worsley into Manchester, and a daily ferry service for
passengers operated the same route. The old buildings at the rear of the pub were originally used as
stabling during the days of the coaches.
Home cooked food, including a daily roast, is available every lunchtime and each evening
till 8.30 (7pm on Sunday) and there is also accommodation.
The guest beers are from the Greenall's list. Although the stocking of guest beers is a
welcome development, licensees tell us that deliveries are rather infrequent and this causes restricted
availability. When available, the guest ales are served through "free-flow" dispensers and fake
barrels, despite the somewhat misleading appearance of being served by gravity direct from the
wood. The pub is trying, with some success, to run a branch of the Real Ale Tasting Society.
Customers pay a joining fee, and receive a T-shirt, and 30p off every pint on a Wednesday
When you are leaving the car park, beware of the hump-backed bridge; the view to the right
is restricted.
◖ ▶ ⯫ ᵬ P ⊗

PORTERS ALE HOUSE
Buttermarket Street
⏰12-11 Mon-Sat; 12-10.30 Sun
Boddingtons B, Cains Traditional B, Greenalls Original, Porters Ale, Theakstons B [H]
Greenall's themed "Alehouse" with wood/flag floors, beams and brown-washed plaster walls. Interesting gabled exterior. Porters Ale believed to be Davenports Bitter from Burton brewery.

POSTERN GATE
No real ale.

RAILWAY
No real ale.

MILLHOUSE
Ballater Drive, Houghton Green
⏰12-11 Mon-Sat; 12-10.30 Sun
Holts Mild, B [H]
Modern estate pub with large bar and lounge. Very popular, good value beer. Food Monday to Friday.

 P

OLD TOWN HOUSE
95 Buttermarket Street
(opposite St Mary's church)
⏰12-11 Mon-Sat; 12-10.30 Sun
**John Smith B, Theakston XB, 2-3 guest beers[H]
up to 3 cask ciders**
Ordinary town pub but an oasis for discerning beer and particularly cider drinkers. Attractive listed Georgian exterior with garden at front (tallest trees in the town centre). Guest beers usually include a mild and usually two real ciders, often Cheshire Cider from Eddisbury (See article).

ORFORD
Gorsey Lane
⏰APH
Greenalls Mild, B, Stones B [H]
Large street corner pub retaining many small rooms and alcoves.

 P

PADDINGTON HOUSE HOTEL
Manchester Road
⏰APH
Courage Directors, Theakstons Best B [H]
Large hotel set back from main road. Quiet comfortable bar. Accommodation.

 P

PENNY FERRY
Thelwall Lane, Latchford
⏰12-11 Mon-Sat; 12-10.30 Sun
Burtonwood Mild, B [H]
Unusual detached pub with through lounge and sunken bar area. Named after the nearby rowing boat ferry over the Manchester Ship Canal. Try the uncommon and tasty Burtonwood mild.

 P

POPLARS
No real ale.

RED LION
Winwick Road
⏰11.30-11 Mon-Sat; 12-10.30 Sun
Greenalls Mild, B, Tetley B [H]
Victorian two-room pub opposite old Tetley-Walker brewery (soon to be demolished). Very much a community pub with three football teams, darts, domino and quiz teams.

RING O' BELLS
Church Street
⏰APH
Greenalls B, Original, guest beer [H]
Old rambling pub now opened out but still retaining several distinct areas. Wood beams and panelling remain but much of atmosphere has now gone. Cobbled forecourt at entrance to parish church.

RING O' BELLS
Dallam
No real ale.

RIVERSIDE
Chester Road (A5060)
⏰11.30-11 Mon-Sat; 12-10.30 Sun
Greenalls B [H]
Seventies pub built on stilts alongside busy main road and River Mersey. Single room which has never been modernised. Bar snacks.
P

ROPE & ANCHOR
Manchester Road, Woolston
⏰APH
Greenalls Mild, B, Original, Tetley B [H]
Recently refurbished lounge split into separate drinking areas. Public bar.

 P

ROSE
No real ale.

ROYAL OAK BRANCH
44 Knutsford Road
⏰3-11 Mon-Wed; 12-11 Thu-Sat; 12-10.30 Sun
Boddingtons B, Greenalls Mild, B [H]
On edge of town near to clubs, but retains a pub atmosphere. Pictures of old Warrington in lounge. Hot snacks Mon-Fri until 5.

SARACENS HEAD
Wilderspool Causeway
⏰11.30-11 Mon-Sat; 12-10.30 Sun
**Greenalls Mild, B, Original,
guest beer [H]**
Large community pub opposite former
Greenalls brewery. Several rooms including
public bar. 'Ale and Hearty' menu
concentrates on good value large portions of
basic pub fare. Bowling green and small
children's 'zoo' to side.

SEVEN WOODS
Westbrook Crescent, Old Hall
Banks B, Camerons Strongarm [H]
Modern pub convenient for multiplex
cinema. Lively and friendly at weekends,
quieter in the week. Oversized lined glasses
for a full pint. Beers unusual for Warrington.

SLOOP
No real ale.

SMITHYS
No real ale.

SPA BROOK
No real ale.

STOCKS
Station Road, Padgate
⏰12-11 Mon-Sat; 12-10.30 Sun
Greenalls Mild, B [H]
Estate pub with strong community links and
sports teams. Separate vault.
Due for refurbishment early 1998 after which
food will be available.

THEATRE TAVERN
1 Scotland Road
⏰12-11 Mon-Sat; 12-10.30 Sun
**Cains Traditional B, Tetley Mild, B.
guest beers [H]**
Street corner pub on edge of shopping area.
Adjacent theatre now demolished. Recently
changed hands, beer range likely to change.
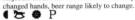

THREE PIGEONS
35 Tanners Lane
⏰ 12-11 Mon-Fri; 12-5, 7-11 Sat;
12-3, 7-10.30 Sun
Courage Directors, Theakstons Mild [H]
Former Tetley pub close to ex Tetley-Walker
brewery. Reputedly the former booking office
for the Warrington & Newton branch of the
Liverpool & Manchester railway. Theakstons
mild is very rare in Cheshire.

WETTENHALL
BOOT & SLIPPER
Long Lane (follow signs to St. David's Church)
⏰12-3, 5.30-11 Mon-Fri; 11-11 Sat; 12-10.30 Sun
Marstons Pedigree, Tetley B [H]
The heart of this busy, family-run free house is a 17th century rural inn, skilfully extended to include
a separate restaurant and four letting rooms. The original building comprises the bar area, and an
interconnected series of small rooms, and has the exposed beams and period furniture that you
expect to find in a country pub. A large open coal fire completes the ambience. The Boot & Slipper
occupies a large plot of ground, with an extensive car park, a delightful rockery/shrubbery and a
beer garden which is totally enclosed so as to be safe for children. A traditional swing, slide and
see-saw are to be found here.
    While catering is an important part of the Boot's trade, with the restaurant having 46
covers, the main bar area is still definitely a pub, and is popular with the locals. The restaurant
benefits from not being one large room, but several rather snug eating areas. There is an extensive
a la carte menu which is changed every two months. Occasional special evenings, such as a
Greek night add variety.
    The name of the pub is a mystery, as there is no local connection to the footwear industry,
and earlier this century, the pub was called the Royal Oak. Oulton Park and an indoor show arena
are nearby, so it can be crowded at certain times. The Boot & Slipper is listed in other prestigious
CAMRA publications; the Good Pub Food Guide and Room at the Inn..

TUT 'N' SHIVE
No real ale.

TYROL HOUSE HOTEL
No real ale.

VILLAGE HOTEL
Centre Park
⏰APH
Boddingtons B, Greenalls B [H]
Large hotel with leisure facilities.

WATERSIDE
1540 Centre Park
⏰APH
**Boddingtons B, Flowers Original,
Marstons Pedigree [H]**
New 'Beefeater' pub with attached travel lodge.

WHEATSHEAF
Orford Road
⏰12-11 Mon-Sat; 12-10.30 Sun
Greenalls Mild, B [H]
Imposing red-brick pub on inner ring-road. Still
retains many original features such as tiled floors
and "Wilderspool Ales" windows. Three separate
rooms. *Beware signs still advertising guest beers
outside.*

WHITE HART
Sankey Street
⏰11.30-11 Mon-Sat; 12-3, 7-10.30 Sun
**Boddingtons B, Greenalls Mild, B,
Tetley B [H] 1-2 guest beers [E & H]**
Large town-centre alehouse. Recently
refurbished. Guest beers usually served from
well-hidden "fake barrel" dispense behind the
bar. Food until 7.30. No food Sunday.
Guest beers are from Greenalls list.

WINWICK QUAY
Woburn Road, Winwick Quay (off A49)
⏰APH
Boddingtons B [H]
Typical 'Brewer's Fayre and Travel Inn' close
to M62. Entrance from A49 northbound.

YATES WINE BAR
Buttermarket Street
⏰APH
**Boddingtons B, Cains Traditional B,
Stones B [H]**
New pub in typical Yates' style, targeting
shoppers in the day and youngsters at night. On
the site of the town's last cinema. Opens from
10-7 for food. Good to see Cains on sale.

TAKE AWAYS

When you want good real beer, there is nothing like visiting a decent pub, but I find that my social life increasingly involves visiting friends at home, or going to parties or barbecues, or more often, watching a game on the box. Once upon a time, this would have meant that drinking beer involved a tin opener, lots of froth, flatulence and a taste like metal polish. Even worse, I have hideous memories of the parties of my youth involving Party Sevens and an old screwdriver. No wonder I'm emotionally scarred.

Luckily, times have changed, and beer at home can involve an altogether more enjoyable experience. Firstly, you can buy up to four pints of fresh Real Ale in one of those excellent plastic containers looking like stone jugs which are sold in some pubs (such as Hogsheads) and off-licences. These keep beer in good condition for a few hours, and properly rinsed, can be re-used regularly. *Every home should have one.*

Your next choice is bottled beer. **Never, ever buy canned beer.** It is always pasteurised, and despite the misleading claims of the less scrupulous brewers, it is not real ale, nor is it draught beer in a can; this is one of the most dishonest and transparent fibs to which they have yet stooped.

Increasingly, off-licences and supermarkets are displaying a wide range of interesting bottled beers from all over the world. Of the British beers, you may be familiar with Greene King Abbot, Morland's Old Speckled Hen and Wadworth 6X. These are bottled versions of draught beers, and you can find a variety of other beers, some with curious names. Most of these are pasteurised to prolong their shelf life, and are not therefore the pinnacle of the style.

In my view, even better and more satisfying are those bottled beers which are the equivalent of Real Ale. These are **Bottle Conditioned Ales** ("BCAs"), which have a small amount of yeast sediment in the bottle, enabling them to continue to ferment, developing considerable character and flavour, and avoiding that sharp, acidic tang associated with most pasteurised bottles. The yeast does of course stay at the bottom of the bottle, unless you shake it, and the beer should not be cloudy. Spotting them takes care, but an examination of the label usually does the trick. Look for the magic words **"Bottle Conditioned", "Yeast", "Sediment",** or **"Secondary Fermentation".** The superior quality is worth a little extra effort. See how many you can find next time you are shopping.

Some of my favourites are **Marstons** *Oyster Stout*, **Hop Back** *Summer Lightning*, **King & Barnes** *Festive*, **Shepherd Neame** *Spitfire*, the strong *Norman's Conquest* from the **Cottage** brewery, and the exquisitely named *Dorothy Goodbody's Stout*, from **Wye Valley**. The award-winning **Fullers 1845** is often seen too. These can be found readily on the shelves of most major supermarkets or off licences. It is worth looking out for **Wood's** *Shropshire Lad*, in its distinctive green bottle, named after the poem by A. E. Housman. *"Ale, man, Ale's the stuff to drink"*

On the subject of our sister county, Shropshire, it is worth noting that **Salopian** brewery is renowned for its adventurous range of BCAs, and its beers are available in Oddbins. Try the wonderfully smoky *Firefly*, or the *Gingersnap,* one of the few beers you can drink with a curry, and still taste!

Tesco has announced a policy which includes promoting BCAs from independent brewers, although first sightings have been patchy. Their own-label **Tesco Stout** is wonderfully dry and full-flavoured. In addition they have a *Pale Ale* and a *Wheat Beer*. The other chains are lagging behind, although *Sainsbury, Asda* and *Booths* can be rewarding. *Marks & Spencer* get the booby prize here, offering nothing for the beer connoisseur.

Of particular interest is a beer which is dear to the hearts of many CAMRA members, **Bass** *Worthington White Shield*. In the dark days of the Seventies, these bottles of naturally conditioned beer were the only form of real ale in some pubs. Having a natural sediment, it needed a steady hand to pour, but the patient were always rewarded with a wonderfully dry, nutty taste. You can still find it, in supermarkets and off-licences, and although its future was in doubt, agreement has been reached Bass to have it brewed by King & Barnes

Foreign beers are a treasure trove, with Belgium, Germany and the Czech Republic boasting great brewing traditions. Anything described as a *Wheat Beer* is likely to be bottle conditioned. This refreshing brew is meant to be cloudy, and an easily found example is *Hoegaarden*. Belgian beers developed by Trappist Monks are fascinating; *Chimay* comes in three strengths, with different coloured caps and is naturally conditioned. *Duvel* (meaning Devil's brew) too, is worth seeking out.

If you see ***Rauchbier***, try it; brewed from malt which has been smoked over beechwood logs, in a parallel to Scotch whisky which uses peat smoke; it has an unsurpassable flavour, an excellent accompaniment to smoked cheese. Curiously, Australia produces more than just fizzy yellow rubbish, and you should try a bottle of (cloudy) **Cooper's Sparkling Ale** and their tasty **Stout**.

Off-licences are worth exploring, as a few sell draught beer either direct from the cask, or from handpumps on the counter, while rather more stock a few bottles of naturally conditioned beer. *Oddbins* has a stated policy of supplying BCAs from independent brewers, and their shelves often contain bottles of interest from Salopian, the King & Barnes range and exotic ales from all over the country.

We are lucky to have a wide choice of real beer styles in bottles, and you should not be afraid to experiment when dining, or for that matter, cooking (see the "Woman's View" article). Some years ago, a very good book on *Cooking with Beer*, by Paul Harris contained many excellent ideas. The first recipe was perhaps a little tongue in cheek. *"Take two pints of lager. Pour lager down sink."*

In conclusion, I can do no more than urge you to experiment. Try beers you have not seen before. Try BCAs above other beers. Look for seasonal and Xmas special brews. Above all, enjoy the choice. *Cheers.*

Readers wishing to pursue this further are heartily recommended to read *The CAMRA Guide to Real Ale in a Bottle*

TEND CAREFULLY, AND WATCH YOUR SALES BLOSSOM...

*A*s welcome as the first budding flowers of spring, Thwaites Bloomin' Ale is a refreshing new cask ale from Daniel Thwaites Brewery.

Golden in colour, its dry, light palate is the perfect compliment to its nutty, bitter finish. The perfect session beer for those long spring evenings, or the perfect accompaniment to a lunchtime snack - Bloomin' Ale.

4.0.% a.b.v.

THWAITES

PROGRESS WITH TRADITION

FOR MORE INFORMATION PLEASE CONTACT
THWAITES CUSTOMER SERVICE ON 01254 54431

WAVERTON
BLACK DOG
Whitchurch Road (off the A41)
⏱12-3, 7-11 Mon-Sat; 12-3, 7-10.30 Sun
Greenalls B, Tetley B, guest beer [H]
An attractive wayside inn with probably the
longest bar in the area. Traditional furniture, a
central fireplace and a plethora of brass and
pottery remind one of the rural setting. The menu
is extensive and refined, but despite this, the
evenings are dominated by the regulars.
Little seating outside, but the patio is a suntrap.
The guest beer is from the Greenall list.

WEAVERHAM
HANGING GATE
Sandy Lane
⏱12-3, 5.30-11 Mon-Thu; 11-11 Fri-Sat;
12-10.30 Sun
Greenall Mild, B, guest beer [H]
Clean well-kept pub in village that is now quiet
since the by-pass was built.
The guest ale is from the Greenalls list.

RING O' BELLS
Northwich Road
⏱12-11 Mon-Sat; 12-10.30 Sun
Greenalls Mild, B [H]
Ordinary local with bowling green.
Food until 7pm. No food Sunday evening.
 P

WHEATSHEAF
High Street
⏱APH
**Theakstons B; Bass Tub Thumper;
2 guest beers [H]**
Recently tastefully renovated with a comfortable
and relaxed atmosphere. No fewer than five real
fires! 'Tub Thumper' is a house beer.
Restaurant and accommodation.

WESTON
WHITE LION
In the centre of the village
⏱11-3, 5-11 Mon-Fri; 11-3, 7-11 Sat;
12-3, 7-10.30 Sun
Boddingtons B, Draught Bass [H]
Low-beamed black & white pub/hotel dating
from 1652. Bowling green.

WETTENHALL
LITTLE MAN
Winsford Road (on long straight road between
the marina and St David's Church).
⏱12-3, 7-11 Mon-Sat; 12-3, 7-10.30 Sun;
**Burtonwood James Forshaws B,
John Smiths B, up to 3 guest beers [H]**
Apparently the only pub of this name in the
country! It can trace its history back to 1673
when it was the Little John Ale House. Very
much a "pub", also serving good solid food. A
strong following for pub games (darts, dominoes
& pool). Popular with the local farming and
equestrian community. Friday evenings can be
very busy. Not open Tuesday lunchtime. **GBG**

WHEELOCK
CHESHIRE CHEESE
466 Crewe Road
⏱12-11 Mon-Sat; 12-10.30 Sun
Banks Mild, B, Morrells Varsity [H]
Friendly local, over 200 years old. The unusual
split-level layout is built up to the road by the
canal bridge. One of only two known outlets in
the county for Morrells of Oxford.

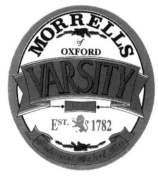

COMMERCIAL HOTEL
Game Street
⏱12-2, 8-11 Mon-Sat; 8-10.30 Sun
**Boddingtons B, Thwaites B,
Marstons Pedigree, guest beer [H]
cask cider [H]**
Listed Georgian building on CAMRA's
National Inventory of Heritage Pubs. Formerly
owned by Birkenhead Brewery, evidence of
which remains. The business has been in the
same family for 75 years. Four distinct
drinking areas including a superbly restored
games room with full-sized snooker table and
table skittles. Open music evenings on
Thursday when a new guest beer is available.
One of the few Cheshire pubs serves
real cider. Also sells the exquisite Marstons
bottle conditioned Oyster Stout.
Note the restricted opening hours. **GBG**

NAGS HEAD
Crewe Road
⏱12-11 Mon-Sat; 12-3, 7-10.30 Sun
**Chesters Mild, Boddingtons B,
Flowers IPA [H]**
Comfortable lounge with vault/games room at
rear of the building.

WHITELEY GREEN
WINDMILL
Holehouse Lane (signposted off the A523 just
south of railway bridge, south of Adlington)
⏱12-3, 6-11 Mon-Sat; 12-10.30 Sun
Marstons Pedigree, Tetley B [H]
A large single-roomed pub, off the beaten
track, with emphasis on food. There is a patio
at the front, and a large garden. Close to the
Middlewood Way and canal towpath, north of
Bollington. Beer range and hours may change,
as this was closed for refurbishment as we
went to press.

WHITLEY
BIRCH & BOTTLE
Northwich Road, Higher Whitley
⏱11.30-3,5-11 Mon-Sat; 12-10.30 Sun
Greenalls B, Original [H]
Multi-roomed country pub with conservatory.

CHETWODE ARMS
Street Lane, Lower Whitley
⏱ 12-3.30,5.30-11.30 Mon-Fri;
12-3.30,6-11 Sat; 12-3.30,7-10.30 Sun
Greenalls Mild, B, guest beer [H]
This is a many-roomed country pub with a
friendly atmosphere. It features a good range
of home-cooked food. Bowling green at the
side of the pub. Greenalls provide the guest
beer from their own lists. However, it has
recently changed hands and is threatened by
development.

MILLSTONE
Grimsditch Lane
⏱APH
Greenalls Mild, B [H]
Spacious, open-plan, rural pub.
Separate public bar with pool table. Function
room.

WIDNES
ALBERT
No real ale.

ALBION
No real ale.

ANGEL
No real ale.

APPLETON ARMS
Appleton Road, Appleton
⏱Not provided
Greenalls Mild, B [H]
Large corner pub knocked into one large room
with separate drinking areas. Live music Fri.

BALL
No real ale.

BIRCHDALE HOTEL
Birchdale Road (off A49, Appleton)
⏱6-11.00 Mon-Thu; 8.30-11.00 Fri-Sat;
8.30-10.30 Sun
Boddingtons B, guest beer [H]
Enterprising hotel with enthusiastic owner.
Large lounge with small pool/darts room.
Licensed restaurant 6-8 Mon-Thu. Oversized,
lined glasses ensure full measure. **GBG**

1 - Angel and Elephant

2 - Appleton Arms

3 - Bowers Park

4 - Bradley

5 - Church View Inn

6 - Commercial

7 - Corner House

8 - Cricketers

9 - Crown

10 - Eight Towers

11 - Grapes

12 - Griffin

13 - Horse & Jockey

14 - Millfield

15 - Moorfield

16 - Prince of Wales

17 - Queens

18 - Ring O'Bells

19 - Simms Cross

20 - Tavern

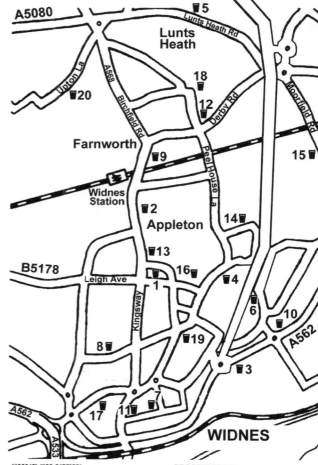

WIDNES

(BLUE JAYS AT THE) BLACK HORSE
No real ale.

BOWERS PARK
Earle Road
⏱APH
Boddingtons B, Flowers IPA [H]
Typical Brewers Fayre establishment.
Menu available in braille.

BRADLEY
38 Albert Road
⏱APH
Tetley B; Walker Mild [H]
Comfortable lounge with separate bar.

CASTLE
No real ale.

CHURCH VIEW
Lunts Heath Road, Farnworth
⏱12-3.30,5.30-11 Mon-Fri; 12-11 Sat;
12-10.30 Sun
Greenalls Mild, B, Original [H]
Half-timbered roadside pub with spacious
interior, open fires and separate vault.
 P

COMMERCIAL
Page Lane
⏱11.30-5,7-11 Mon-Wed;11-11 Thu-Fri;
11.30-11 Sat; 12-3,7-11 Sun
Matthew Brown Mild [H]
Two-roomed estate pub. Mild brewed by
Scottish Courage in Bristol and rarely seen in
Cheshire.
P

CORNER HOUSE
1 Alforde Street
⏱11-11 Mon-Sat; 12-6.30 Sun
Tetley B [H]
One large split-level room

CRICKETERS
170 Milton Road
⏱12-11 Mon-Sat; 12-10.30 Sun
Tetley B [H]
Popular locals pub with pool table and
satellite TV. Accommodation.

CROWN
Birchfield Road, Appleton
⏱11-3.30, 5.30-11 Mon-Thu; 11-11 Fri-Sat;
12-10.30 Sun
Greenalls B; Tetley B [H]
Long, narrow pub catering for young on
Fridays.

DERBY
No real ale.

DOCTORS
No real ale.

NATIONAL BLANDS

One of the regrettable trends in recent years has been the increasing emphasis placed on "brands" in the selling of goods and services. We do not need to go into the psychology of marketing here, but clearly many businessmen are convinced that a brand name or identity is as important as (or more important than) such matters as the quality of the product itself.

This is something we see increasingly in the brewing industry, where traditional brewers are snapped up by larger predators simply to obtain a name. *Old Peculier, Old Speckled Hen, Ruddles County* and *Boddingtons* are examples which spring to mind. It matters not to the bean counters that these long-established firms have thousands of appreciative customers, hundreds of employees, scores of licensees and a string of distinctive local beers. All they want is a marketable name. Inevitably, the local brewery is closed down, most of the beers discontinued and the "brand" produced elsewhere, often to a blander different recipe.

Those of us a little long in the tooth remember when *Boddingtons* brewed two milds and a winter strong ale, as well as a delightful hoppy bitter. Now the strong ale is only a memory, one mild has gone, the other is hard to find, and the bitter is a heavily advertised national "bland", deflavoured so as to avoid offending palates across the UK, and looking for all the world like a keg beer.

Given the choice, we would choose an independent brewer's ale every time.
They care about their products, and so do we.

EIGHT TOWERS
Wheates Close
⏱APH
Banks Mild [E], B [H]
New pub on outskirts of town with fine view of Fiddler's Ferry power station! Children's play area outside. Food all day Sun to 6. Oversized, lined glasses for a full measure.

GRAPES
38 Widnes Road
⏱11-11 Mon-Sat; 7-10.30 Sun
Boddingtons B, Cains Traditional B
Tetley B, 2 guest beers [H]
Comfortable front lounge and back bar with pool table. Full range of bitters not always available.

GRIFFIN
Farnworth Street, Farnworth
⏱APH
Greenalls Mild, B [H]
Basic street-corner local retaining original vault.

GROSVENOR
No real ale.

HILLCREST
No real ale

HORSE & JOCKEY
Birchfield Road, Appleton
⏱11.30-11 Mon-Sat; 12-10.30 Sun
Greenalls B, Tetley B, guest beer [H]
Cosy one-room local with keen licensee. Snacks available. Greenalls list guest beers.

MAIN TOP
No real ale.

MAJORS ARMS
No real ale.

MERSEY
No real ale.

MILLFIELD
Millfield Road
⏱11-11 Mon-Fri; 11-5, 7-11 Sat;
12-4,7-10.30 Sun
Websters Yorkshire B [H]
Back street local with comfortable lounge and smaller bar.

WILDBOARCLOUGH
CRAG

In the village centre (1 mile north of A54 Congleton - Buxton road on a minor road which follows the river)

⏰12-3, 7-11 Mon-Sat; 12-4 (12-6 in summer)Sun

Worthington Draught B, guest beers [H]

Named after the nearby Shutlingsloe "crag", one of the Peak District's true "peaks", this building, dating from the early seventeenth century became a hostelry about 150 years ago. The plain, farmhouse exterior belies the comfortable and cosy atmosphere within. The bar room is furnished with timbered ceilings, inglenook windows, wooden settles. The room is adorned with gleaming brass and copper, numerous stuffed birds, animals and even antlers (which were hunted long ago, we convince ourselves in this modern, politically correct climate). To continue the theme there are various farm and racing pictures as well as a plate rack which encompasses the whole room. Two roaring log fires provide a welcoming sight in winter for the multitude of walkers, who are also provided with over-shoes in the porch if they wish to retain their boots. A piano is also available for voluble visitors to entertain (!)

The popular menu includes a carvery on Sunday lunchtime. There is also a separate restaurant, with a non-smoking area. Children are welcome in the dining room or garden, but dogs are not permitted inside. Camping facilities can be found nearby for the hardier amongst us. The guest beers is unimaginative, comprising beers from major breweries only. If the choice was more adventurous, the Crag would be even more of a draw.

◖ ◗ ● P

MOORFIELD ARMS
Moorfield Road

⏰12-11 Mon-Sat; 12-10.30 Sun

Greenalls Mild, B, Stones B, Tetley B [H]

Large two-roomed pub.

● ⇌

PRINCE OF WALES
Kent Street

⏰APH

Boddingtons B, Greenalls Mild, B [H]

Large and recently refurbished. Very busy at weekends. Disco on Friday and Saturday.

◖ ● P

QUEENS ARMS
4 Moor Lane

⏰12-11 Mon-Sat; 12-10.30 Sun

Greenalls Mild, B [H]

Large lounge and separate bar. Latter is dominated by large screen TV showing Sky Sports. Road access easier via Rose Street.

RING O' BELLS
97 Farnworth Street, Farnworth

⏰APH

Greenalls B, guest beer [H]

Popular local with comfortable seating area. Regular entertainment, including live music. Guest beer is from Greenalls list.

P

SIMMS CROSS
100 Widnes Road

⏰12-11 Mon-Sat; 12-10.30 Sun

Greenalls B, Tetley B, Clubhouse B [H]

Popular local refurbished in "Clubhouse" theme. Pool table in bar. House beer believed to originate from Carlsberg-Tetley.

◖

SWAN
No real ale.

UPTON TAVERN
288 Upton Lane, Farnworth

⏰12-2.30, 5-11 Mon-Thu; 12-11 Fri-Sat; 12-10.30 Sun

Walkers B, Tetley B [H]

Pleasantly furnished large open-plan room. Welcoming local on housing estate.

◖ ● P

VICTORIA
No real ale.

WELLINGTON
34 Prescot Road

⏰12-11 Mon-Sat; 12-10.30 Sun

Greenalls Mild, B, Stones B, Tetley B [H]

Cosy two-roomed pub. Functions catered for.

● ⇌ P ⊗

SMILE, YOU'RE IN GREENALL WHITLEY LAND?

Eleven years ago, when the last edition of this guide was produced, there was a brewer called Greenall Whitley. Its pubs and beers dominated much of Cheshire. They were the largest regional brewer in Britain, with plants in Birmingham, Wem and Nottingham as well as their native Warrington. Many places had 70% Greenalls pubs, and indeed there had been 100% monopolies until some forced sales of pubs. This was an unhealthy state of affairs, as Greenalls were showing little commitment to real ale. Many of their pubs did not sell the real thing, and their dominance of the market led to a number of "*real ale deserts*".

Thanks to the efforts of CAMRA, traditional beer then reasserted itself across the UK, and the attitude of Greenalls improved. They replaced *keg or tank beer* with real ale in many outlets, handpumps appeared in profusion, and they launched a new cask beer, "Thomas Greenall's Original"

Greenalls then transformed themselves from brewer to pub-owning company. They closed their remaining breweries and subcontracted the brewing to other companies. They also took over the pubs owned by the former Manchester independent, Boddington. Some feel that this change of emphasis brought an unwelcome detachment, and they have been criticised for lack of sensitivity. Critics point to their closure of local breweries, tasteless modernisation of historic pubs and a cavalier approach to conservation. They reached a notorious low point early in the Nineties. Refused permission to demolish the famous and popular Tommy Duck's pub in central Manchester in order to build an office block, they brought in a bulldozer in the middle of the night. Enraged town planners could only fine the giant a paltry £1500 for this cynical and callous act.

The current position is that Greenalls is a pub chain and not a brewer. While ¾ of its pubs stock real ale, and one in five supply a guest beer, many of the guests are uninspired choices from national brewers. *Various restrictions are imposed on licensees.* They must choose from a list, rather than selecting any beer that they or their regulars want. Infrequent deliveries often mean that the availability of these guest beers is sporadic. On the brighter side, their guest beer policy, despite its limitations, is very welcome. Some of the beers are from small independents, and the latest development is a range of ales specially brewed in Essex by Ridleys. We feel that they would please their customers if they developed this aspect of their trade.

They have spent heavily on their pubs, food, family and disabled facilities score well, but in imposing themes, they have lost the character of some lovely old pubs. Some of their low turnover outlets have been sold, with the licences spitefully removed. In a curiously out-of-step move, they have introduced the so-called *"smooth" keg beer*, just at a time when other brewers were seeing demand for this fad begin to fall. Their continued dominance in some areas means that the availability of cask ale to the local population is entirely in their hands. Déjà vu?

Love them or hate them, Greenalls cannot be ignored in this part of the world, and some people have little option but to rely on the company's goodwill to real ale and its pubgoers.

WILLEY MOOR LOCK

WILLEY MOOR LOCK TAVERN
Tarporley Road (400 yards off the A49, around 1½ miles north of Whitchurch)
⏰12-2.30, 6-11 Mon-Sat; 12-3, 7-10.30 Sun
Theakstons Best B, 2-4 guest beers[H]
This is a delightful former lock keeper's cottage, with five beamed rooms and a real fire. As the name suggests, it is adjacent to the Shropshire Union Canal, and indeed, you have to cross this by a footbridge to reach the pub. Getting to the Lock takes a little planning; and access is from the A49, where a clear inn sign points you down the driveway. You may see signs on the A41 for Willey Moor, but there is no way through by road from that direction.
A collection of unusual teapots and toby jugs adorns the rooms, alongside a variety of canal pictures. It has been in the same family for twenty years, and the friendly landlord is a 'Grand Master' cellarman, so you should be guaranteed a good pint. The Lock is popular with diners, and with those wishing to enjoy the open air. It has seating by the towpath as well as a large fenced beer garden with a lawn and a play area for children. Waterborne arrivals can use the moorings. Walkers using the Sandstone Trail will be able to enjoy the hospitality of this inn without going out of their way. Regrettably, access for wheelchairs is difficult, due to the narrow footbridge.
Guest beers increase in number during summer. Most come from independent breweries, as evidenced by the many pumpclips displayed behind the bar (only the tip of the iceberg according to the licensee). The Willey Moor Lock Tavern is a haven for real ale drinkers.
◖◗ 🐎 ● P

WILDBOARCLOUGH

CAT AND FIDDLE
Buxton New Road (A537 Macclesfield to
Buxton road, near the county boundary with
Derbyshire)
⏰11-4, 7-11 Mon-Fri; 11-11 Sat;
12-10.30 Sun
Robinsons Best B [E]
At 1690 feet, England's second highest pub.
Built by John Ryle (see Ryle's Arms, Sutton
Lane Ends) in the late 18th century. Large
lounge and separate, more basic wood-
panelled room for muddied walkers.
A welcome sight in the middle of good
moorland walking country; the warming coal
fire has lifted many a damp spirit. Also
popular with motor-cyclists. Gets cut off by
snow in winter, and the posters in the rear hallway show how dangerous the road can be.
Separate dining room. Often open all day in
Summer. The Best Bitter is served by electric
pumps, but is real ale.
◖◗ 🐎 ●

WILLASTON
(Bebington)
NAGS HEAD
Hooton Road (B5133, on the village square)
⏰APH
**Boddingtons B, Flowers IPA,
guest beer [H]**
This friendly locals' pub features a separate
dining area. No food Monday, evenings only
Tue-Sat, lunch only Sunday. Bar snacks are to
be had at all other times.
The guest beer is from the Whitbread list.
◖◗ 🐎 ♿ ● ≢ P

POLLARD INN
Hooton Road
(just off village square, opposite Nag's Head)
⏰APH
**Boddingtons B, Cains Traditional B,
Draught Bass, Greenalls B, Tetley B [H]**
A plush one bar pub with attached restaurant.
Food all day Sunday. Bar meals also.
◖◗ 🐎 ♿ ● ≢ P

WILMSLOW

1 - Blue Lamp

2 - Boddington Arms

3 - Carters Arms

4 - Farmers Arms

5 - George & Dragon

6 - Horse & Jockey

7 - Kings Arms

8 - Kings William

9 - New Inn

10 - Rectory

11 - Riflemans Arms

12 - Samuel Finney

13 - Swan

WILLASTON (Nantwich)

HORSESHOE
Newcastle Road (A500, at Wybunbury Road)
⌚12-3, 5-11 Mon-Thu; 12-11 Fri-Sat;
12-10.30 Sun
**Robinsons Best B, Old Stockport,
Hartleys XB [H]**
Once a brewery and smithy, now a welcoming
two-roomed pub. A children's play area and
good value home-cooked food add to its
appeal. No food on Sunday/Monday evenings.
Tuesday night quiz, and a meeting place for
veteran car club.
 P

LAMB
12 Wistaston Road (near the level crossing)
⌚12-11 Mon-Sat; 12-10.30 Sun
Greenalls Mild, B [H]
A large two-roomed pub with a strong local
following. Adjacent to Willaston White Star
football ground.
 P

PEACOCK
Crewe Road (outskirts of town at A534/A500
bypass junction)
⌚APH
Greenalls B, Original, guest beer [H]
Huge, characterless barn, catering for families
and passing traffic. Darts room with satellite
TV. Opens 7am for breakfast. Majoring on
accommodation. Food all day. Guest beer,
which can be from independents, changes
monthly.
Playground in garden.

WILMSLOW

BLUE BELL
Manchester Road (A34, at Dean Row Road)
⌚APH
Boddingtons Mild, B [H]
Two room pub at busy crossroads across the
street from BMW garage. One of the very few
places where Boddington's Mild is still found.
P

BLUE LAMP
Green Lane
⌚11-11 Mon-Sat; 12-3, 7-10.30 Sun
Banks B, Marstons Pedigree [H]
Large open plan pub in town centre.
Food served Tue-Sat evenings only.

BODDINGTON ARMS
Altrincham Road (A538)
⌚APH
Boddingtons B, Castle Eden Ale [H]
Huge, open plan, food-based, family pub,
situated by Lindow Moss. Accommodation.

CARTERS ARMS
22 Chapel Lane (corner of Bourne Street)
⌚11.30-3, 5.30-11 Mon-Fri; 11.30-11 Sat;
12-10.30 Sun
Courage Directors, Wilsons Original [H]
Small busy local just off roundabout.
No food served on Sundays.
P

FARMERS ARMS
71 Chapel Lane
⌚APH
Boddingtons Mild, B [H]
Characterful local with a number of separate
rooms, including a vault, secreted behind the
finely etched front windows. The front lounge
contains a large, Boddington's mirror
(from the good old days!) and a working
piano. The rear lounge displays three
fascinating paintings of Wilmslow,
Macclesfield and Cheshire and another piano.
The darts room is lined with wooden-panelled
benching and the main wall is adorned with an
ancient pair of skis. Try a taste of the *real*
Cream of Manchester here -
the super Boddington's Mild! **GBG**
P

GEORGE & DRAGON
51 Church St
⌚ 12-3, 5-11 Mon-Tue; 12-11 Wed-Sat;
12-10.30 Sun
Draught Bass [H]
Large town centre pub.
Meals noon till 5 Sat & Sun.
 P

DRIVEN TO DRINK

As this guide went to press, there were strong indications that the "Drink Driving Limit" was to be reduced from 80mg to 50mg units of alcohol per ml of blood. Many people have strongly held views on this subject. Some argue that any reduction can only be a good thing, while others counter that this would only affect those drivers who have attempted to drink sensibly within what they see as a reasonable limit. Arguably, the change does little to combat the serious 'problem of the reckless drunk driver who is well over any legal limit.

CAMRA loves pubs, but certainly does not condone drink-driving. We do not propose to dicuss this particular issue here, but there is a closely allied point which concerns us equally. Many of the pubs in a rural county such as Cheshire are reliant on customers arriving by car. If we leave out of account the foolish minority, most of the drivers will be staying within the current alcohol limit, say 1½ to 2 pints. The new rule could reduce this to one pint or less. The hapless driver could in fact be over the 50mg limit on a single pint of a stronger beer. Licensees are afraid that they will lose customers as their regulars choose to stay at home. Many of our best pubs are not goldmines, and they could go under. Traditional pubs may make even more of a move toward the restaurant/bistro concept which has threatened the character of so many examples of our heritage.

How can the responsible driver, who likes a drop of ale deal with this? We offer the following suggestions:

1) **Have someone else drive.** Make arrangements so that several people can travel in one car, with one taking a turn to be the non-drinking driver. A long-standing tradition is that the driver does not pay, and whatever they have is bought by their passengers. We know of some pubs which offer free soft drinks to drivers.

2) **Use public transport.** We admit this is easier said than done, but some of our best pubs can still be reached by bus or train. It is worth finding out.

3) **Use a taxi or private hire 'minicab'.** For door to door transport, these are ideal, and sharing the cost between say, four passengers could work out cheaper than driving. Keep your licence; get a cab.

4) **Take advantage of the pub's own scheme.** Some pubs provide a get-you-home service. The Bull's Head in Mobberley, for instance, has a dedicated minibus taxi service for customers.

5) **Cycle or walk!** Especially at weekend, or on summer evenings. Twenty minutes' gentle exercise is good for your waistline, the environment and your driving licence!

HORSE & JOCKEY
144 Gravel Lane (off Knutsford Rd)
⌚2-11 Mon-Fri; 12-11 Sat; 12-10.30 Sun
Greenalls Mild, B, Original [H]
Large brick multi-room Victorian pub on edge
of town. Real fire. Quiz night Monday.
🍻 ● P

KINGS ARMS
Fulshaw Cross (A34/B5085 roundabout).
Robinsons beers
*Landlord does not want pub to appear in a
CAMRA guide. Draw your own conclusions.*
P

KING WILLIAM
35 Manchester Rd
⌚12-3, 5-11 Mon-Fri; 12-3, 6.30-11 Sat,
12-3.30, 7-10.30 Sun
Robinsons Hatters Mild, Best Bitter [H]
Very pleasant town centre drinkers' pub with
paved outdoor drinking area and birdcages!
Children only at lunchtimes.
Meals 12-2 every day.
◖ ≢ P

NEW INN
Alderley Road
(old A34, immediately south of town centre)
⌚11.30-3, 5.37-11 Mon-Sat;
12-3, 5.30-10.30 Sun
Hydes Billy Westwoods B [H] Light , B [E]
A comfortable, plush, refurbished pub with a
large car park, handy for the shopping centre.
Photos of turn of the century Wilmslow and
bookshelves grace the walls. Children are
admitted, but only if using the family dining
area. Meals are served weekdays 12-3;
Thursday to Saturday 6-9. Thursday is Singles
Night. One of the few outlets for this brewery
in the county.
◖ ▶ ≢ P ⊗

RECTORY
Station Rd
⌚12-11 Mon-Wed, 12-12 Thu-Sat,
12-10.30 Sun
Draught Bass, guest beer [H]
Modern pub right next to station. Food 12-9
Sun-Wed, 12-8.30 Thu-Sat. Thursday to
Saturday are lively, with guest DJs and a
supper menu. No entry on these days after
10.30.
◖ ▶ ● ≢ P

B.T. TAXIS
WILMSLOW

FORD GRANADAS
MINIBUSES

CONTRACTS/AIRPORTS

24 HOUR SERVICE
DISTANCE NO OBJECT

01625-527272/3

RIFLEMANS ARMS
Moor Lane (continuation of Chapel Lane)
⌚11.30-3, 5-11 Mon-Sat; 12-3, 7-10.30 Sun
Boddingtons Mild, B, Stones B [H]
Airy, 1950's estate pub encompassing vaults
and sprawling lounge, due for refurbishment
shortly. Quiz night on first Thursday of each
month. Regular charity events. Dominoes and
darts played. Try some Boddington's Mild
before it disappears altogether!
● P

SAMUEL FINNEY
Alderley Road (A34)
⌚12-11 Mon-Sat; 12-10.30 Sun
**Boddingtons B, Courage Directors,
2 guest beers [H]**
Recently built into part of the old Rex Theatre,
this town centre pub gets very busy at times.
Real fire. You can keep an eye on your car
from the balcony which overlooks the car
park! Dress restrictions apply Thursday to
Saturday evenings.
Guest beers usually from major brewers.
◖ ▶ ≢ P ⊗

SWAN
2 Swan Street
(just west of the Station Road traffic lights)
⌚11-11 Mon-Sat; 12-3, 7-10.30 Sun
**Boddingtons B, Taylors Landlord,
guest beers [H]**
Newly opened, comfortable pub in the town
centre, with the best selection of guest beers
around, normally from independent breweries.
The alehouse theme is not overdone, and a
mixed clientele is the result. The Swan is an
ex-Boddington's pub, as evidenced by the
attractive, etched windows and is very popular
with the office crowd at lunchtimes.
Also handy for station and shops. Food is
served from noon till 8pm Monday to
Thursday, till 6pm otherwise. Open fire. Quiz
nights Wednesday. Patio seating in summer.
Beer is the main focus here, with a
Beer Festival in late summer. The management
is very keen, and obtains the three regularly
changing guest beers from independent
sources. An interesting feature is the Real Ale
Tasting Society. RATS members pay £5 to
join and receive a T-shirt and 30p off every
pint of real ale on Thursdays. Real cider is
expected to join the portfolio in 1998. Some of
the beers have been kept on a cask breather
system, although we believe this is to be
discontinued; opinion is divided as to whether
this method of cellar practice is within the
spirit of Real Ale.
◖ ● ≢ P

WILMSLOW FLYER
Dean Row Road
⌚APH
Marstons Pedigree [H]
New pub in shopping precinct, just off the by-
pass.
P ⊗

WIMBOLDSLEY
VERDIN ARMS
Nantwich Road
(A530, near the railway bridge)
Robinsons Best B [H]
Large, isolated, roadside pub near the
Shropshire Union Canal, relying on food trade. It
has 14 clocks, 6 of which chime!
◖ ▶ ● P

WINCHAM
BLACK GREYHOUND
Hall Lane
(A559, 1 mile NW of Lostock Gralam)
⌚12-11 Mon-Sat; 12-10.30 Sun
Boddingtons B, Tetley B [H]
A family oriented pub with an attended indoor
play area for children and safe enclosed
garden.
Meals served from noon until 9.30pm daily.
◖ ▶ 🍻 ● ≢ P ⊗

WINCHAM HALL HOTEL
No real ale.

WINSFORD
ARK
Market Place, Middlewich Road (A54)
Greenalls Mild, B [H]
Authentic timber-framed alehouse that once
slaked the thirst of salt-makers and boatmen
P

BRIGHTON BELLE
Middlewich Road (A54)
⌚APH
**Burtonwood B, Forshaws B,
seasonal beers [H]**
Two rooms; one large open plan lounge and a
games room. Pullman coach serves as a restau-
rant but this is to go in the impending
refurbishment.
◖ ▶ ● ≢ P

WINCLE

SHIP

Nearly 2 miles south of A54 Congleton to Buxton road, through Wincle, heading towards River Dane.

⏰12-3, 7-11 Tue-Sat; 12-4, 7-10.30 Sun

2 varying beers[H]

A destination popular with walkers and diners alike. Set in stunning countryside and just inside the Peak District National Park near the meandering River Dane, Gritstone Trail and local trout fishery (note the menu!). The name comes from the Shackleton's Arctic expedition ship, the Nimrod, seen on the sign outside.

The 16th century long, stone building has three small rooms; a flagged vault/family room (or for muddy booted ramblers!) and two lounges. The barrelled bar is flanked by two old navigation lamps and festooned with old pumpclips, testament to past beer glories! This goes some way to explaining the Good Beer Guide listing. At present one of the regular beers is from the superb Congleton brewery, Beartown. The far room houses a red sandstone fireplace with an unusual smiling stone face, as well as hop-decorated beams. The Ship is a welcome example of a quiet pub, with no intrusive music; only the buzz of conversation. In addition to the good, home-made food, they sell ice cream in the Summer! Beware that the pub is closed on Mondays from November to March. **GBG**

◖ ◗ ● P

WINSFORD

DENBIGH

No real ale.

GATE

Delamere Street, Over

Draught Bass, Worthington Draught B, Stones B [H]

Characterless suburban pub.

◖ ● P

GEORGE & DRAGON

No real ale.

GOLDEN LION

High Street

⏰ 11-3, 7-11 Mon; 11-11 Tue-Sat; 12-10.30 Sun

Boddingtons B, Greenalls Festival, guest beer [H]

Fairly basic but neat and tidy local. Large beer garden. Bar snacks occasionally.

● P

KNIGHTS GRANGE

No real ale.

ODDFELLOWS ARMS

Station Road

⏰12-3,7-11 Mon-Wed; 12-4, 7-11 Thu-Sat; 12-3,7-10.30 Sun

Chesters Mild, Whitbread Trophy [H]

Neat & tidy local with lounge and pool table. Good to see real Chesters mild.

⇌ P

OLD STAR

No real ale.

PRINCES FEATHERS

Station Road (Wharton)

⏰11.30-3,6-11 Mon, Wed, Thu; 12.30-3, 6-11 Tue; 11.30-11 Fri; 11-11 Sat; 12-10.30 Sun

Cains Traditional B, Chesters Mild; Flowers IPA or Whitbread Castle Eden, Weetwood Old Dog; 1-2 guest beers [H]

A lively two-room town pub, with boxing memorabilia in the bar. Local CAMRA Pub of the Year 1996. An excellent local with best range of beer for miles. Weetwood is a Cheshire micro-brewery based in Tarporley. Regular £1 a pint promotion on selected beer Tuesday evenings. Food is available on Saturday lunchtime only.

⇌ P

WALKING IN CHESHIRE

Cheshire is dominated by its lush plain, providing easy rambling especially suitable for family excursions. However, there is some surprisingly varied scenery, including hill-walking, for the more intrepid walker. There are numerous publications describing, on the whole, circular walks within the county. Some of these are based around visits to rural pubs, although personally I haven't always been impressed by the authors' choices and the accuracy of information. I hope you will find Out *Inn* CHESHIRE more useful in choosing your
refreshment stops.

There are also a number of linear walking routes in Cheshire. These include the Sandstone, Gritstone/Mow Cop and Longster Trails, the Delamere, Salter's, Baker, Eddisbury and Middlewood Ways and the **Cheshire Ring Canal Walk** (the first canal circuit to be recognised as a long distance footpath). The routes are shown in various publications, with most also included in the Ordnance Survey's Street Atlas of Cheshire.

In addition, the **SANDSTONE** and **GRITSTONE/ MOW COP TRAILS** and Cheshire Ring are detailed in leaf-lets produced by Cheshire County Council (available from Tourist Information Centres). Pubs to visit on the latter route are given in the Cheshire Ring Canal article within Out *Inn* CHESHIRE. For the former Trails, there are two useful books to supplement the official guide leaflets. These describe short circular walks along the routes, and have been produced by Ruth and Carl Rogers. Both Trails are clearly way-marked and provided with Trail information boards at various points. For walkers
attempting them, here are a number of recommended "staging posts" on, or near, the routes to help you on your way. On with your walking (& drinking) boots!

SANDSTONE TRAIL (West Cheshire) - 32 miles from Frodsham to Whitchurch following the great sandstone ridge, in classic Cheshire dairy farming country.

Frodsham	***Netherton Hall*** and ***Helter Skelter***
	(note: **The Delamere Way** shares its start with the Sandstone Trail)
Alvanley	***White Lion*** (also convenient for **Longster Trail**)
Mouldsworth	***Goshawk*** (also for **Baker** & **Eddisbury Way**)
Hatchmere	***Carriers*** (also for **Delamere Way**)
Kelsall	***Boot*** [near Boothsdale]
	(& for **Eddisbury Way**, passing the **Weetwood** microbrewery and Eddisbury Fruit Farm, home of **Cheshire Cider**)
Tarporley	***Rising Sun*** and *The Swan*
Beeston	***Shady Oak***
Burwardsley	***Pheasant*** [see under Higher Burwardsley]
	(& for **Eddisbury Way**)
Willey Moor Lock	***Willey Moor Lock Tavern***

GRITSTONE TRAIL (East Cheshire) - 18.5 miles from Lyme Park to Rushton Spencer, along the western fringes of the Peak District National Park, extendable by 8.75 miles as the **MOW COP TRAIL**. The route traverses some of Cheshire's more impressive, upland areas
of moors, woodland and rocky outcrops.

Disley	***Dandy Cock*** (Trail starts at Lyme Hall)
Bollington	***Church House*** & ***Poachers*** (also for **Middlewood Way**)
Rainow	***Rising Sun***
Walker Barn	***Setter Dog***
	(Gritstone Trail passes through Tegg's Nose Country Park near here)
Langley	***Leather's Smithy***
Sutton Lane Ends	***Hanging Gate Inn*** [area known as "Higher" Sutton]
Wincle	***Ship***
Timbersbrook	***Coach & Horses***
Newbold	***Horseshoe Inn***
Mow Cop	***Cheshire View***
Harriseahead (Staffordshire) -	***Royal Oak*** (excellent range of guest beers)

WINCLE

WILD BOAR

On main A54 Congleton to Buxton road (near, though not in, the village)
11-3, 7-11 Mon-Fri; 11-11 Sat; 12-10.30 Sun
Robinsons Hatters Mild, Best B [H]

The Boar is a typical, multi-roomed country pub, much involved in country sports (local clay pigeon and pheasant shooting societies meet here). It is also frequented by walkers and commands excellent views over the surrounding hills. The many-roomed and heavily beamed interior is adorned with brasses, dried flowers and pine settles, but the main feature is the large wild boar skin adjacent to the bar! This is because the pub is named after the legend that the last wild boar in England was killed in the nearby Macclesfield Forest during the eighteenth century. The main, bar room houses a warming open fire in a stone fireplace, with crossed swords and a wild boar bust above. There are also copper-topped tables, a large, pine farmhouse dresser and an old Robinson's dray photo (it must have been a tough job for those horses to deliver up here!). Board games and darts, dominoes and cards are all played.

The friendly, Scottish landlady serves a varied range of dishes including wild boar steak and sausages and traditional "stovies". Food is served whenever the pub is open. There is no music in the separate dining room. The well-equipped children's room has games, videos and cartoons. Wheelchairs are welcome, with good access to the pub and a handrail in the ladies toilet, but getting to the garden can be difficult. There is a real fire even in summer! The Robbies Mild is regrettably not always available in winter, due to low turnover.

RED LION
Wharton Road
Greenalls Original [H]
A timber-framed survivor. Real ale hangs on amongst a depressing forest of keg fonts. By canal. Function room. Accommodation.

RIFLEMAN
Weaver Street
Greenalls B [H]
Town local with some 30's style architectural merit. Light oak panelling has survived.

P

SAXONS
No real ale

TOP HOUSE
Wharton Road (Wharton)
APH
Boddingtons B, Chesters Mild, guest beer [H]
Town local at top of hill from market. Country style décor and loud music.
Next to Winsford United FC.

WHARTON PARK
Weaver Valley Road
APH
Boddingtons B, Flowers IPA [H]
Typical theme pub. Uninspiring.

WHITE LION
Delamere Street (Over)
Boddingtons B, Chesters Mild [H]
Large estate pub with lounge and pool room. Loud music. The "Nathanial Frogget" theme consists of an old bike, a stuffed fish and two shovels! Does somebody actually get paid to think them up?

WHITE SWAN
Wharton Road, Wharton
APH
Chesters Mild [H]
Large estate pub, happily still with cask mild.

WINTERLEY

FORESTERS ARMS
473 Crewe Road
12-11 Mon-Sat; 12-10.30 Sun
Tetley Dark Mild, B, guest beers [H]
Addlestones Cider [H]
Cosy country local with low beams and a long, narrow bar with a fireplace at each end, decorated with wood carvings by local craftsmen. One of the few Cheshire pubs serving traditional cider.

HOLLY BUSH
499 Crewe Road
12-3, 5.30-11 Mon-Fri; 12-11 Sat; 12-10.30 Sun
Greenalls Mild, B, Original [H]
Much extended, end-terrace building with restaurant, though retaining public bar. Children admitted if eating.

WINWICK

SWAN
1 Golborne Road
(near church and M6/M62 junction 22)
APH
Theakstons Best B, XB [H]
Large, open-plan pub. Big garden with play area. Food is available daily until 10pm.

WISTASTON

RISING SUN
130 Earle Street
(opposite Grand Junction retail centre)
11.30-11 Mon-Sat; 12-10.30 Sun
Boddingtons B, Chesters Mild [H]
Two roomed pub with Sky TV in the bar.

WOODSIDE
Woodside Lane (at Valley Road junction)
12-11 Mon-Sat; 12-10.30 Sun
Greenalls Mild, B [E], Original [H]
A large, welcoming open plan pub with recently added restaurant area, non-smoking during serving times. Good food at fair prices.

WOODBANK

YACHT INN
Parkgate Road (A540, 4 miles from Chester)
APH
Greenalls B, Original, Tetley B, guest beer [H]
Largo open plan roadside eatery, typical of its style for this chain. Popular with dining families; food all day. Well-appointed and tasteful, but the muzak can be intrusive.

WOOLSTANWOOD

FARMHOUSE
Woolstan Road
(by roundabout at Marshfield Bank)
APH
4 guest beers [H]
Built in 1996, two-roomed bar and Beefeater restaurant. Original farmhouse is retained as staff quarters. Landscaped gardens with pond and enclosed children's play area. The beers are from the Whitbread portfolio.

WRENBURY
DUSTY MILLER

Cholmondley Road (by the canal bridge)
⏰11-3, 6-11 Mon-Sat; 12-3, 7-10.30 Sun (winter)
Robinsons Hatters Mild, Best B, Frederics, with Old Stockport B, Hartleys XB and Old Tom alternating with the season [H]
A classic waterside inn, housed in an old mill building once owned by the current landlord's great grandfather and only becoming a pub in the late 1970's. The inside has been sympathetically decorated with a tiled bar floor, hop-strewn beams, wooden settles and rural artefacts including the odd butter churn! The beam above the bar is formed from a single tree trunk! The main lounge features excellent views over the canal and the lifting road bridge. The upstairs dining area is something special with polished wooden tables and chairs, real-candle candelabras, bare boards and rattan rugs, with an over-all rustic millhouse feel.
       The excellent food choice is all freshly cooked and includes set meals as well as daily specials. The speciality cheeses come from the nearby Tattenhall "Cheshire Cheese Experience". Menus are to be found in a bicycle basket attached to one of the supporting beams! The range of food is impressive and the cuisine excellent, if a little pricey. The canalside garden set by the old mill race, is reached via a wooden causeway. Moorings are available for waterborne arrivals. Many hours can be spent here watching the narrowboats sliding by under the draw-bridge on a warm, sunny day. These hours may be extended in summer. Wheelchair friendly.

⊄ ◗ ⛷ ● ⇌ P

WORLESTON
ROYAL OAK
Main Road (B5074, in middle of village)
⏰11.30-3, 6.30-11 Mon-Sat;
12-4, 7-10.30 Sun
Boddingtons B, Greenalls B [H]
A converted 18th century farmhouse, now comfortably smart with an emphasis on meals.

⊄ ◗ ⛷ ● P

WRENBURY
COTTON ARMS
Cholmondley Road (near the canal)
⏰12-3, 6-11 Mon-Fri; 12-11 Sat;
12-10.30 Sun
Greenalls Mild, B, guest beer [H]
A comfortable country pub with an open fire.
Bowling green and enclosed garden.

⊄ ◗ ⛷ ● ⇌ P ⊗

WYBUNBURY
RED LION

5 Main Road (opposite church at foot of hill)
⏰11-11 Mon-Fri; 12-11 Sat; 12-10.30 Sun
Greenalls Mild, B [H]
Large red brick pub with a comfortable interior, although being single roomed, it has lost most of its character.
Why must they do this?

⛷ ⛸ ● P

SWAN INN
Main Rd. (next to church)
⏰12-11 Mon-Sat; 12-10.30 Sun
Marstons B, Pedigree, guest beers [H]
Spacious, beamed village pub. Food all day until 9pm Sunday.
At least two guest beers.
A good note on which to finish our guide!

⊄ ◗ ⛷ ● P ⊗

In these pages, we have flagged up the best of Cheshire's pubs. We hope you will enjoy visiting them as much as we enjoyed describing them. The task was completed on St. George's Day 1998
Simon Scott, George Symes

OVER THE BORDER

While this is a guide to Cheshire's pubs it would be churlish to ignore some very good pubs just on the other side of the boundary line. We think it would be helpful to give you a rundown of the highlights of our neighbouring areas.

Starting at the top of the map, and working clockwise, we have **ALTRINCHAM**, a market town of some significance, and a cluster of pubs to interest the visitor. Turning right out of the Bus, Metro and Rail Interchange, a short stroll will reveal the *Old Mill* on the right, a young person's pub selling the legendary Holt's Bitter and Coachman's Best Bitter from the Coach House brewery in Warrington. More or less opposite is the *Railway* where Marston's Bitter and Pedigree can be enjoyed in comfort. A little way up Victoria St is a pub of special merit, the *Malt Shovels* renowned for Jazz and Sam Smith's Bitter. Further up the hill is a rarity for the town, a multi-roomed pub, the *Old Roebuck*, a John Smith's outlet. Crossing the busy A56 with care you will observe a cluster of food takeaways and two final pubs.
Very prominent is the *Hogshead*, one of a chain of themed Alehouses from Whitbread, and we must admit they do it well. It offers an impressive range of up to ten real ales and a draught real cider (Old Hazy). It also features bare boards and a no-smoking room at the back on the right of the bar. Directly on the market place, behind the market cross and next to a highly recommended Indian Restaurant (and therefore a good spot to wait for your takeaway) is the *Orange Tree*. This is a family-run local with a friendly bar and a no-smoking room. It is a long-

standing entry in CAMRA's Good Beer Guide, usually stocking a guest beer from an independent brewery as well as more mainstream products from its bank of handpumps.

Outside Altrincham, but worthy of mention are two pubs with the same name. the *Railway* at Broadheath, on the A56 is a classic pub saved from demolition by the concerted action of CAMRA and the locals. It is listed on CAMRA's National Inventory of Heritage Pubs, and sells Holt's Mild and Bitter at their renowned low prices, as well as Boddington's Bitter. To the south of the town, in Hale, you will find another pub called the *Railway*, on Ashley Rd. Despite its urban location, it has the atmosphere of a village pub, with no machines or jukeboxes to spoil the buzz of conversation. It is a classic multi-roomed local, and all are welcome. In nearby Hale Barns is the lovely **Bull's Head**, a sympathetic all refurbished Georgian building, retaining many small, intimate rooms. Along with its popular menu, it serves a wide range of well-kept Robinson's beers.

Our next port of call is **MANCHESTER AIRPORT**, where travellers will be cheered by real ale available in each terminal. Terminal 2 arrivals level has *Busby's* with four handpumped ales including one interesting guest, while Terminal 1 has the *Donkey Stone*. Earthbound spectators can take solace in the *Tatton Arms* at the eastern end of Ringway Road, or at the *Airport Hotel* at the eastern end of the runway, with well-kept Robinsons. Developing the aviation theme, we come to **WOODFORD**, home of British Aerospace. Here the cosy *Davenport Arms*, known locally as the Thief's Neck, after its inn sign, has the air of a farmhouse, helped by the geese and goats wandering the yard. The Robinsons beers are good enough to have won it the CAMRA Regional Pub of the Year award in 1996, and we cannot do justice to it in these few lines.

Moving eastward, we come to **STOCKPORT**, dominated by its famous railway viaduct (the largest brick-built structure in Europe) and Robinson's Brewery. One of the results of the latter is that more than 95% of the pubs in the town serve real ale, and over half sell cask mild. The beer-lover is spoilt for choice, but a good spot to start our tour is the old market place. The magnificent market hall was modelled on the Crystal Palace, and is surrounded by several recommended water-ing holes. *Bakers Vaults* is well known for its food and live music, and the confusing continental-style fonts serve electrically-pumped traditional Robinsons Bitter and Mild. Opposite, is the *Boar's Head*, another venue in the town's thriving music scene and a source of Sam Smiths Old Brewery Bitter. At the narrow end of the market hall, opposite the church can be found the *Pack Horse,* a multi-roomed inter-war pub with a mock Tudor exterior and the relatively rare Tetley Dark Mild alongside the Bitter. Down the side of the church runs Millgate, at the foot of which is one of Stockport's most famous pubs, Robinson's *Arden Arms*. Despite some controversial modernisation in recent times, this still features what is arguably the best pub room in the town. The snug is reached by walking directly through the bar, through the midst of the staff serving your fellow drinkers. This wonderful, intimate room is everything a visit to the traditional British pub should be, and should not be missed.

Handy for shoppers in the precinct are two other traditional Robinsons pubs. The *Swan with Two Necks* is on Princess Street, parallel to Merseyway. It has a distinctive frontage and attractive wood-panelled interior with a pre-war feel; the back lounge alone is worth the visit, despite the limited opening hours. Nearby on Tiviot Dale is one of the few really traditional pubs in the centre, the *Tiviot,* serving good value food at lunchtime.

The old coaching route through Stockport ran up Underbank and Hillgate, and this is unsurprisingly the most heavily-pubbed area apart from the Market Place. Before Christmas, many locals indulge in the Hillgate Crawl along here. Almost under the old iron bridge is the *Queen's Head,* known locally as *Turner's Vaults* after its former use as a tasting room for a wine merchant. An essential rebuild was carried out so well by Sam Smiths that in 1991 it won a CAMRA award for its sensitive refurbishment; a lesson which could be learned by many of our less imaginative pub chains. Famous for its unique spirit taps and the newsroom with neatly folded papers on a rack, this is one pub that the visitor must see.

Fringing the main shopping area, at opposite ends, are two excellent houses for lovers of beer. The *Crown* on Heaton Lane, almost underneath the viaduct, and famously illustrated on the cover of our sister publication *Viaducts & Vaults,* is a tremendously popular alehouse, with at least 6 independent real ales from micro-breweries always on tap. Regrettably, its owners, Greenalls are threatening to sell the goose that lays the golden egg. Opposite the Peel Centre at the eastern end of town is the *Railway,* selling a full range of Porters beers from Rossendale. This is wonderful beer, at prices that are very easy on the pocket. Clearly the lucky burghers of Stockport have a healthy pub scene, and you can find full details of them all in the award-winning local guide, "Viaducts & Vaults 2", available from the Stockport branch contact listed separately. Every year around the end of May, CAMRA holds a Beer & Cider Festival in the "wedding cake" Town Hall, and it improves every year!

The **HIGH PEAK** fringe of Cheshire provides much good walking, and as most walkers need a little rest and refreshment, it is worth mentioning a few of the better inns. On the north-eastern tip of the county is Strines, between Marple and New Mills, where the *Sportsman's Arms* provides a warm welcome and impressive views over toward Mellor. Amongst the ales on offer are those from Cain's of Liverpool. Above Marple on the back road, you will find Mellor, and the *Oddfellows Arms.* Another Good Beer Guide entry, this provides high quality Marston's beers and guest ales in an elegant three-storey building in a picture postcard setting, while there is a strong accent on quality food. The *Little Mill* at Rowarth is certainly worth seeking out, too. It has a working water wheel and possesses considerable character in its many rooms. With a campsite nearby and rooms available, there is a temptation to stay for the excellent beers. As well as guest beers, the regulars are from Banks, Camerons, Hardy & Hansons and Marstons. Heading south to Hayfield, famous for its summer festival of music, we find the *Royal Hotel.* This is a gem, with oak panelling and pews, in a former vicarage on the banks of the River Sett, hard by the church and cricket ground. Again a guest beer policy supplements the Pedigree and John Smiths. Just outside Whaley Bridge is the only remaining canal tramway interchange at Buxworth, and here you will be pleased to find the *Navigation.* This is an excellent multi-roomed pub with an extensive restaurant, and guest beers to add to the choice of Landlord and Pedigree. Back down into Whaley takes you to the *Shepherd's Arms,* at the terminus of the High Peak canal. This is an ageless local, with a quiet lounge contrasting with a convivial vault, complete with scrubbed tables and a flag floor. Banks and Marstons provide the beers for this, our sixth Good Beer guide entry in the High Peak area.

STOKE and its environs are just over the Staffordshire border, and Good Beer Guide listed pubs include the *Royal Oak* at Harriseahead, close to Mow Cop, with the best choice of guest beers in its area. Burslem has the George Hotel, with Marstons beers and Morland's Old Speckled Hen, as well as a highly recommended restaurant. Further south-west, Bignall End has the *Plough* with a range of at least five guest beers and good value food served in a former Potteries CAMRA Pub of the Year. The *Rising Sun* at Shraley Brook, near junction 16 of the M6, no longer brews its own beer, but it still offers a range of real ales, food and folk music in a traditional country inn setting. The Shropshire town of **MARKET DRAYTON** boasts the *Stag's Head,* a friendly three-roomed town pub next to the Shropshire Union Canal.

THE WIRRAL was part of the county until local government reorganisation, and boasts a number of pubs of note. The *Traveller's Rest* in Higher Bebington dates from 1792. The apt inn sign shows some weary travellers of times gone by, taking a well-earned rest, and you could do a lot worse than follow their example. The window boxes are attractive, but the beer range is better, with eight cask ales, including guest beers from a variety of interesting breweries. It was Wirral Pub of the Year for 1998 and is an entry in the national Good Beer Guide. The *Rose & Crown* in Lower Bebington was built in 1732 and serves Thwaites beers to shoppers and office workers at lunchtime and locals at night. Originally a coach house,it retains its traditional public bar. Moving along the estuary, the *Cleveland Arms* in New Ferry is another Thwaites house. It is a popular and friendly open plan local. It has seen some changes since it was built in 1859, now being situated in a pedestrianised area.

BIRKENHEAD is well off for great pubs. The *Old Colonial* was rebuilt and refurbished to a magnificent standard by Robert Cain's Brewery of Liverpool in 1997, using wooden floors from the brewery and carefully salvaged traditional fittings from demolished pubs. They introduced marble fireplaces and even converted wooden bed heads from Liverpool's famous Adelphi Hotel into mirrors. It is set in the Hamilton Quarter which is renovating Birkenhead's historic heart. The nearby Transport  Museum hosts CAMRA Wirral's annual Beer Festival, while the Mersey Ferry gives views of the Pier Head. The "OC" features live music on Saturdays as well as offering the full range of Cain's excellent beers, including a traditional Mild, and seasonal brews. Additionally there are two guest beers. Meanwhile, the *Crown Ale House* in Birkenhead's Conway Park, opposite the bus station, has been tastefully refurbished to retain many of its Victorian characteristics, including a polished wooden floor and a splendid Cheapside Brewery bar mirror. Its traditional bar provides five guest beers and traditional cider in addition to the Cain's and Greenall's regulars. It has won two CAMRA Wirral Pub of the Year awards and the Birkenhead Beer Festival Pub of the Year award 1997. The *Stork Hotel* on Price Street is a lovely Victorian pub with a protected interior and Threlfall's Salford Ales windows. The island bar serves two lounges, a public bar and a 'newsroom'. The regular beer is Flowers, but the guest is often one of Liverpool's Passageway Belgian-style beers or one of the fine products from the Hart Brewery in Eccleston, Lancashire.

Along the coast at **NEW BRIGHTON** your best bet is the *Clarence Hotel,* on Albion Street, offering six real ales including two guests from the more unusual micro-breweries and a quality 'house beer' from Hart. With home-cooked food, this is a good spot to combine with a visit to the July Wirral Show. **WALLASEY** is well-served by the *Farmer's Arms*, another former Pub of the Year and a Good Beer Guide entry. Amongst the Cain's and Whitbread products is a hand-pump in the front bar for a guest beer. The licensee has been in charge for over a decade and this produces an active social aspect, so the pub appeals to all groups. **GREASBY** has an excellent country pub in the *Irby Mill* standing on the site of an ancient windmill. An attractive sandstone building, it was formerly Lumsden's Café but is now one of Wirral's best pubs, with cask Mild and eight real ales in tip-top condition. Its numerous awards include CAMRA Regional Pub of the Year. Finally, **IRBY VILLAGE** has a focal point in the *Shippons Inn*, converted from cowsheds in the 1990s. It retains many original ancient timbers and stone flagged floors. The interior is divided by wooden partitions into separate drinking areas and there is a cosy inglenook. The five real ales include one imaginative guest, and there is a range of over sixty malt whiskies. Monday Folk, Wednesday Quiz and regular theme nights are a credit to the enthusiasm of the staff.

As you can see, there is no shortage of excellent pubs in Cheshire's hinterland. Enjoy them, but...

"Y'all come back now!"

The Little Mill, Rowarth

READER'S FLAGSHIP RECOMMENDATION

Name of town, village or area:

Name of pub:

Address:

Opening hours:

Beers and dispense method:

Food details:

Children admitted?	<1 mile to railway station?
Disabled facilities?	Car park?
Garden?	No-smoking room?

Narrative description:

Your name: Date of survey:

(This form may also be used to notify updates and corrections to CAMRA branches)

INDEX OF ARTICLES

INDEX OF PUBS IN CHESHIRE
(Flagships shown in bold)

Chester Bells	Chester
Chester Road Tavern	Macclesfield
Chetwode Arms	Whitley
Chichester Arms .	Chester
Childe of Hale	Hale
Chimneys	Hooton
Cholmondeley Arms	Cholmondeley
Church Green	Lymm
Church House	Bollington
Church House	Sutton Lane Ends
Church Inn	Congleton
Church Inn	Mobberley
Church View	Widnes
City Arms	Saltney
Clarendon	Runcorn
Clavertons	Chester
Coach & Horses	Bradfield Green
Coach & Horses	Chester
Coach & Horses	Timbersbrook
Coachman	Elworth
Coachman	Hartford
Cock & Pheasant	Bollington
Cock & Trumpet	Hale Bank
Cock Inn	Henbury
Cock o' Budworth	Great Budworth
Combermere Arms	Burleydam
Comfortable Gill	Glazebury
Commercial	Wheelock
Commercial	Widnes
Commercial Hotel	Chester
Community Centre	Grappenhall
Congleton Leisure Centre	Congleton
Copper Mine	Broxton
Corner House	Widnes
Cotton Arms	Wrenbury
Cotton Tree	Bollington
County	Alderley Edge
Crabwall Manor	Mollington
Crag	Wildboarclough
Crescent	Disley
Crest Hotel	Runcorn
Cricketers	Sandbach
Cricketers	Widnes
Crompton Road Tavern	Macclesfield
Cross Keys	Crewe
Cross Keys	Knutsford
Cross Keys Hotel	Chester
Crown	Bollington
Crown	Crewe
Crown	Goostrey
Crown	Lower Peover
Crown	Lymm
Crown	Macclesfield
Crown	Nantwich
Crown	Sandbach
Crown	Tarporley
Crown	Widnes
Crown & Cushion	Penketh
Cuerdley Cross	Cuerdley
Dandy Cock	Disley

Davenport Arms	Calveley
Davenport Arms	Marton
(Congleton)	
de Trafford	Alderley Edge
Dee Miller	Chester
Delamere Arms	Crewe
Dixon Arms	Chelford
Dog	Over Peover
Dog & Dart	Grappenhall
Dog & Partridge	Bollington
Dog & Partridge	Warrington
Dolphin Inn	Macclesfield
Dray	Runcorn
Drovers Arms	Allostock
Drum & Monkey	Comberbach
Dublin Packet	Chester
Duke of Bridgewater	Crewe
Duke of Portland	Lach Dennis
Duke of Wellington	Ince
Dukesfield	Runcorn
Dun Cow	Ollerton
Dunham Arms	Dunham-on-the-Hill
Durham Heifer	Broxton
Durham Ox	Congleton
Durham Ox	Macclesfield
Dusty Miller	Wrenbury
Dysart Arms	Bunbury
Earl of Chester	Crewe
Earl of Crewe	Crewe
Egerton Arms	Astbury
Egerton Arms	Broxton
Egerton Arms	Chelford
Egerton Arms	Chester
Egerton Arms	Runcorn
Eight Farmers	Crewe
Eight Rights	Chester
Eight Towers	Widnes
Elephant & Castle	Shavington
Elms	Pickmere
Ermine Hotel	Chester
Express	Crewe
Fagins	Chester
Falchion & Firkin	Chester
Falcon	Chester
Famous King & Queen	Warrington
Farmers	Warrington
Farmers Arms	Congleton
Farmers Arms	Huxley
Farmers Arms	Lymm
Farmers Arms	Poynton
Farmers Arms	Ravensmoor
Farmers Arms	Rudheath
Farmers Arms	Wilmslow
Farmhouse	Wollstanwood
Farndon Arms	Farndon
Fat Cat	Chester
Faulkner	Hoole
Feathers	Warrington
Ferry	Penketh
Fiddle i' th' bag	Burtonwood

Filigree & Firkin	Macclesfield
Fishpool	Delamere
Flower Pot	Higher Hurdsfield
Flower Pot	Macclesfield
Flying Lady	Crewe
Fools Nook	Oakgrove
Forest View	Oakmere
Foresters	Congleton
Foresters	Glazebury
Foresters	Tarporley
Foresters	Winterley
Foresters Arms	Kelsall
Fortress & Firkin	Chester
Four Topped Oak	Hough Green
Fourways	Delamere
Fox	Elworth
Fox	Haslington
Fox & Barrel	Little Budworth
Fox & Grapes	Macclesfield
Fox & Hounds	Sproston
Foxcote	Little Barrow
Foxfields Country Inn	Ellesmere Port
Franklin	Macclesfield
Freemasons	Handforth
Freemasons	Knutsford
Freemasons	Northwich
Friars' Gate Tavern	Warrington
Frog	Upton
Frog & Ferret	Nantwich
Frozen Mop	Great Warford
Gamekeeper	Chester
Gardeners Arms	Boughton
Gate	Winsford
General Elliot	Croft
George	Crewe
George & Dragon	Chester
George & Dragon	Great Budworth
George & Dragon	Higher Hurdsfield
George & Dragon	Holmes Chapel
George & Dragon	Macclesfield
George & Dragon	Tarvin
George & Dragon	Wilmslow
George Hotel	Sandbach
Globe	Nantwich
Globe	Scholar Green
Golden Eagle	Chester
Golden Fleece	Lymm
Golden Lion	Ashton
Golden Lion	Frodsham
Golden Lion	Macclesfield
Golden Lion	Middlewich
Golden Lion	Warrington
Golden Lion	Winsford
Golden Pheasant	Plumley
Goshawk	Mouldsworth
Grace Arms	Ellesmere Port
Grapes	Runcorn
Grapes	Widnes
Green Dragon	Heatley

Old Hall Hotel	Sandbach	Queens Arms	Bollington
Old Harkers Arms	Chester	Queens Arms	Bosley
Old Kings Head	Gurnett	Queens Arms	Widnes
Old Kings Head	Macclesfield	Queens Head	Congleton
Old King's Head	Chester	Queens Head	Frodsham
Old Millstone	Macclesfield	Queen's Head	Threapwood
Old Quay	Parkgate	Queen's Hotel	Macclesfield
Old Town House	Warrington	Queensgate	Alderley Edge
Old Transporter	Runcorn		
Old Vaults	Nantwich	Railway	Chester
Old White Lion	Congleton	Railway	Congleton
Olde Vaults	Chester	Railway	Handforth
Orford	Warrington	**Railway**	Heatley
Orient Express	Crewe	Railway	Helsby
Ox-Fford	Macclesfield	Railway	Mobberley
		Railway	Nantwich
Pack Horse	Broken Cross	Railway	Runcorn
Pack Horse	Culceth	**Railway View**	Macclesfield
Paddington House	Warrington	Rake & Pikel	Huntington
Park Tavern	Macclesfield	Rake Hall	Little Stanney
Parkgate	Over Peover	Rams Head	Congleton
Parkgate Hotel	Parkgate	Rams Head	Grappenhall
Parr Arms	Grappenhall	Ram's Head	Disley
Peacock	Chester	Raven	Crewe
Peacock	Nantwich	Raven	Darnhall
Peacock	Willaston	Raven	Glazebury
Peel Arms	Macclesfield	Red Admiral	Runcorn
Penny Ferry	Warrington	Red Bull	Church Lawton
Pheasant	Higher	Red Bull	Kingsley
	Burwardsley	Red Cow	Knutsford
Pickering Arms	Thelwall	**Red Cow**	Nantwich
Pied Bull Hotel	Chester	Red Fox	Tiverton
Piper	Hoole	Red House	Chester
Plough	Alsager	Red Lion	Bollington
Plough	Christleton	**Red Lion**	Dodleston
Plough	Croft	Red Lion	Eaton
Plough	Eaton		(Tarporley)
	(Congleton)	Red Lion	Frodsham
Plough	Houghton	Red Lion	Goostrey
	Green	Red Lion	Handbridge
Plough	Marton	Red Lion	Hartford
	(Northwich)	Red Lion	Holmes Chapel
Plough & Flail	Mobberley	**Red Lion**	Little Budworth
Plough (Prestbury Rd)		Red Lion	Little Sutton
	Macclesfield	Red Lion	Lower
Plough (Station St)	Macclesfield		Withington
Ploughboy	Disley	Red Lion	Malpas
Poacher	Gorse Covert	**Red Lion**	Moore
Poacher	Gorse Covert	Red Lion	Nantwich
Poachers	Bollington	**Red Lion**	Parkgate
Poachers Pocket	Tattenhall	Red Lion	Penketh
Poacher's Pocket	Alsager	Red Lion	Pickmere
Pollard Inn	Willaston	Red Lion	Preston Brook
Porter's Ale House	Warrington	**Red Lion**	Stockton Heath
Preston Brook	Preston Brook	Red Lion	Tarvin
Prince Albert	Macclesfield	Red Lion	Warrington
Prince of Wales	Crewe	Red Lion	Winsford
Prince of Wales	Macclesfield	Red Lion	Wybunbury
Prince of Wales	Widnes	Redway Tavern	Bollington
Prince's Feathers	Winsford	Ridgegate	Macclesfield
Princes Hotel	Ellesmere Port	Rifleman	Nantwich
Priory	Wilmslow	Rifleman	Wilmslow
Prospect	Runcorn	Rifleman	Winsford
Puss in Boots	Macclesfield	Rigger	Elton

Ring o' Bells	Christleton	Salamanca	Smallwood
Ring o' Bells	Daresbury	Salt Barge	Marston
Ring o' Bells	Overton	Samuel Finney	Wilmslow
Ring o' Bells	Stretton	Sandpiper	Sandbach
Ring o' Bells	Warrington	Saracen's Head	Warrington
Ring o' Bells	Weaverham	Scruffy Murphy's	Chester
Ring o' Bells	Widnes	**Setter Dog**	Walker Barn
Ring Of Bells	Sandbach	Seven Woods	Warrington
Rising Sun	Gawsworth	Shady Oak	Tiverton
Rising Sun	Rainow	Shakerley Arms	Congleton
Rising Sun	Scholar Green	Ship	Macclesfield
Rising Sun	Tarporley	Ship	Parkgate
Rising Sun	Wistaston	Ship	Styal
Riverside	Acton Bridge	**Ship**	Wincle
Riverside	Warrington	Ship Inn	Handbridge
Robin Hood	Congleton	Ship Victory	Chester
Robin Hood	Helsby	Shrewsbury Arms	Little Budworth
Robin Hood	Rainow	Shrewsbury Arms	Mickle Trafford
Roebuck	Mobberley	**Shroppie Fly**	Audlem
Roebuck	Northwich	Shropshire Arms	Chester
Rookery Tavern	Ettiley Heath	Silkman	Macclesfield
Rookery Wood	Crewe	Simms Cross	Widnes
Rope & Anchor	Warrington	Slow & Easy	Lostock Gralam
Rose & Crown	Allgreave	**Smoker**	Plumley
Rose & Crown	Arclid	Spinner & Bergamot	Comberbach
Rose & Crown	Congleton	Spinners	Bollington
Royal Oak	Alderley Edge		
Royal Oak	Bollington		
Royal Oak	Hoole		
Royal Oak	Rode Heath		
Royal Oak	Runcorn		
Royal Oak	Worleston		
Royal Oak Branch	Warrington		
Royal Oak Hotel	Kelsall		
Ryans	Chester		
Ryles Arms	Sutton Lane Ends		

STOCKPORT AND SOUTH MANCHESTER CAMRA

No:167
Volume 14
Issue 3

FREE

6,500 CIRCULATED FREE EVERY MONTH

MARCH 1998

Opening Times is the award-winning free newsletter produced by the Stockport & South Manchester branch of CAMRA, the Campaign for Real Ale. It includes news and views of pubs in North East Cheshire as well as articles on Cheshire and items of general interest to pub-goers. It can be found in a number of pubs in Knutsford, Mobberley, Bollington and Macclesfield.

As we go to press, the suggestion has been made that an occasional newsletter on similar lines for the county of Cheshire might be well received. We would welcome comment on this, from anyone who would wish to advertise in, stock, or contribute to "Out *Inn* CHESHIRE" - the newsletter. Please call your branch contact listed on page 2.

CAMRA – THE CAMPAIGN FOR REAL ALE...

...is the most successful consumer organisation in Europe. Aside from a small administrative staff, it is run entirely by volunteers. More than 50,000 people, all very different but united by a love of good beer and good pubs. Independent of brewers or pub-owners, it is the fearless voice of the pub-goer.

We welcome new members regardless of age, race, gender or favourite football team! If you wish to join us, you will find a membership form overleaf. You can find out more about what CAMRA does, and what fun it is to be part of it, by reading the Good Beer Guide, visiting a CAMRA Beer Festival or calling your local branch contact as listed on page 2.

Aside from saving real ale from being consigned to the dustbin of history, CAMRA has been instrumental in extending opening hours and promoting legislation on full measure. Local issues have included the listing and saving of many historic pubs, and persuading licensees to sell tasty beers from independent local brewers.

DRAWINGS:

The pen & ink drawings of the Red Lion, Shroppie Fly, Holly Bush and Foxcote are by Rosemary Wignall. Rosemary lives in Stockport and has produced other line drawing of local views and pubs. She also works in "watercolour". Should anyone be interested in obtaining some of her work, she can be contacted on Tel: 0161-432-2509.

We acknowledge the drawings of the Davenport Arms, Queens Arms and the Mill, originally drawn for Viaducts & Vaults – the Stockport Pub Guide by Beryl Baguley.

This guide was prepared by the Campaign for Real Ale
Why not join us ?

What do you get as a CAMRA member?
- What's Brewing, the independent monthly newspaper for the beer drinker
- an information-packed Member's Handbook
- discounts on many products, including CAMRA's best-selling, annual Good Beer Guide
- up-to-date information about new beers and breweries, take-overs, closures and campaigns
- advance notice of beer festivals around the country, and discounted admission

What can you do as a CAMRA member?
- you can join in CAMRA's local and national campaigns
- you can participate in branch activities such as socials, beer festivals and brewery visits - there is a branch near you !
- you can play a part in CAMRA's Great British Beer Festival, the country's biggest extravaganza

APPLICATION FOR CAMRA MEMBERSHIP

NAME: ....

ADDRESS...

....POSTCODE....................

TELEPHONE NUMBER(S)...

I/We wish to join the Campaign for Real Ale Limited and agree to abide by the Memorandum and Articles of Association of the Campaign.

Rates are : Full Single £14, Joint £17, Disabled, Retired, Unemployed or Under 26. £8.

Method of payment (Please delete as appropriate)

1. I/We enclose remittance of £........ for membership for one year.

(Cheques payable to CAMRA)

2. Please debit my VISA/MASTERCARD card with the amount of £........

Card Expiry Date.. Card Number...

SIGNED..

Please post to:
THE MEMBERSHIP SECRETARY, CAMRA, 230 HATFIELD ROAD, ST ALBANS, HERTS AL1 4LW

If you have any queries, you can contact CAMRA HQ by phone on (01727) 867201; By e-mail on camra@camra.org.uk
Visit the CAMRA web site at http://www.camra.org.uk